IMAGES
of America

SMYRNA

ON THE COVER: Photographed in the 1920s, Waller Bros. and King Mercantile store was built on the south end of the Jefferson Square in the town neighboring Smyrna. It was owned by Sidney and Claiborne Waller until 1930, when Sam Hall took over operations. In this image, R.S. "Sidney" Waller stands under the Coca-Cola sign, and Claiborne Waller is to the right, next to his wife, Ollie. Howard, sitting in front of Sidney, and Everett, standing in front of Ollie, were the children of Claiborne and Ollie. The Wallers were well-respected figures in Smyrna. Claiborne became a member of the First Baptist Church of Smyrna in 1934, and Sidney drove a school bus for Smyrna High School for 25 years, from 1925 to 1950. (Courtesy of the Rutherford County Archives.)

IMAGES
of America

SMYRNA

Christina Runkel

ARCADIA
PUBLISHING

ISBN 978-1-4671-1190-4

Published by Arcadia Publishing
Charleston, South Carolina

Printed in the United States of America

Library of Congress Control Number: 2013952886

For all general information, please contact Arcadia Publishing:
Telephone 843-853-2070
Fax 843-853-0044
E-mail sales@arcadiapublishing.com
For customer service and orders:
Toll-Free 1-888-313-2665

Visit us on the Internet at www.arcadiapublishing.com

To my mom, who shared her love of history with me, and to the many people who shared their photographs and knowledge to make this book possible.

Contents

Acknowledgments

The publication of this book is only the first step in preserving Smyrna's rich history. With these photographs made public, others will no doubt come to light, and I would like to thank every person who helps make Smyrna the amazing town that it is.

I am deeply thankful to my loved ones, who have encouraged me throughout my life. A special thanks to my Smyrna-native friend Kelsey Jensen, who first showed me the fascinating history of my adopted town. Huge thanks to John Lodl at the Rutherford County Archives and Jerome Azbell at the Smyrna Public Library for providing me with their extensive knowledge and photographs of the town. Many thanks to David Bucher for his expertise on Smyrna's past, particularly about Sewart Air Force Base, and the driving tour of Smyrna to show me the exact locations of the structures.

I wish to also thank the numerous residents, past and present, who searched through family albums and keepsake boxes for photographs. John Moore, James "Toby" Francis, Ginny Williams, Chuck Clark, Robert "Bud" Raikes, and the family of Katherine Haynes Walkup provided many of the amazing images on the following pages and shared the stories behind each one. Lisa Ramsay; Barry Lamb; Bethany Hall at the Rutherford County Office of Information Technology, GIS Division; Hal Loflin at the Smyrna Golf Course; and Nissan North America also provided a glimpse into Smyrna through their images. Gloria Christy of Shacklett's Photography allowed me access to the numerous wonderful images in their archives, and I am deeply grateful to the Shacklett family for use of the photographs and for doing their part to preserve history. The Sam Davis Memorial Association had a treasure trove of photographs in their possession related to the Davis family. The organization does an amazing job each day of keeping history alive.

I hope that you enjoy this book and remember that your photographs help tell the story of a time forgotten.

INTRODUCTION

Rutherford County was organized in 1803 when several hundred settlers came to Middle Tennessee from the east in search of farmland. Many settled in the area surrounding a river that ran south from Nashville, today known as Stones River. In honor of Pres. Thomas Jefferson, they named the town Jefferson; it later became the county seat in 1804. The town grew, but a few families established farms outside of town in a community they named Stewartsboro.

With the South booming in the mid-1800s, the Nashville & Chattanooga Railroad decided to build a way station between Nashville and Murfreesboro. The railroad saw potential in the area and sold land near the rail line, dividing it into residential and commercial lots, and those who settled there took the name of a nearby church, Smyrna Presbyterian Church. Of the lots, 64 went to public auction in 1855, and a town was created in the next few years. With this new means of transportation, many farmers were able to sell more food and other crops and thus increased the size of their profit, which in turn led to larger farms and plantations.

Soon after the town of Smyrna was established, the country was ravaged by the Civil War. Many Smyrna boys and men joined the Confederate forces. The 20th Tennessee Regiment was organized in Smyrna and led by a local man, Col. J.S. Gooch. Between Union-held Nashville and Confederate fortifications of Murfreesboro, Smyrna was often caught in the crossfire with both armies using the roads passing through the small town. The Battle of Stones River was fought less than 10 miles from Smyrna on December 31, 1862, and January 1 and 2, 1863. Local boy Sam Davis fought in the battle. Davis joined the Confederate forces just after the Battle of Fort Sumter and later served as a Coleman Scout. In November 1863, he was captured, tried as a spy, and hanged. His body was brought back to his home in Smyrna the following month, and his story garnered attention in the late 1800s when a newspaperman heard of it and wrote it in the *Confederate Veteran* magazine. By 1927, Sam Davis was well known enough for the family to sell 168 acres and the house in which Sam had lived before his death to the State of Tennessee; the structure still exists as a historic house museum: the Historic Sam Davis Home & Museum. After the Civil War came to an end, Smyrna farmers declined in wealth and stature, as did much of the South.

For many years, Smyrna continued farm life, growing corn, wheat, cotton, and other crops well into the late 1900s. Nearby Jefferson also saw growth. The town was surrounded by water on three sides and served as a major shipping port for the area. Throughout the history of both towns, the Stones River provided shipping opportunities; however, industry soon began to outpace agriculture, and the buzz of the sawmills faded away. As automobiles became more popular, so did highways. The Dixie Highway, which linked the north (up to Canada) with the south (down to Miami, Florida), served as a major road through the Smyrna. The road was organized in 1914 in Chattanooga, and construction began shortly after. Many visitors came through town on this highway and stopped at favorite hot spots, including the New Majestic Café; R. O. Davis Grocery, Meat, and Ice; Payton Clothing Co.; Gambill Service Station; and the Regal Theater, among others.

The small Tennessee town grew rapidly when the Air Force decided to build a base a few miles near downtown. Smyrna beat out three other towns to win the honor of housing long-range bombers, including the B-24. The state resolved to acquire land for federal government purposes in 1941. Most of the residents were on board, though a few that had homes on or surrounding the new proposed military site were not pleased. At the time, Smyrna had fewer than 500 residents. The base took 2,996 acres of land that had previously been devoted to growing corn, hay, and small grains; the land was flat with few trees and therefore perfect for military flight operations. The base saw opportunity in the workforce of nearby Nashville as well as opportunities in shipping with the railroad hub in the city.

Building of the base began in January 1942 and was completed by July that same year. The town saw an increase in nearly every sector. More schools were built for the children of military servicemen, businesses opened to accommodate the growing population, and more houses were constructed. Soldiers had access to miles of runways, several hangars, and other amenities. Men and their families came to the Smyrna Army Airfield, as it was named, in droves, and the town nearly doubled, seemingly overnight. The Combat Crew School was activated, and men began learning the intricacies of B-24s, B-17s, and other bombers. By the end of the first year of American involvement in World War II, the airfield was a center for training hundreds of officers. Throughout the war, the base sent hundreds of men overseas, and airline flight attendants and pilots of commercial planes used the base facilities for training. After the war, the base was placed on an inactive list, but by September 1948 it was reactivated. Nearby, Murfreesboro provided a Middle Tennessee State College, where former servicemen could use their new GI education benefits and stay in the area.

The base was renamed in 1950 to commemorate a local soldier who was killed in 1942. Maj. Allan J. Sewart Jr. grew up in Nashville and was killed in combat over the Solomon Islands. On March 25, 1950, the military held a ceremony to rename the base to Sewart Air Force Base. With the Korean Conflict, the base saw action again. The 9th Air Force's 314th Troop Carrier Wing trained in Smyrna and traveled to Korea and later Vietnam. In June 1970, the base was deactivated for good. The land was split among four organizations, and much of what remained of the base is used as an airport and National Guard training quarters today.

After the military men left the area, Smyrna worked hard to remain a thriving community, but it could not keep up the same level of growth and industrial advancement. Not until the 1980s did Smyrna again prosper. Cumberland Swan (now Vi-Jon), Nissan North America, and other companies decided to place manufacturing plants in town. Nissan broke ground in 1981, and by June 1983 the first truck rolled off the assembly line. The company hired over 1,500 employees when it opened, which was a huge boost to the local economy. The original factory covered over 5.1 million square feet, and the company has continued to expand through other buildings on the site and others in Smyrna throughout the years.

Today, Smyrna embraces agriculture as well as industry and continues to grow.

One

Street Scenes

With the Nashville & Chattanooga Railroad expanding in the 1850s, it was decided that a way station would be built near the old Smyrna Presbyterian Church between Nashville and Murfreesboro. The railroad bought land near the line and subdivided it into residential and commercial lots, 64 of which went up for public auction in 1855. Streets were created to be perpendicular to one another, with the flat land making this possible.

Horse-drawn buggies first beat down the ground on Smyrna roads before automobiles and paved roads came onto the scene. Smyrna had its first paved street in 1928. The early residential streets were named for presidents, and there were few bridges in the early years. Toll roads helped pay for street care, and in 1915 Smyrna was incorporated as a town, with local taxes helping pay for maintenance.

A highway connecting the Midwestern and Southern states was planned in 1915 by the Dixie Highway Association. The Dixie Highway, or US 41-70, passed through Smyrna on its way to Miami from Chicago and later extended to Canada. Prior to this road, residents and visitors could only get into Smyrna via Hazelwood Drive on Old Nashville Highway. The Dixie Highway ran right through the center of town, and residents relied on it for everyday travel around the community and to Nashville and Chattanooga, Tennessee. Today, the road (known as Lowry Street in Smyrna) serves as a means of getting from one part of town to the other relatively quickly. Most of the businesses that popped up along the Smyrna portion of the Dixie Highway when it first passed through town are gone, but the memories of them remain. Interstate 24 was constructed in the area between 1962 and 1968 and extends from southern Illinois to Chattanooga. It runs west of the center of town. The early 2000s saw huge growth along the Smyrna exits, with many large retail stores setting up shop.

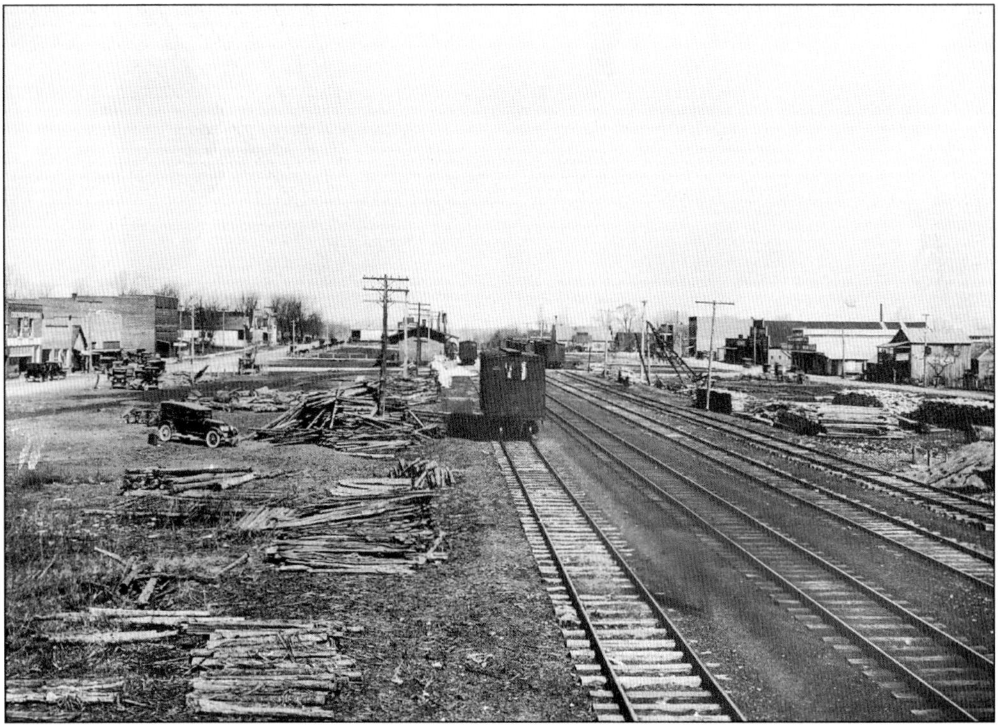

The business district flanks both sides of the train tracks in this 1920s photograph. On December 11, 1845, the State of Tennessee granted a charter to the Nashville & Chattanooga Railroad for Smyrna. The railroad was to connect Middle Tennessee with the South Atlantic seaports, including Charleston and New Orleans. (Courtesy of Shacklett's Photography.)

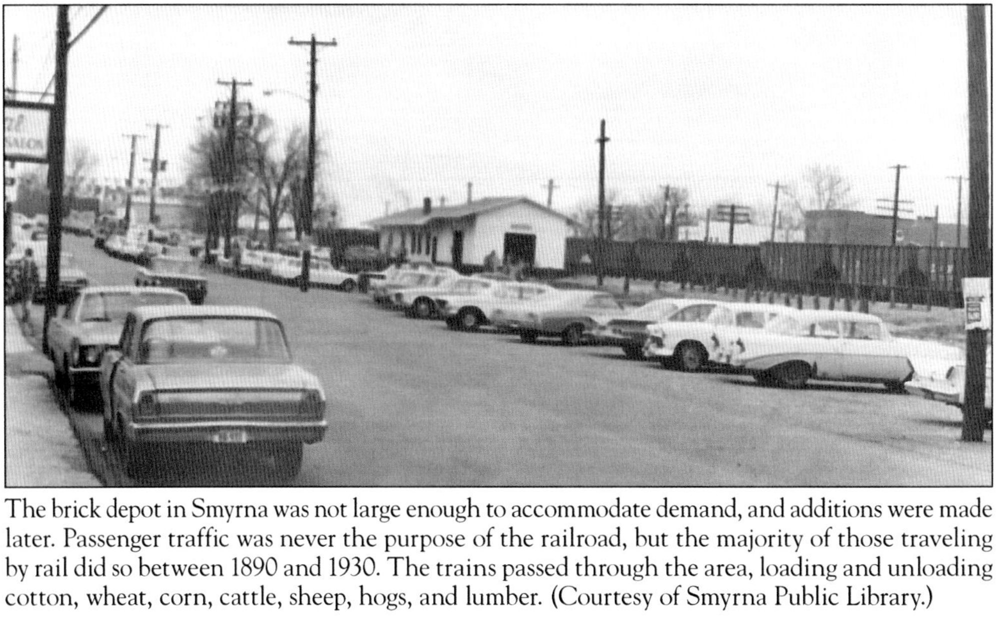

The brick depot in Smyrna was not large enough to accommodate demand, and additions were made later. Passenger traffic was never the purpose of the railroad, but the majority of those traveling by rail did so between 1890 and 1930. The trains passed through the area, loading and unloading cotton, wheat, corn, cattle, sheep, hogs, and lumber. (Courtesy of Smyrna Public Library.)

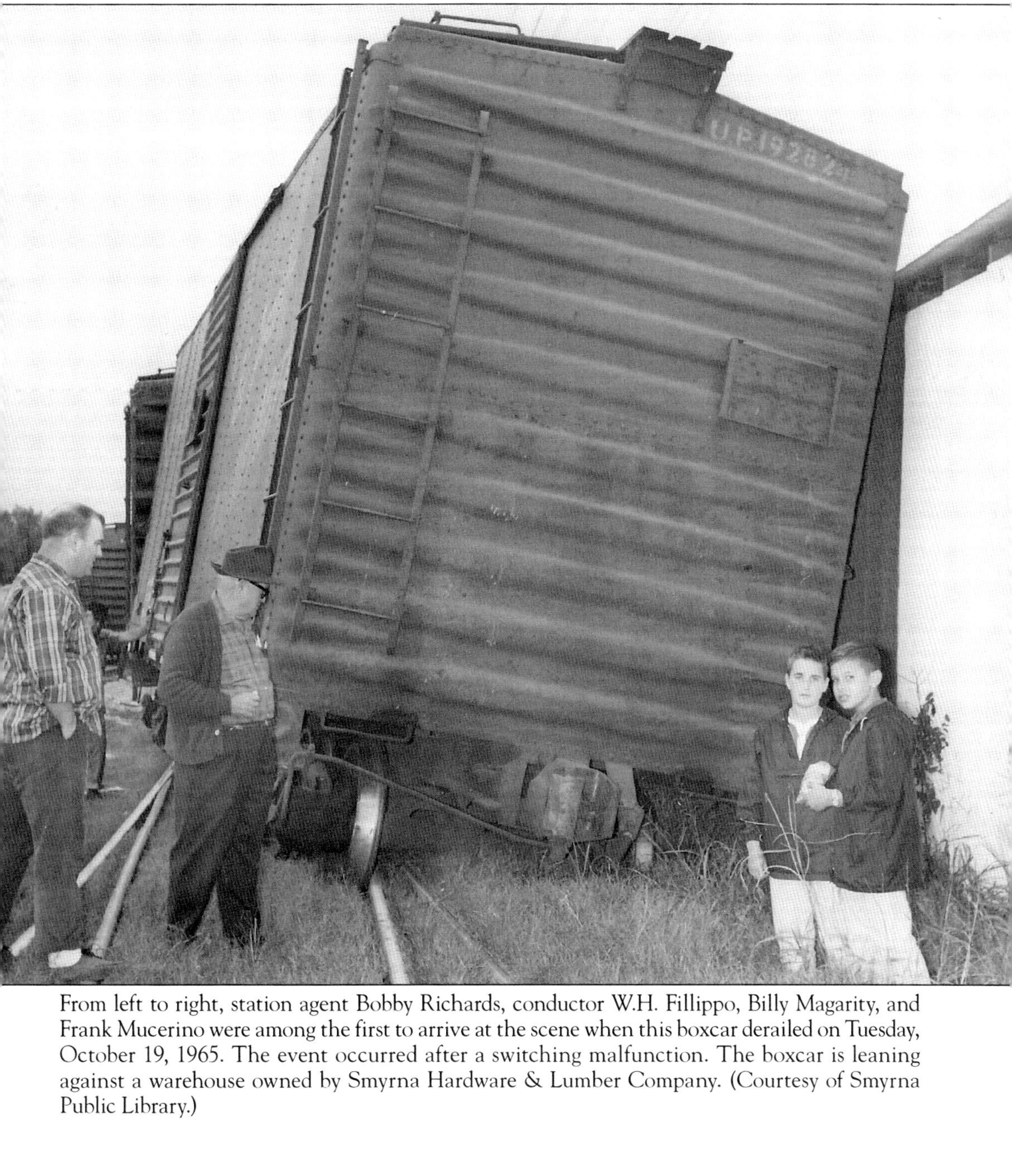

From left to right, station agent Bobby Richards, conductor W.H. Fillippo, Billy Magarity, and Frank Mucerino were among the first to arrive at the scene when this boxcar derailed on Tuesday, October 19, 1965. The event occurred after a switching malfunction. The boxcar is leaning against a warehouse owned by Smyrna Hardware & Lumber Company. (Courtesy of Smyrna Public Library.)

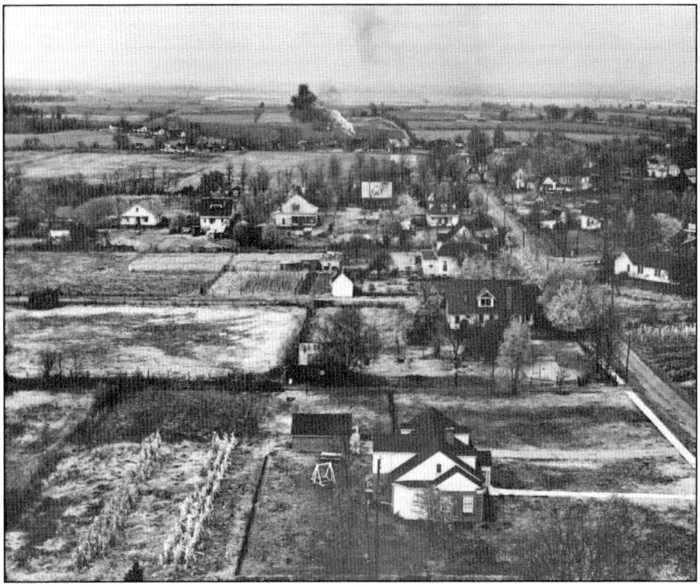

This early-1900s photograph shows a few of the homes and farms in downtown Smyrna. In the early 1900s, fewer than 1,000 people lived here; by 1950, the population rose to just above 1,500. By 2000, over 25,000 people called Smyrna home. (Courtesy of Shacklett's Photography)

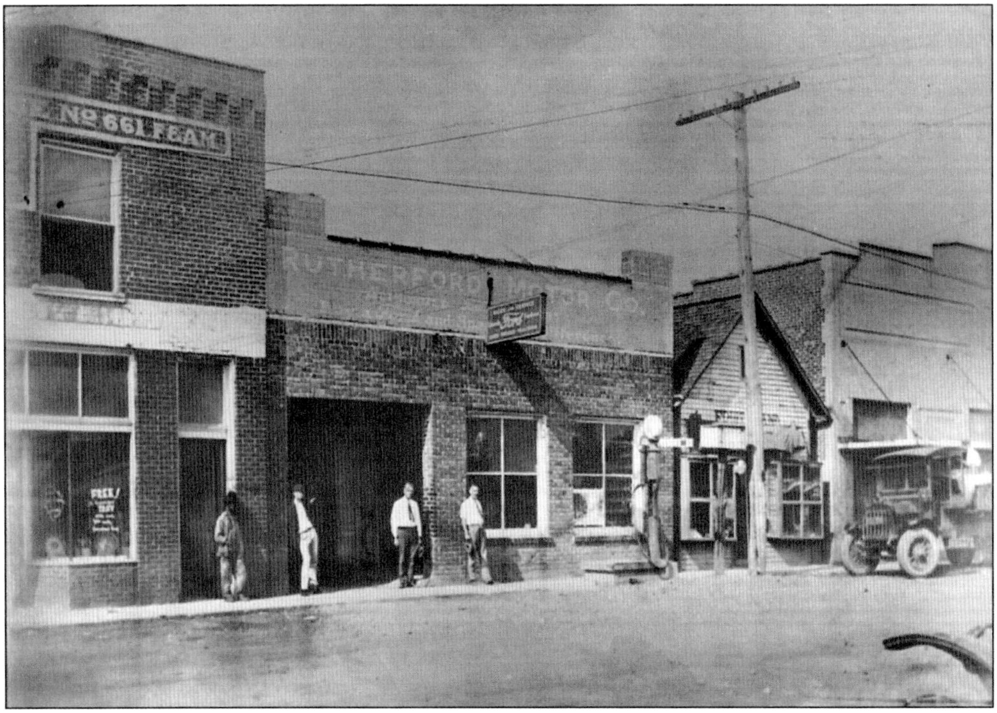

The Rutherford Motor Company is pictured in 1922, two years after opening at 108 South Front Street. B.S. Flowers and his wife sold Ford vehicles. The company lasted only six years, and the building burned in 1931. Also shown here are the Sam Davis Lodge, Ridley-Engles-Lawrence Grocery, Chambley's Fruit Stand, and Robert Davis Store and truck. Davis carried meats, vegetables, fruits, stock feed, and more and delivered the items to customers' doors with a Federal truck rather than the horse-drawn wagons customary of the day. (Courtesy of Shacklett's Photography.)

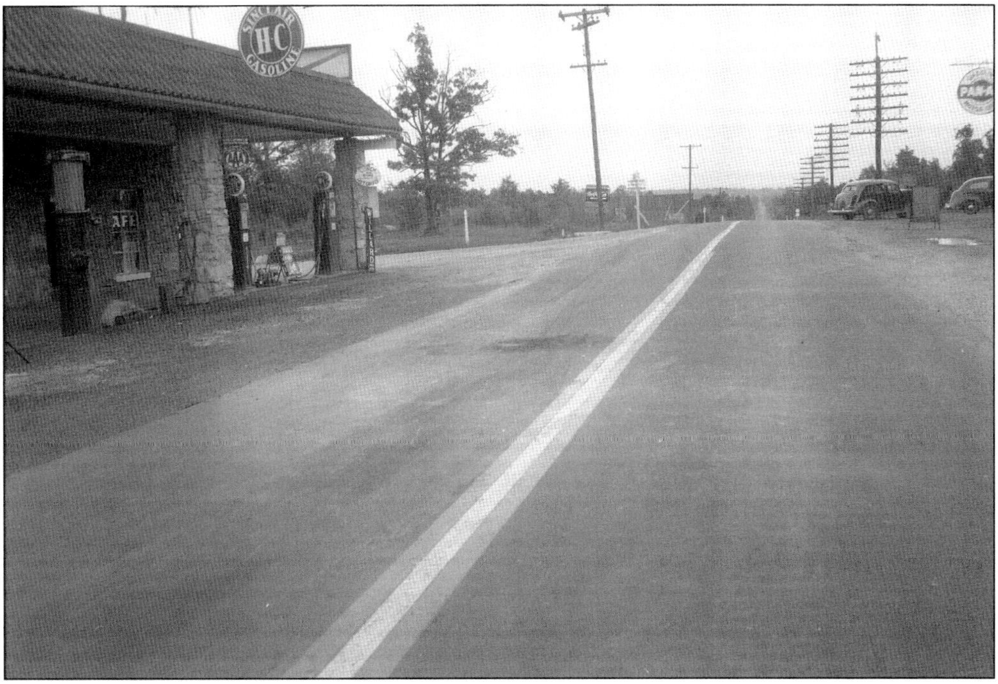

Located in the Hilltop community at Highway 102 and Dixie Highway, the Sinclair station was a popular local stop, as shown here in the 1940s. Hilltop was primarily the African American section of town. Across from the station was Fat Gambill's Garage. (Courtesy of Shacklett's Photography.)

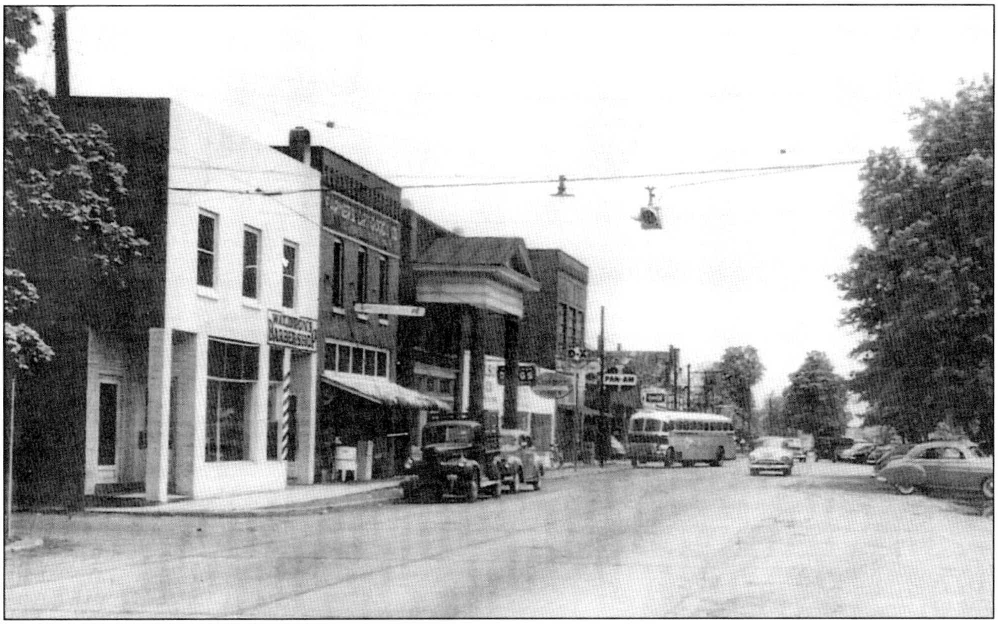

This photograph shows downtown Smyrna around 1940. The bus is similar to the one the Smyrna High School football team used for road trips during the 1970s. (Courtesy of Robert "Bud" Raikes.)

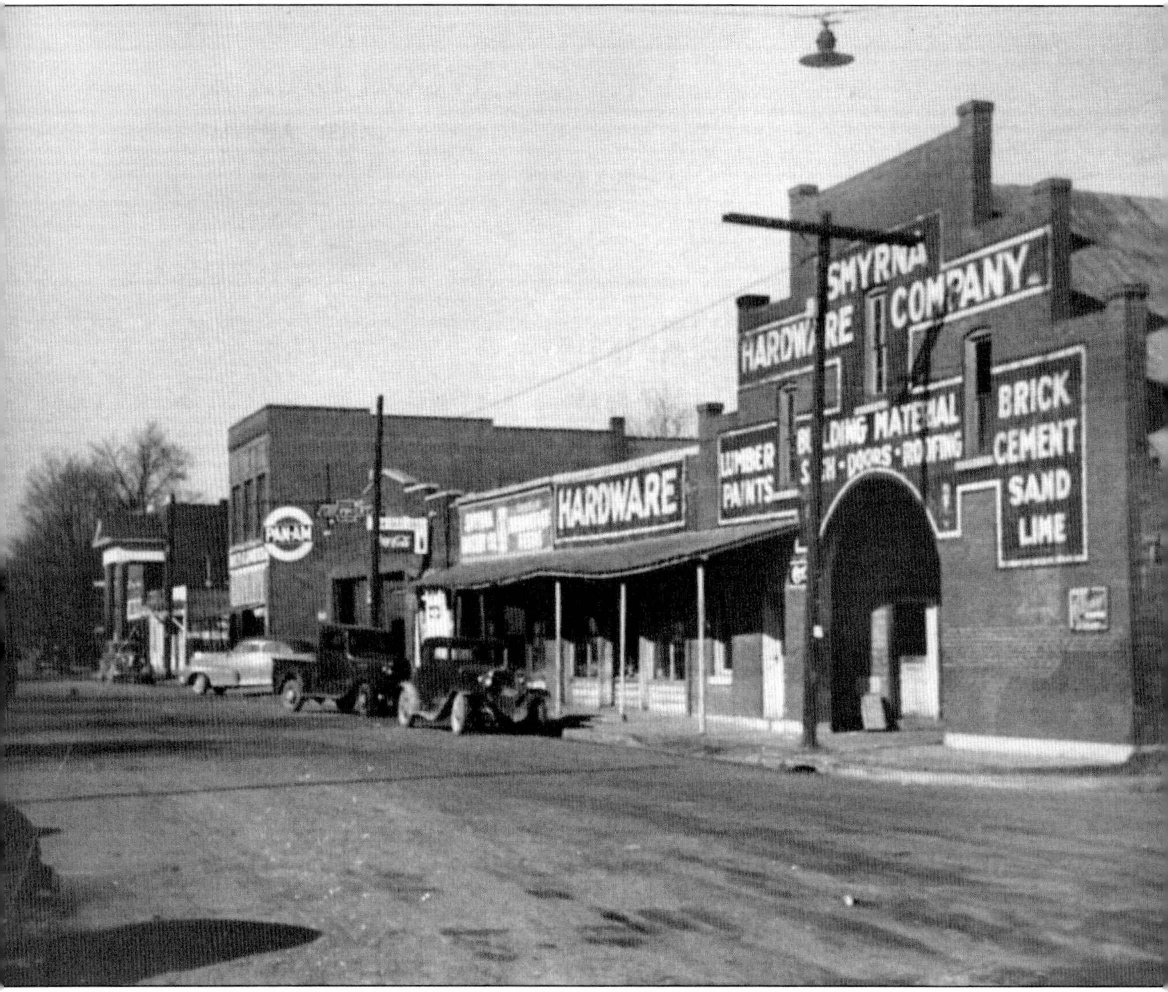

This 1948 photograph of Front Street shows the First National Bank at the end of the street, with Smyrna Hardware Company in the foreground. In 1916, W.A. Hutton owned the hardware business. At the same time, Horace Pruitt and Walter Hibbett operated a lumber shed, where there was a large planning mill. By the 1950s, the New Nashville Highway would pass along Lowry Street in front of these buildings. (Courtesy of Shacklett's Photography.)

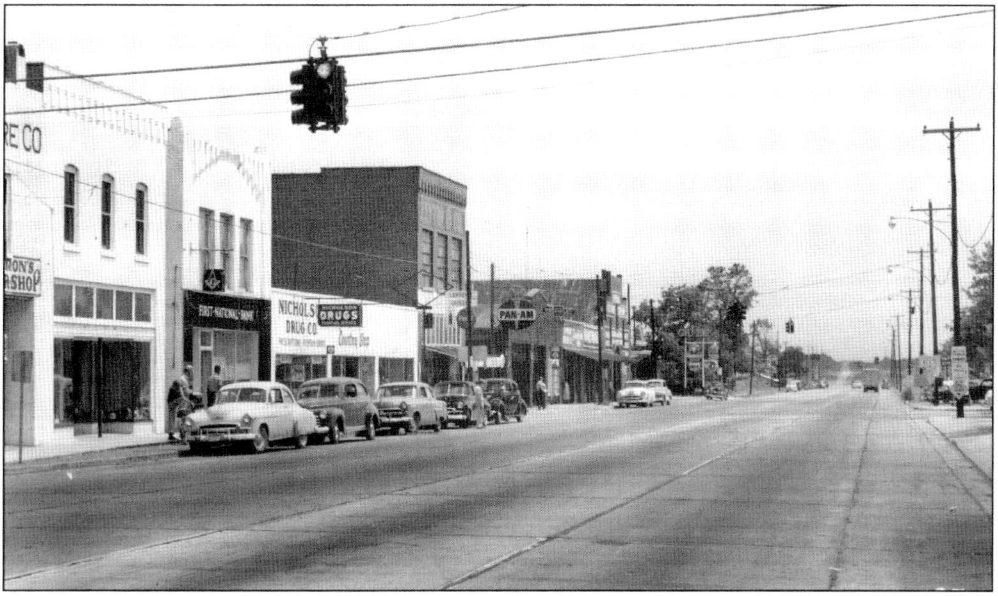

This 1960s photograph shows downtown Smyrna on Lowry Street. The First National Bank (to the left of the Nicholson Drugs sign) began as the Peoples Bank of Smyrna in 1911. J.N. Barnett became the cashier in 1914 and held the job for over 50 years. The front of the bank was remodeled in 1950 to include the black stone and glass facade seen here. Several robberies occurred over the years, including the February 12, 1923, heist in which robbers cut a hole in the vault door with a flame torch and took everything of value. (Courtesy of Lisa Ramsay.)

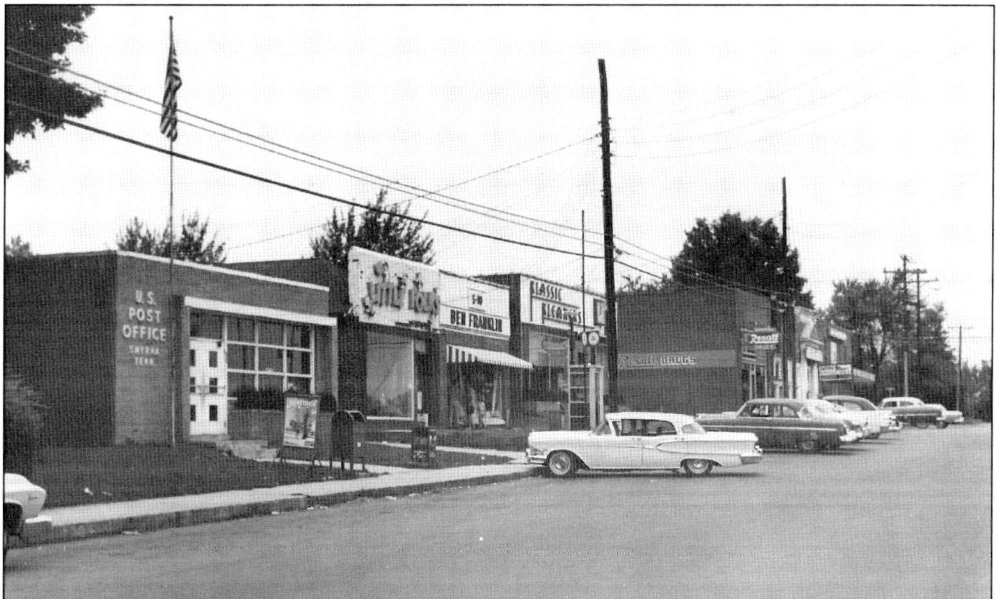

The federal post office, Little Folks Shop, Ben Franklin Store, Rexall Drug, and other Smyrna businesses are shown here in the 1950s. Smyrna got its first post office in 1852. Prior to this, residents received their mail at a general store according to oral legend. The Little Folks Shop and the Ben Franklin Store began operating in the mid-1950s. (Courtesy of Smyrna Public Library.)

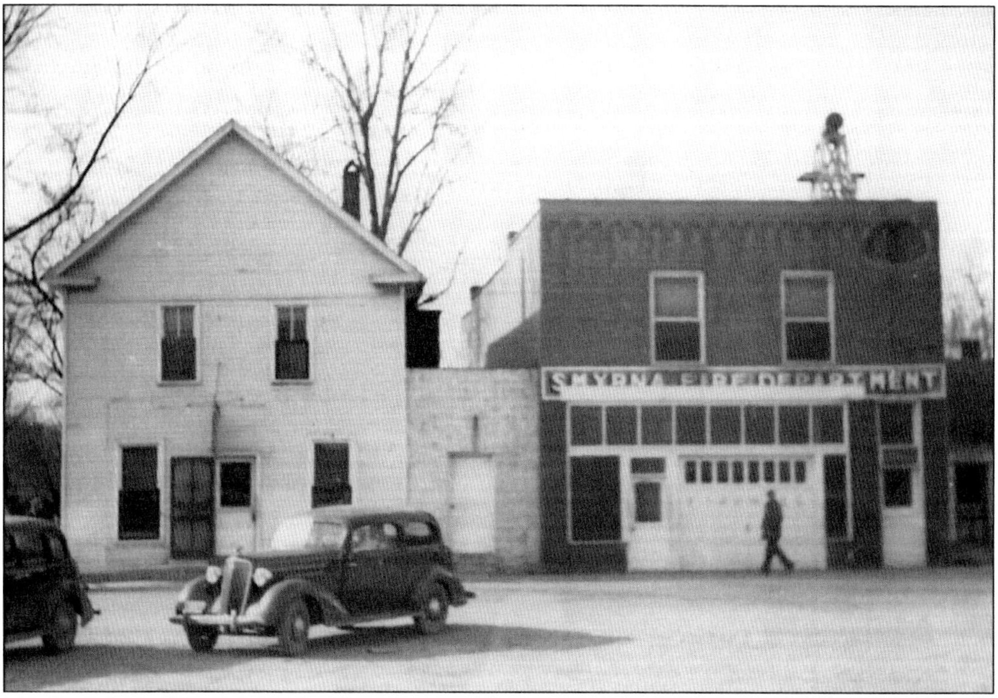

The Smyrna Fire Department building was on Front Street, as shown in this 1948 photograph. Before 1916, Smyrna had no firefighting equipment, and many buildings were destroyed. John Haber Sr. saw the need of the town and built his fire engine. Not until 1924 did Smyrna receive money to create a fire department through local taxes. (Courtesy of the Sam Davis Memorial Association.)

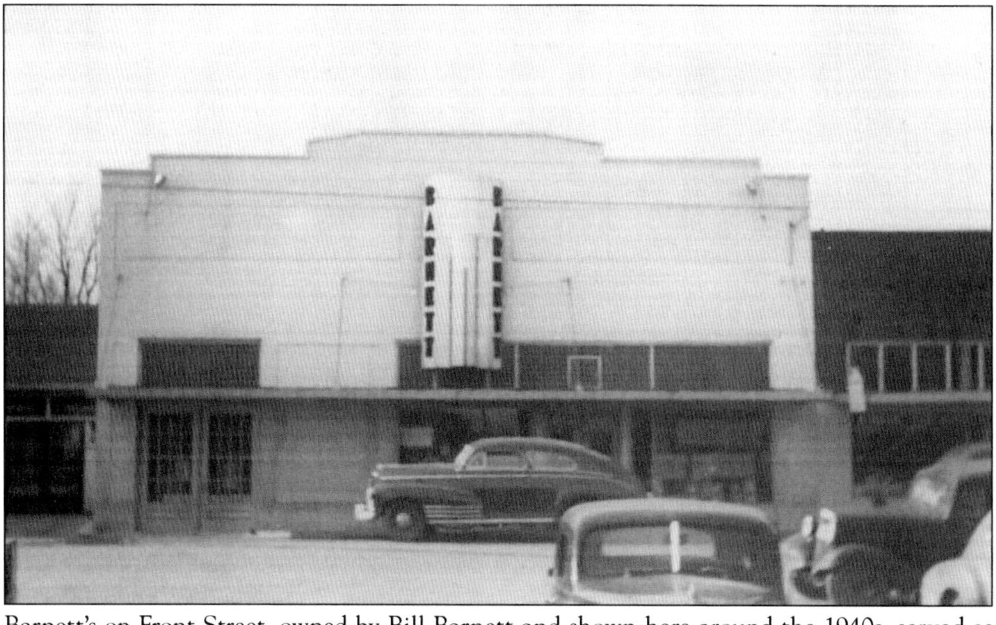

Barnett's on Front Street, owned by Bill Barnett and shown here around the 1940s, served as cold storage for people who did not have a freezer at home. Later, the building served as a Bi-Rite Supermarket owned by Thurman Francis. To the right of the building is Moore's Market, and to the left is a tavern known as the Snakepit. (Courtesy of the Sam Davis Memorial Association.)

Two

Business and Industry

Smyrna's business origins began when the Nashville & Chattanooga Railroad claimed the area next to the Smyrna Presbyterian Church for its new rail station. The land was near waterways, and because it was flat it was perfect for rail lines.

After the lines were set, people began moving to the area in droves to set up farms. Land was cheap, and the soil was fertile. Corn, wheat, and cotton grew abundantly. Until emancipation, most of the laborers were enslaved African Americans. In 1860, all of Rutherford County had 1,644 farms, with a portion of them in Smyrna. By 1920, the county had 5,264 farms, but by 1950 there were only 3,672. The cotton gins disappeared, and large machinery took their place.

Businesses were spurred by the arrival of the Dixie Highway and Air Force base in the early and mid-1900s. By the 1950s, local hot spots such as Goodall Clinic, Barnett Furniture Company, Gil's Supermarket, Smyrna Dairy Dip, and Smyrna Pan-Am Service popped up. The early 1980s saw further industrial growth when Nissan North America selected the town to host a new manufacturing plant. Nearby airports and a large workforce encouraged many companies to set up shop in Smyrna, including Taylor Farms, Asurion, and Vi-Jon. Today, the town combines agriculture with industry as it continues to grow and prosper.

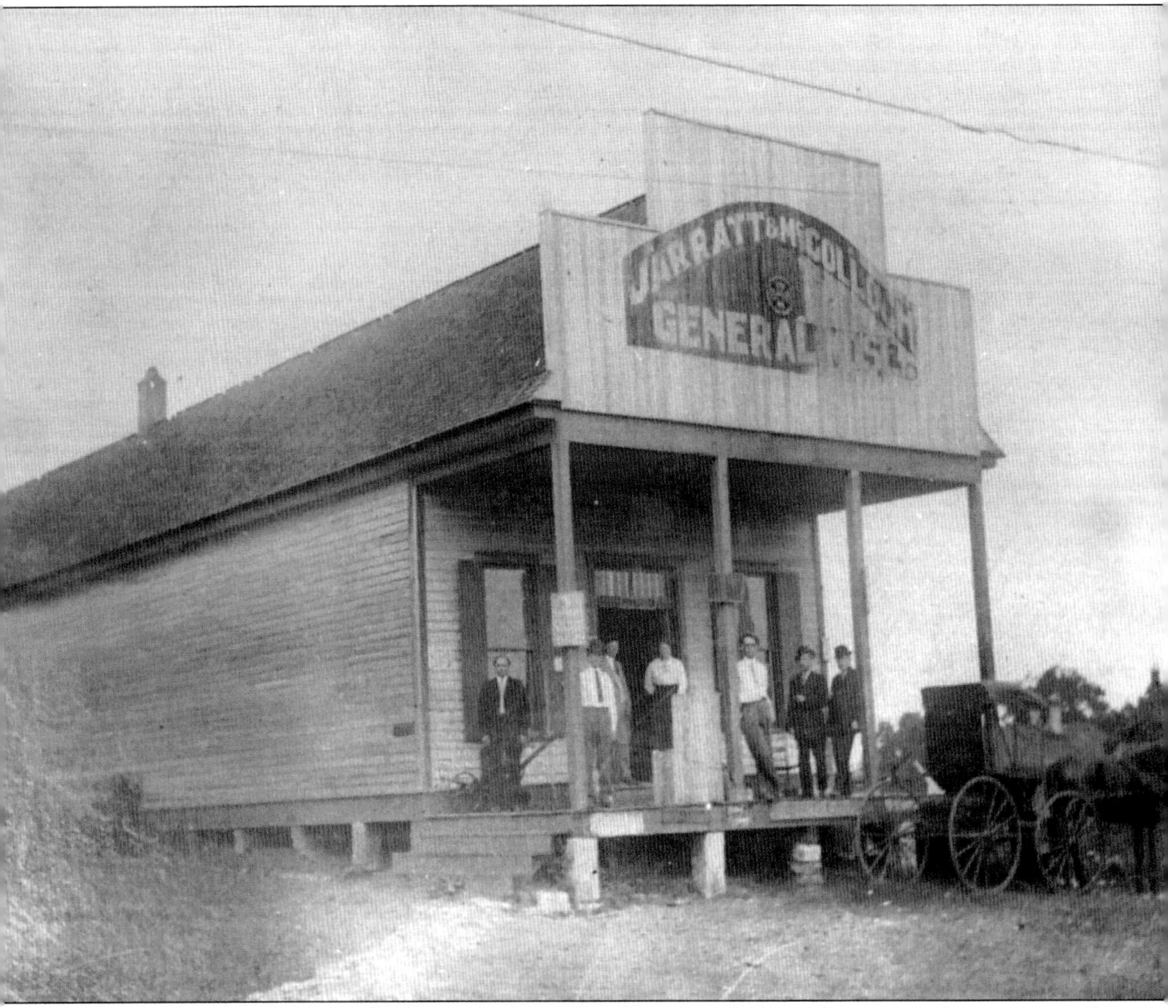

This is Jarratt and McColloch General Merchandise around 1900. The earliest known general store in Smyrna was opened prior to the Civil War by Maj. Houston Dudley. In 1885, the store was purchased by the Jarratt brothers: Dudley and Will. In 1908, the business became known as Jarratt and McColloch after Bob McColloch bought a half interest in the store. It went out of business in the late 1920s, and the building burned down in 1930. (Courtesy of Shacklett's Photography.)

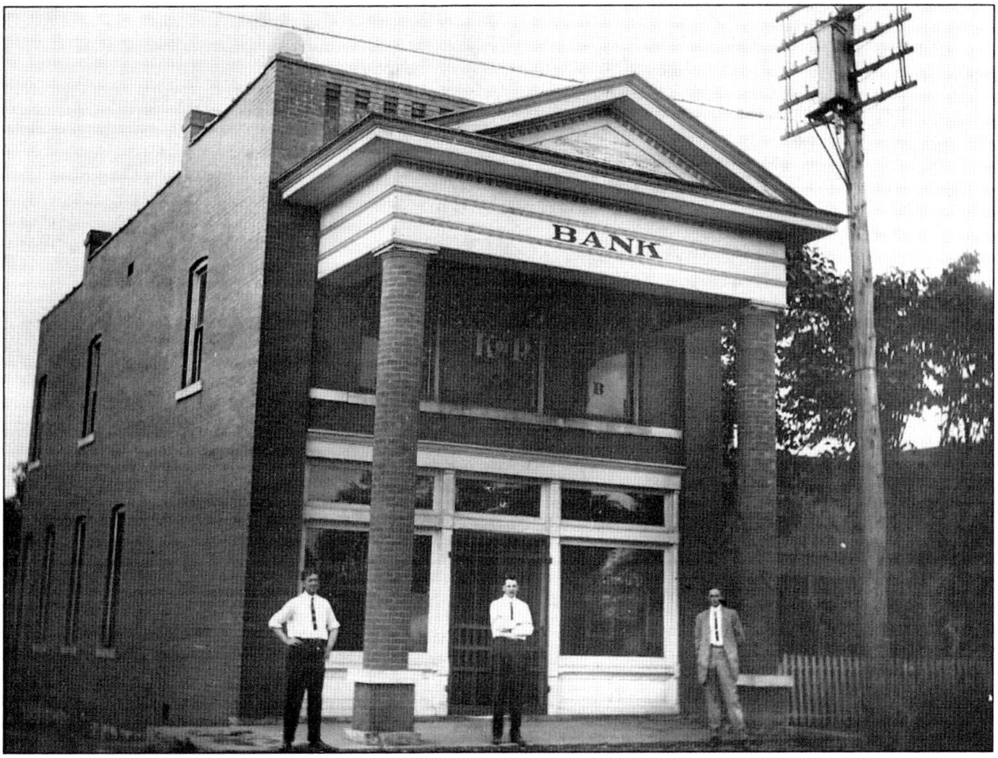

From left to right, Silas Hudson, Jack Ewing, and Jack Batey stand in front of the First National Bank in Smyrna in 1911. The Bank of Smyrna opened in 1904; in 1910, a new building was constructed, and the name was changed to First National Bank the following year. (Courtesy of Shacklett's Photography.)

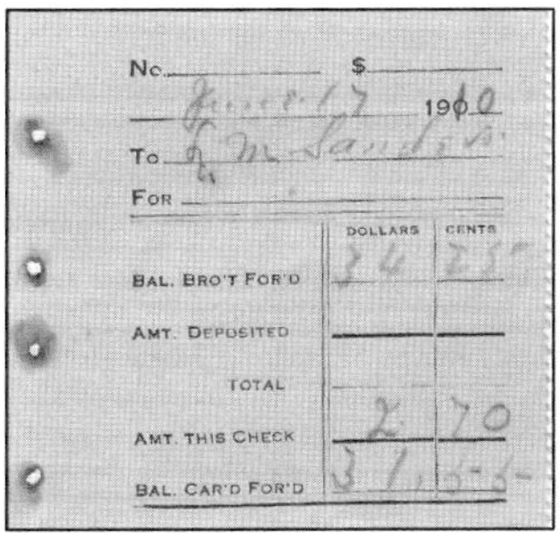

No. $

190

To

For

	DOLLARS	CENTS
BAL. BRO'T FOR'D		
AMT. DEPOSITED		
TOTAL		
AMT. THIS CHECK		
BAL. CAR'D FOR'D		

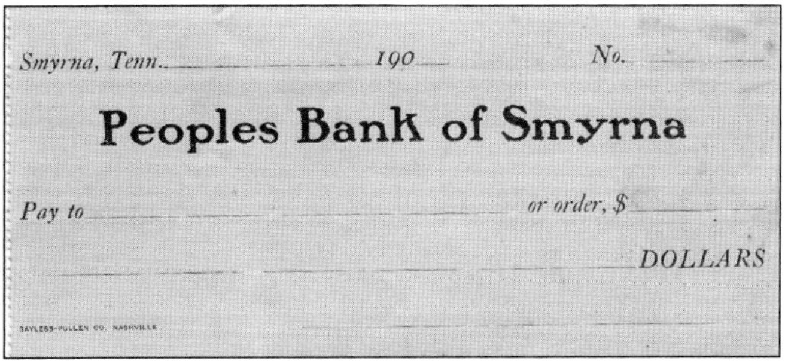

Smyrna, Tenn. 190 *No.*

Peoples Bank of Smyrna

Pay to *or order,* $

DOLLARS

BAYLESS-PULLEN CO. NASHVILLE

This deposit form and slip are from the Peoples Bank of Smyrna. In the early 1900s, the Bank of Smyrna opened and was the only bank in the area. In 1908, it changed its name to the Peoples Bank of Smyrna, and two years later it expanded to finally allow a walk-in vault and lockboxes. These would have been in place in the bank when the deposit, shown here, was made in June 1910 by L.M. Sanders. (Courtesy of Smyrna Public Library.)

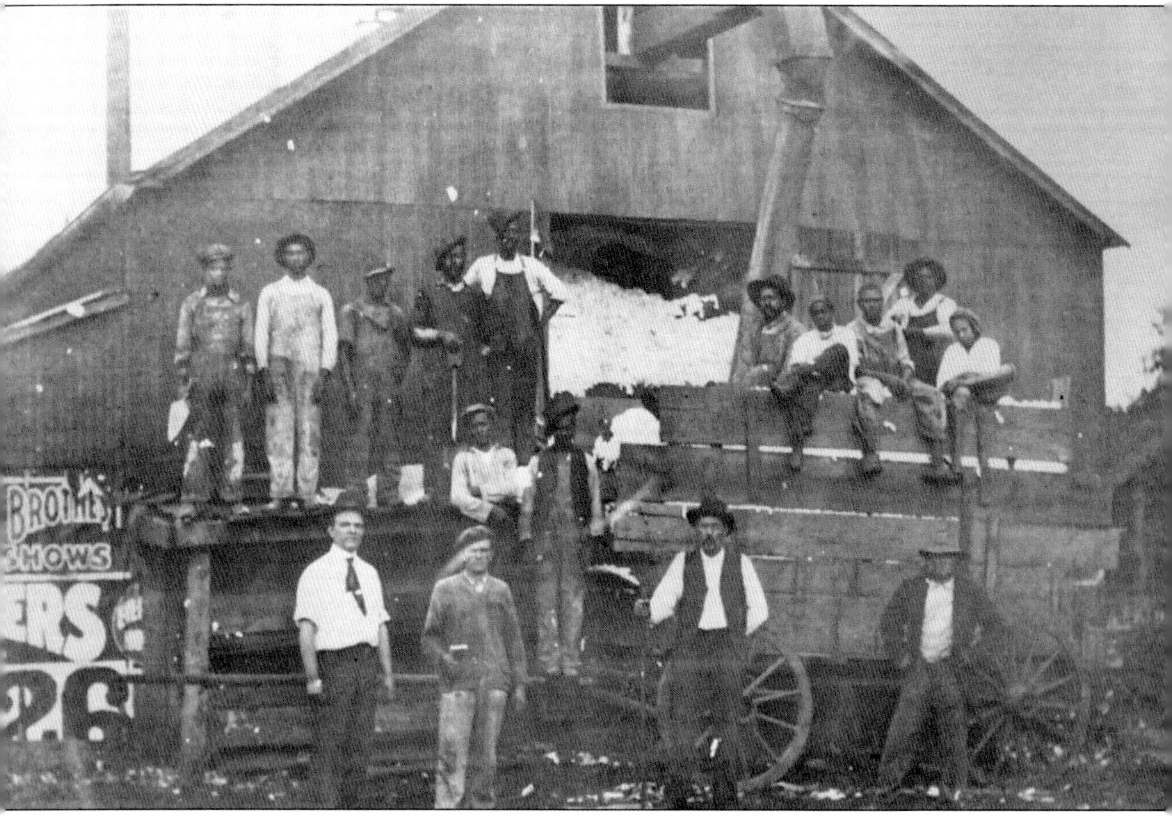

This c. 1915 photograph shows men outside the S.E. Hager cotton gin. Huger built this cotton gin in 1882, and it stayed in business until the late 1920s. (Courtesy of Shacklett's Photography.)

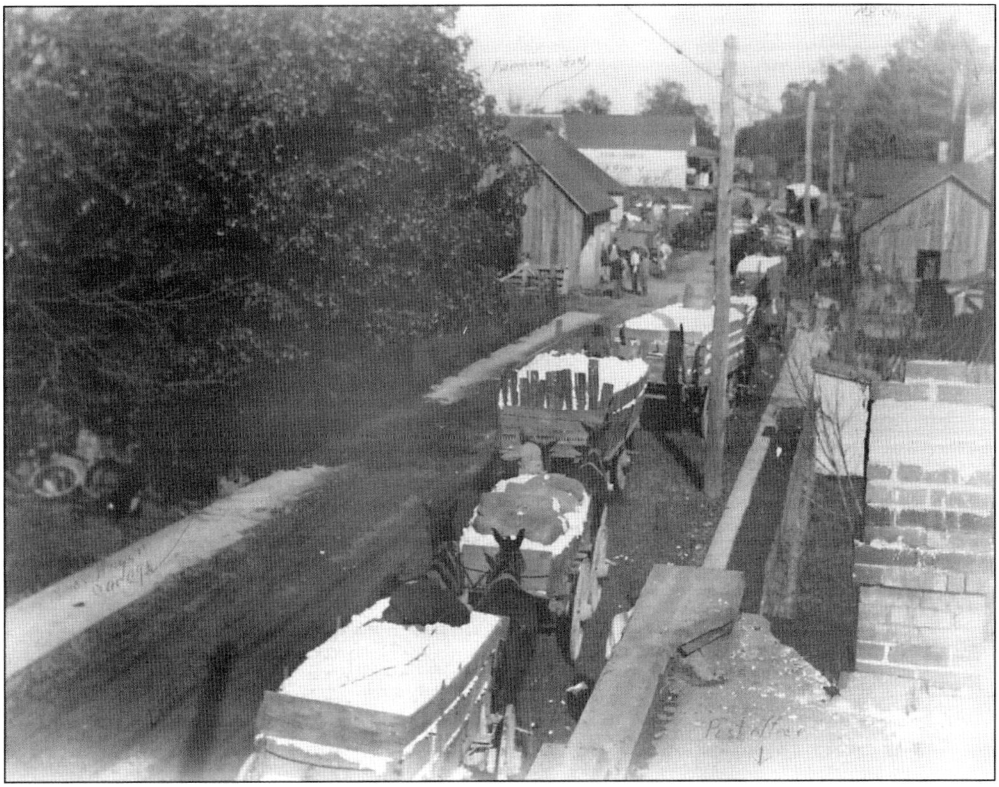

These wagons full of cotton are making their way to S.E. Hager's cotton gin around 1920. Hager was born in November 1851. One of his first jobs was working in a local general store before opening the S.E. Hager General Merchandise Store. (Courtesy of Shacklett's Photography.)

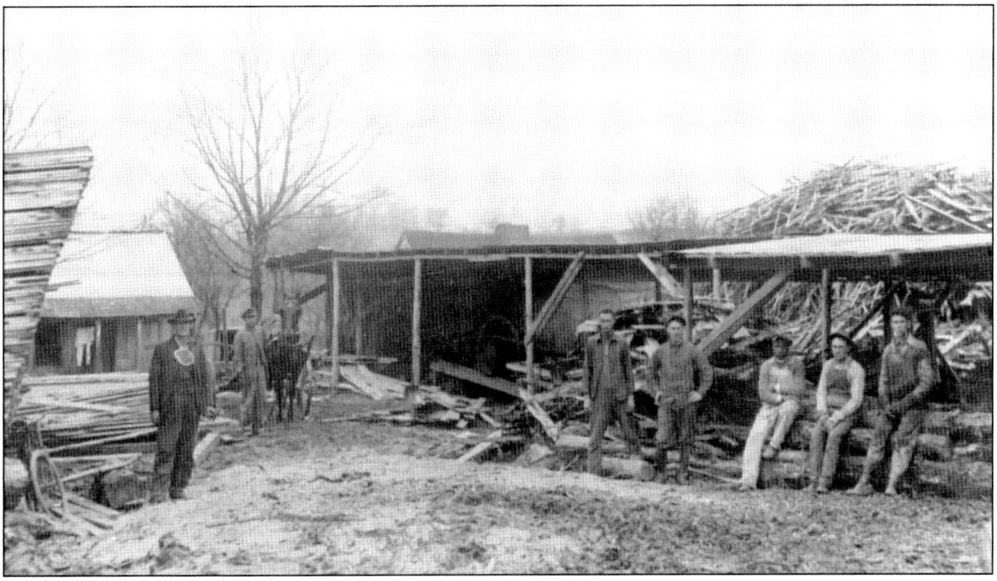

E.E. Nance opened a lumberyard in Smyrna on Hazelwood Drive in 1918. This c. 1920 photograph shows several men taking a break from work. In the 1920s, Nance moved the lumberyard to Madison Street. (Courtesy of Shacklett's Photography.)

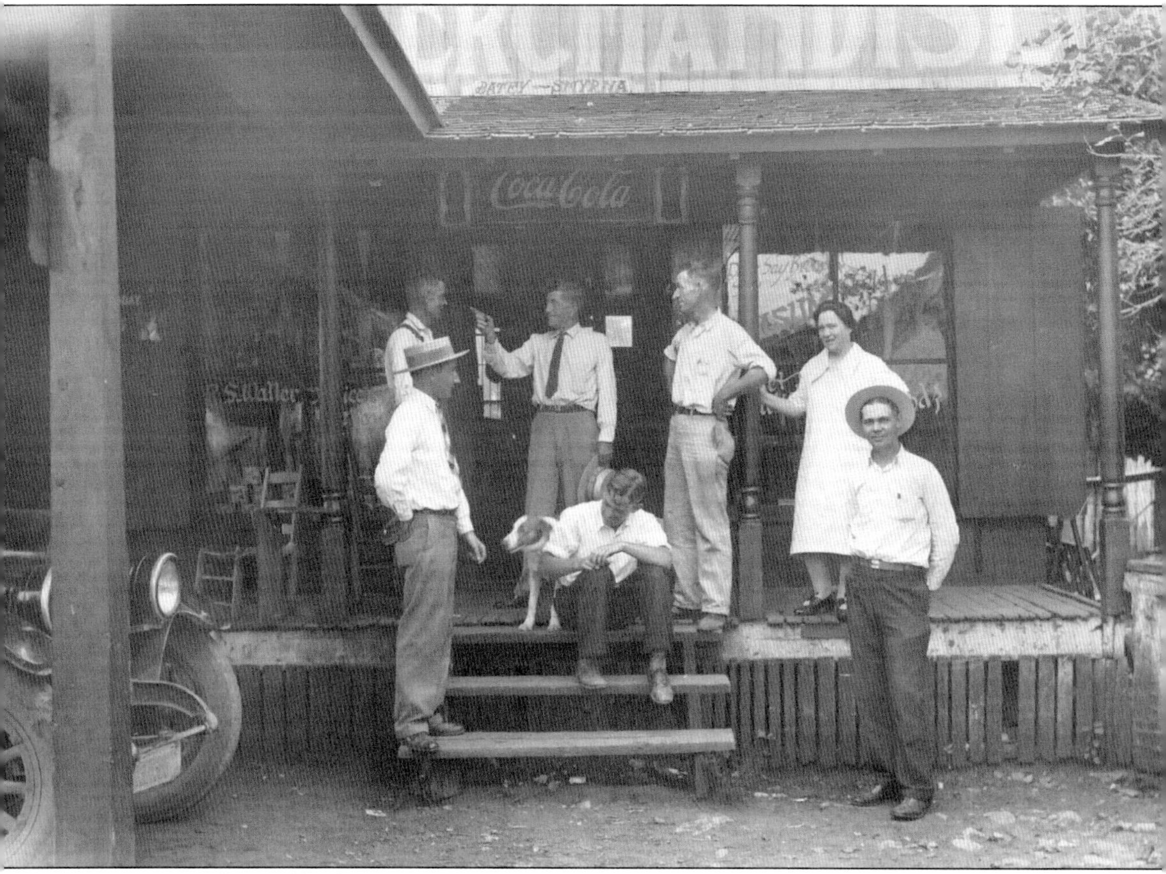

Sidney Waller and his brother Claiborne opened the Waller Bros. and King Mercantile Store in Jefferson, the town neighboring Smyrna. In 1930, Sam Hall took over operations. In this 1920 photograph, R.S. "Sidney" Waller stands under the Coca-Cola sign, and Claiborne Waller is on the right next to his wife, Ollie. Howard, sitting in front of Sidney, and Everett, standing in front of Ollie, are the children of Claiborne and Ollie. (Courtesy of Rutherford County Archives.)

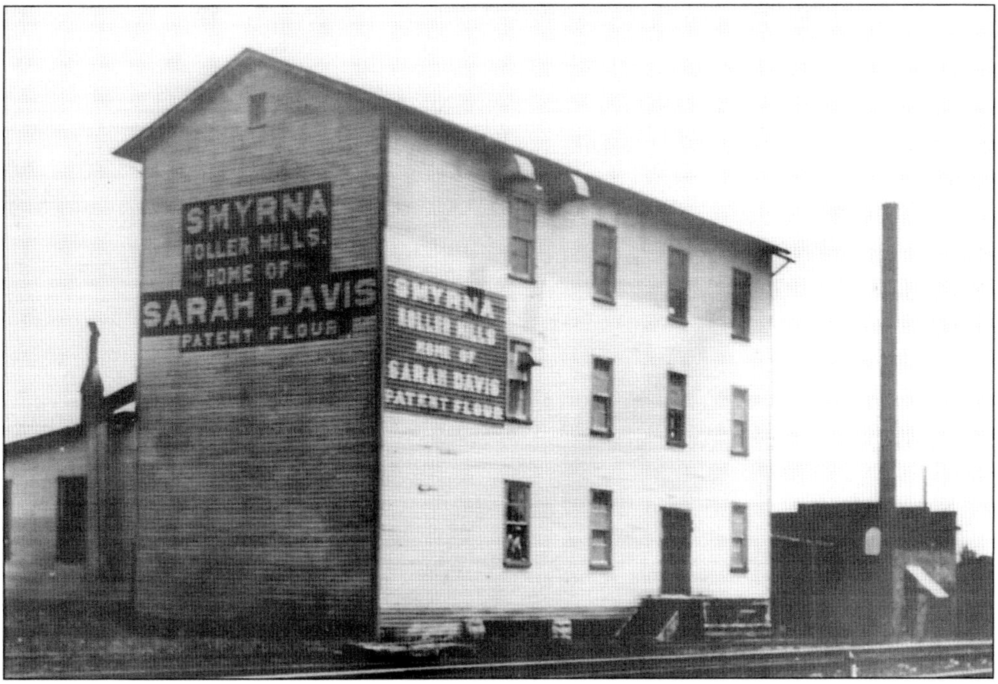

The Sarah Davis Flour Mill began operation in the early 1900s in downtown Smyrna near Lowry Street. Robert Davis took over a mill from his father, William Davis, who was the half brother to the famous Sam Davis. By the early 1900s, Robert and a relative built the Davis Roller Mills, where Sarah Davis Flour was sold in bags with a picture of Robert's daughter Sarah on the front. (Courtesy of the Sam Davis Memorial Association.)

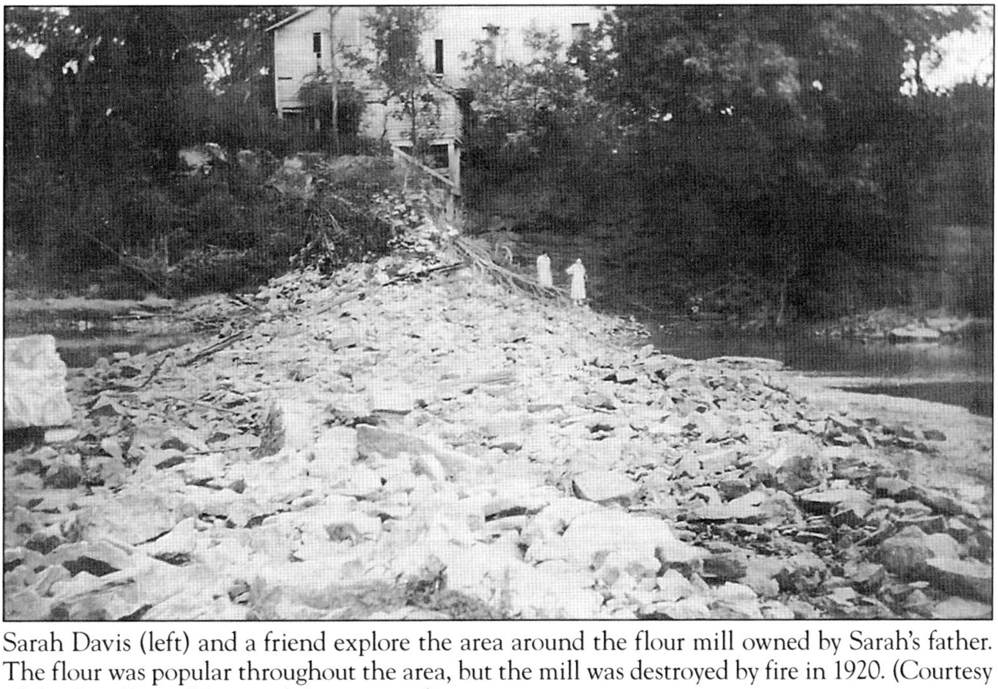

Sarah Davis (left) and a friend explore the area around the flour mill owned by Sarah's father. The flour was popular throughout the area, but the mill was destroyed by fire in 1920. (Courtesy of the Sam Davis Memorial Association.)

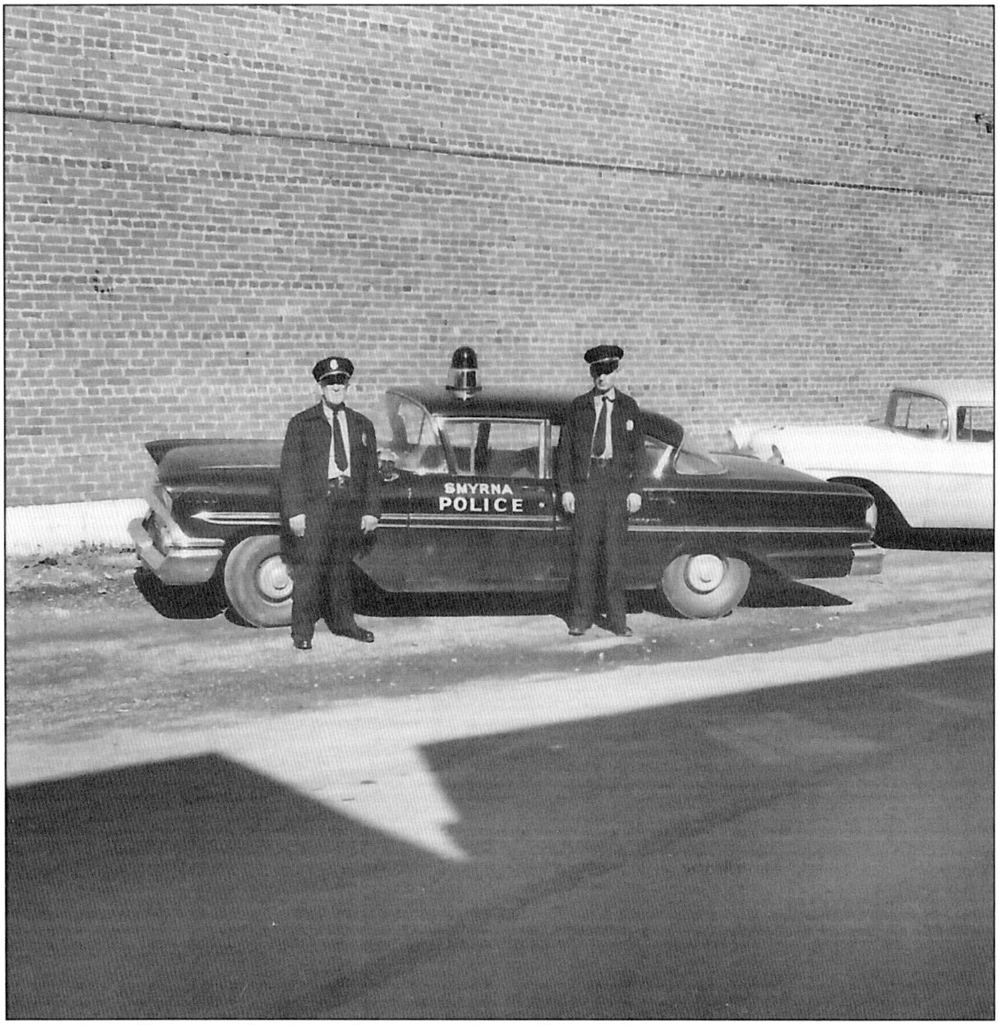

Two police officers stand in front of the town's first official police car in December 1957. (Courtesy of John Moore.)

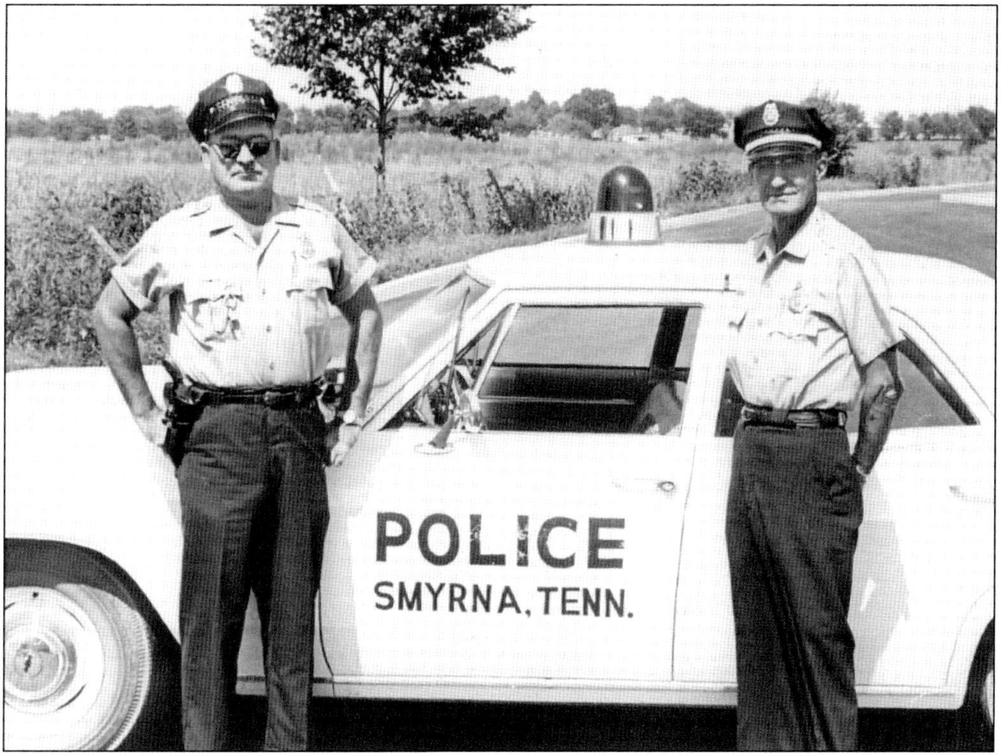

New patrolman William R. Baty (left) stands beside one of Smyrna's police cars before going on patrol with Harry Beddingfield in August 1965. Baty joined the force on August 1, 1965, and Beddingfield had recently been promoted to assistant police chief. (Courtesy of Smyrna Public Library.)

Chief Joyner (left) and Officer Westmoreland look over a report in the mid-1960s. Chief Robert Joyner was originally from West Tennessee but moved to the area and served as the town's police chief for several years. (Courtesy of Smyrna Public Library.)

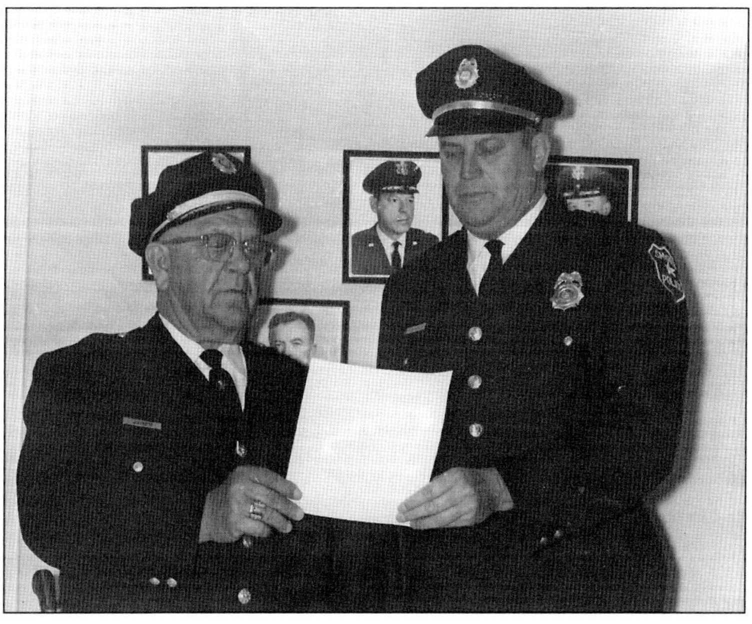

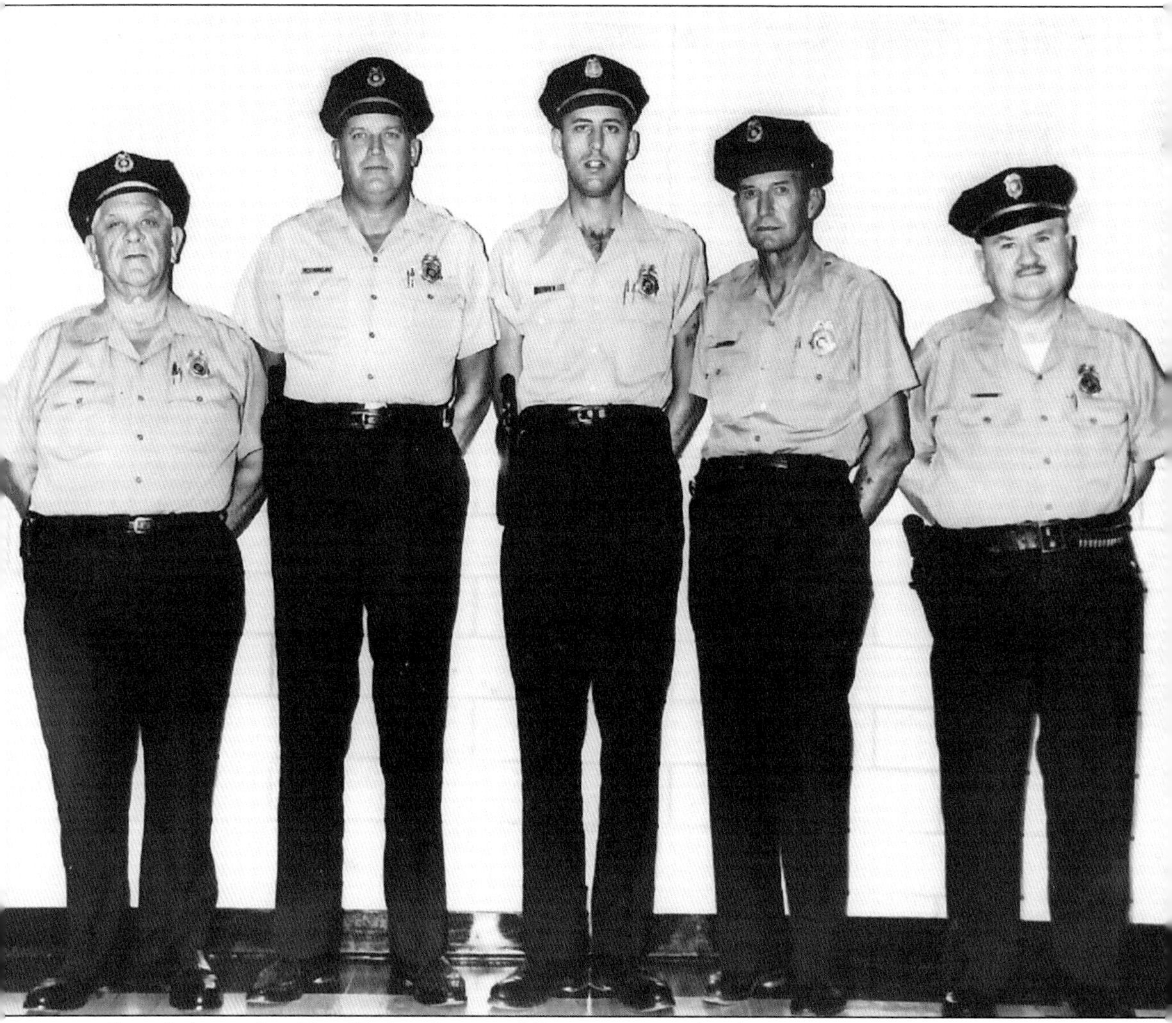

From left to right, Chief Robert Joyner, Officer Westmoreland, "Preacher" Lee, unidentified, and Officer Morrison pose for a photograph in the mid-1960s. These men worked as Smyrna policemen, patrolling the streets for miscreants. (Courtesy of Smyrna Public Library.)

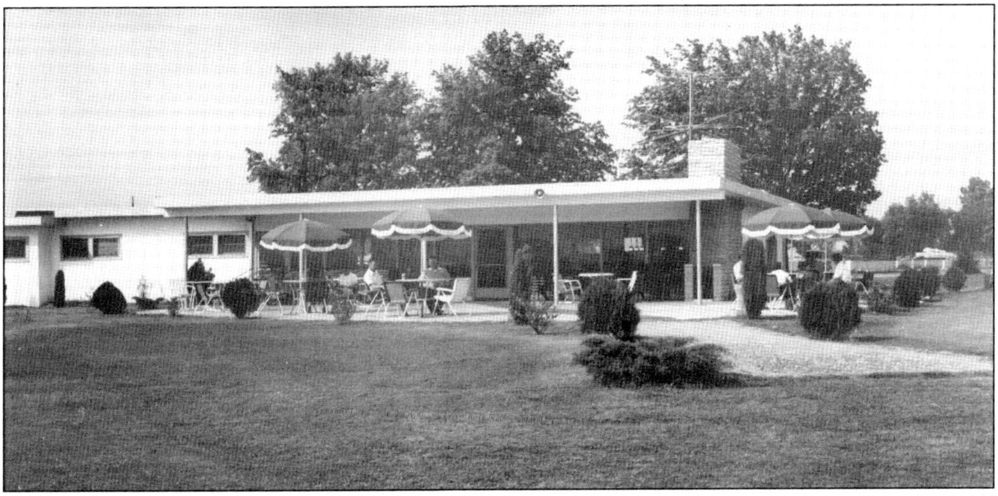

A few men enjoy a beautiful day at the Smyrna Golf Course clubhouse in the 1960s. The golf course was built by Sewart Air Force Base in the late 1940s and had nine holes. Nine more holes were added in the 1950s, and this building was used as the clubhouse until 1986 when a new one was built. (Courtesy of Smyrna Golf Course.)

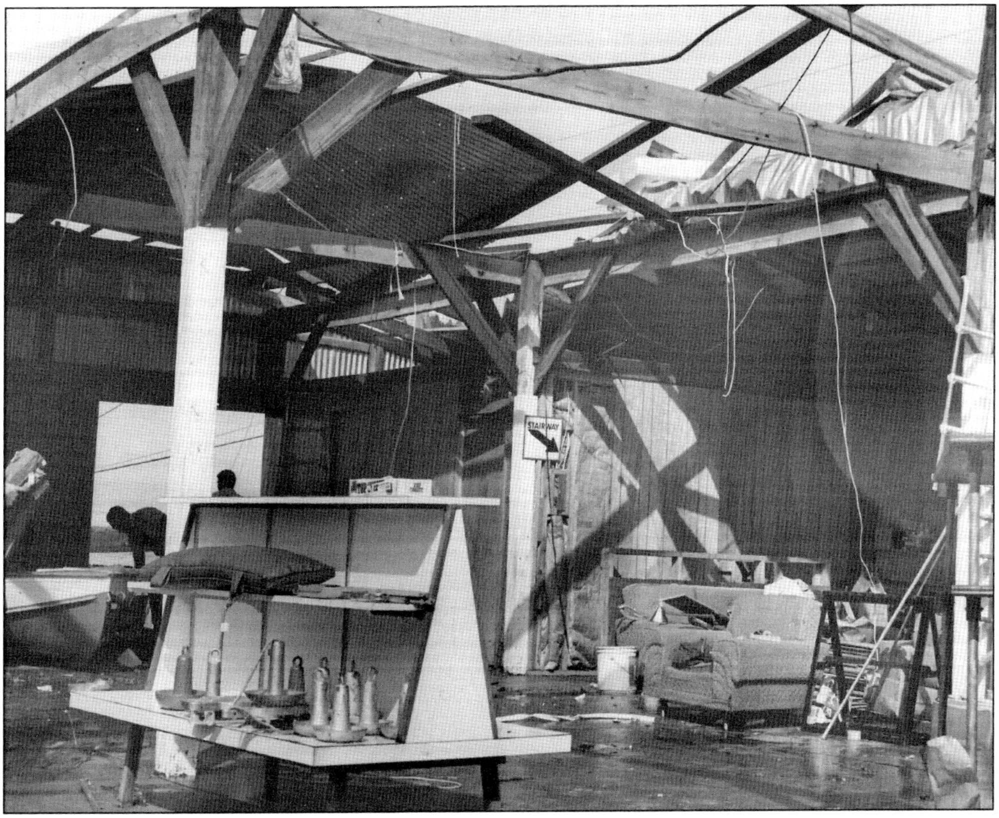

Strong winds ripped the roof off the Sportsman's Grill on June 24, 1969. George Franklin's restaurant was not the only building damaged; several houses along Avondale, Belaire, Clearview, McNickle, and Prindle Streets were also affected. A number of people reported a small twister that moved from west to east. (Courtesy of Smyrna Public Library.)

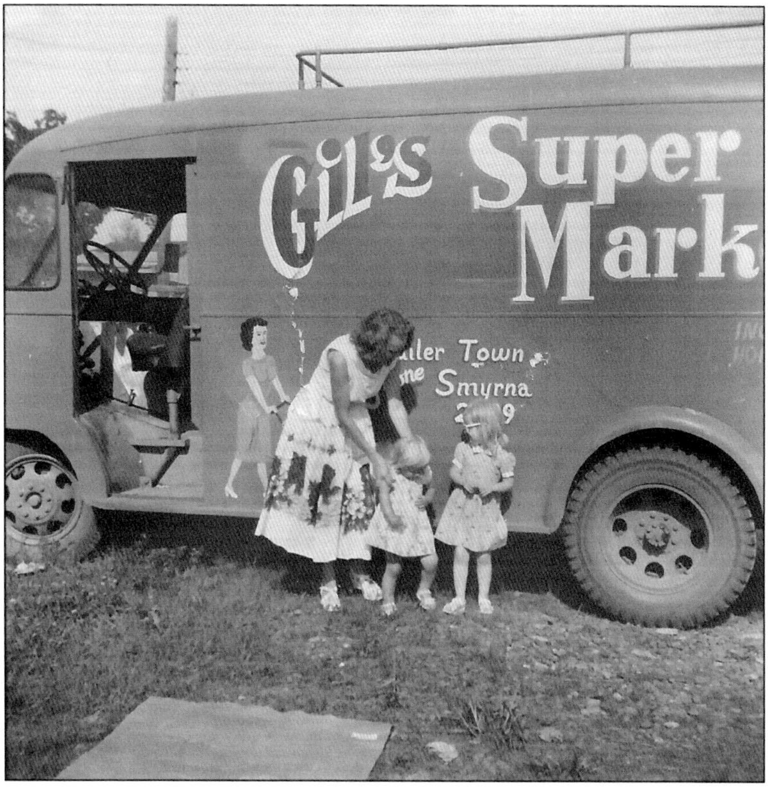

In May 1956, Mavis "Rusty" Olerud readies her daughters Candy (center) and Ginny in front of the family's grocery store delivery truck. The Olerud family owned Gil's Supermarket, the first supermarket in Smyrna. (Courtesy of Ginny Williams.)

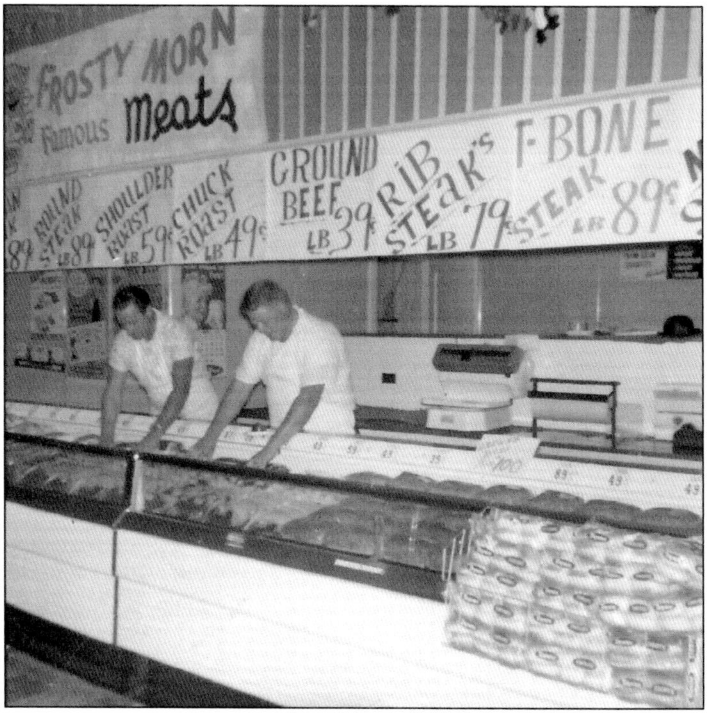

Marvin Barrett (right) and a fellow meat cutter stock the counter for a big meat sale at Gil's Supermarket, then located at the corner of Sam Davis Road (now Sam Ridley Parkway) and Jefferson Pike. Note the August 1961 prices for T-bone steak at 89¢ per pound and ground beef at 39¢ per pound. Later, owner Gilbert Olerud took out advertisements in local papers promoting the meat and launched "Round-Up Days," in which the store clerks dressed in Western outfits. (Courtesy of Ginny Williams.)

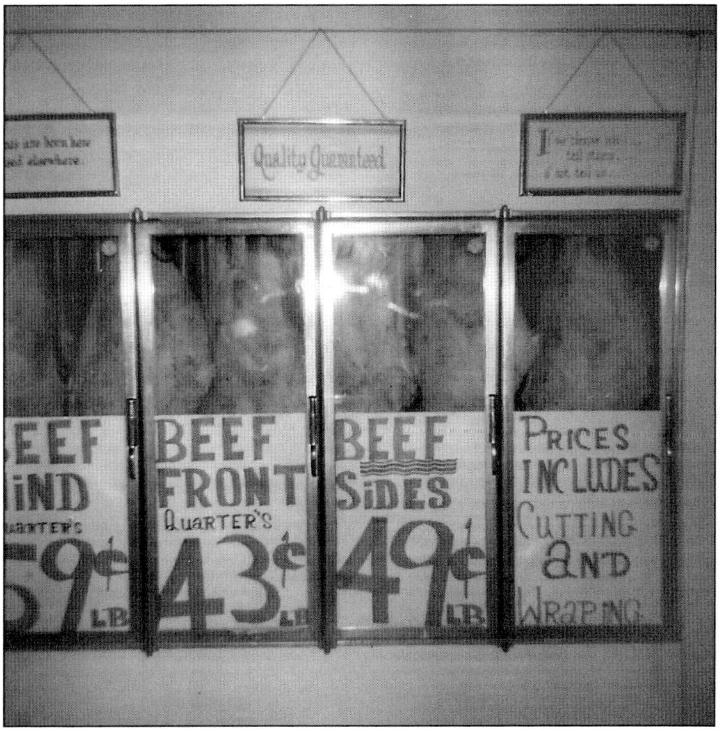

Customers who visited Gil's Supermarket were able to select the best-quality meat. Gil put his meat on display, as shown in this 1961 photograph of meat hanging inside the freezer. A few of the signs in the store read, "Prices are born here and raised elsewhere," "If we please you . . . tell others . . . if not, tell us," and "Quality Guaranteed." (Courtesy of Ginny Williams.)

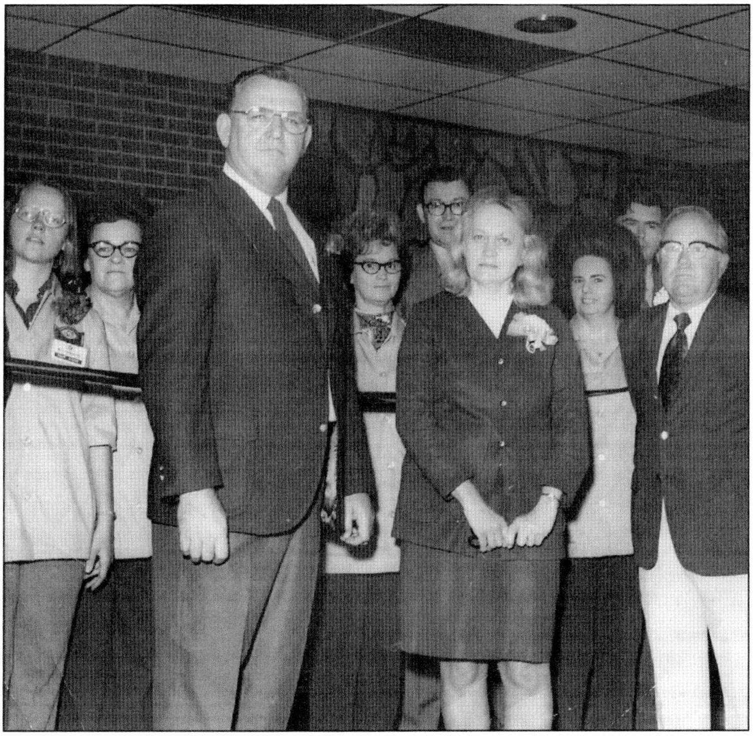

Gilbert Olerud (front left) opened Gilsville Family Center in 1972 and gave away a new car at the grand opening. In this photograph, Gil and Mavis Olerud (front center) and Mayor Sam Ridley (front right) prepare to cut the ribbon for the grand opening. The clerk in the back left is the Oleruds' daughter Candy. (Courtesy of Ginny Williams.)

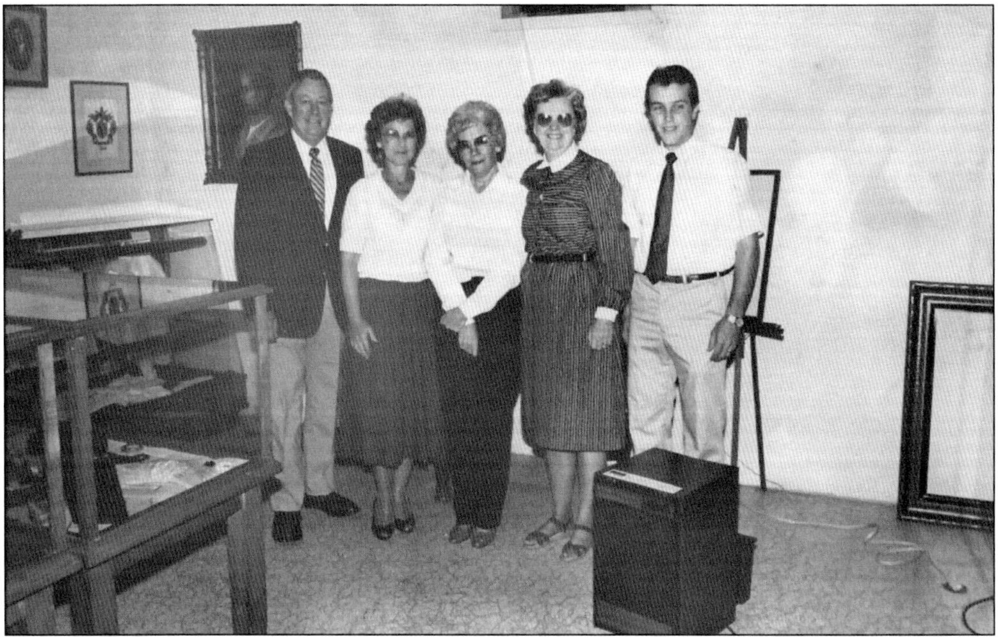

The Sam Davis Home had limited museum space but made the most of what was available. Katherine Walkup (second from the right) worked tirelessly throughout her life to promote the historic site. (Courtesy of the Sam Davis Memorial Association.)

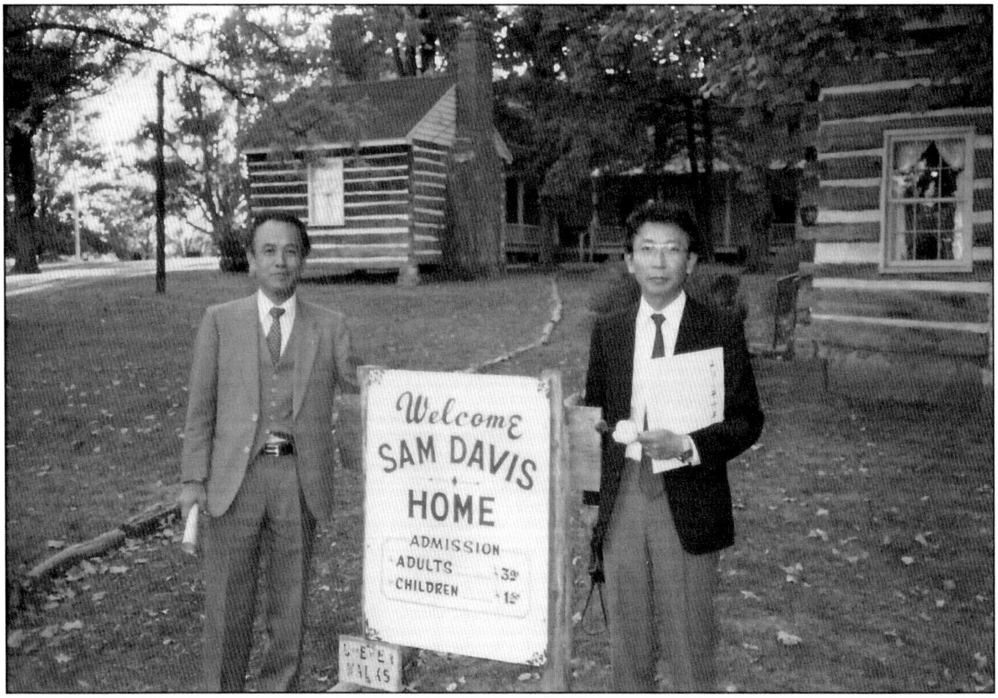

With Nissan building a plant in Smyrna in 1984, several Japanese families moved to the area. In order to get to know the area better, many visited the Sam Davis Home. During this 1987 tour, the admission was $3 for adults and $1.50 for children, and the museum was housed in the building on the right. (Courtesy of the Sam Davis Memorial Association.)

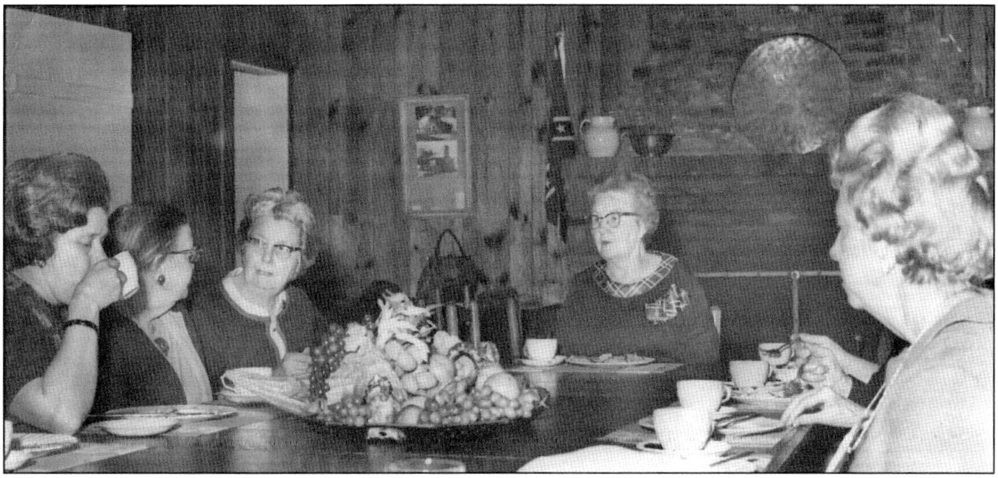

The United Daughters of the Confederacy met often Jane Simmons Tea Room at the Sam Davis Home to discuss club matters. The Smyrna chapter was organized in December 1927, and the women first met at Mrs. Allen Gooch's residence. They voted to name the chapter the Sam Davis Home Chapter. The club moved its meetings to the Jane Simmons Tea Room after a year and sponsored many pageants for the historic home, including the popular play *Son of This House*, written by member Adeline King. (Courtesy of the Smyrna Public Library.)

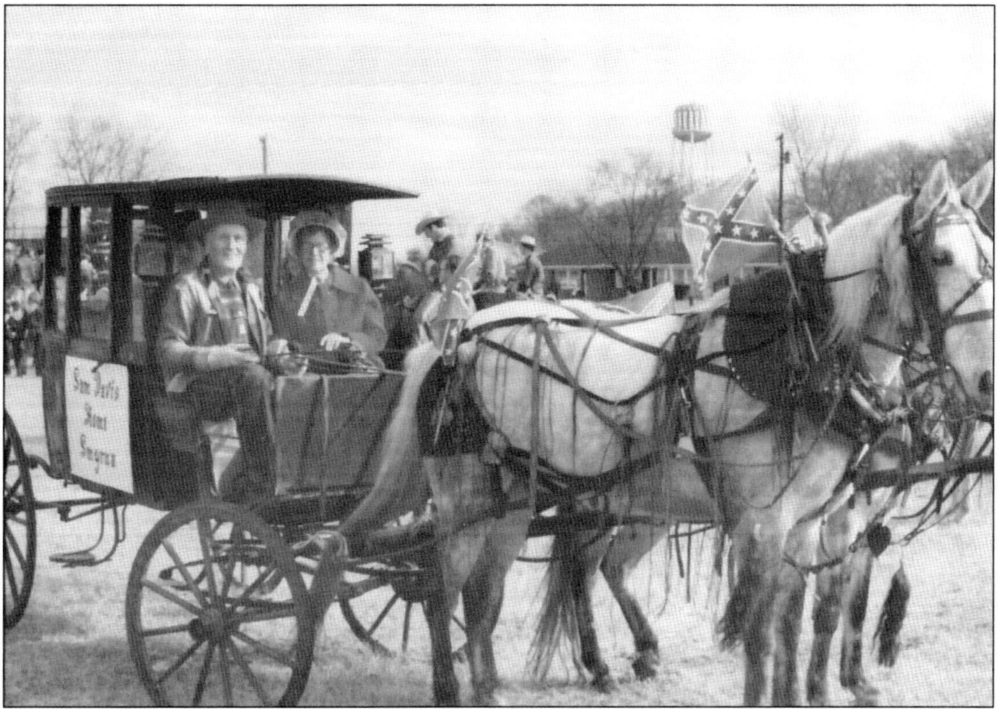

The Sam Davis Home staff, volunteers, and board kept active in the community. In this 1977 parade, the Sam Davis Home shows its spirit with a reproduction wagon. (Courtesy of the Sam Davis Memorial Association.)

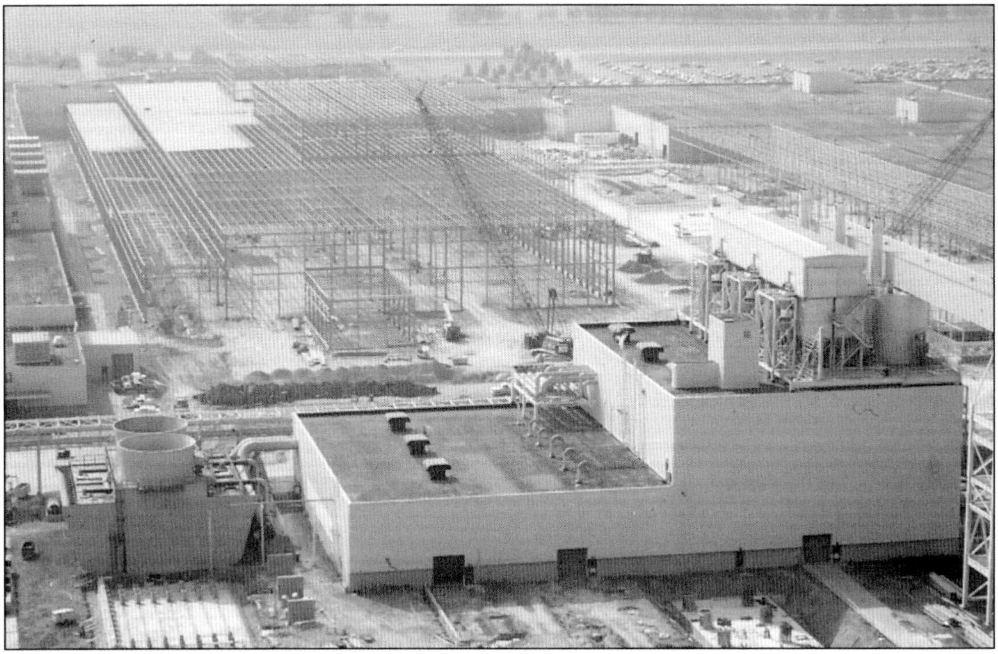

Nissan North America broke ground on the Smyrna plant in February 1981, with Marvin Runyon as president and chief executive officer of the company. Middle Tennessee's affordable labor, transportation networks, location, and right-to-work laws enticed the company to locate in Smyrna. The building spans over 5.9 million square feet. By 2013, it had a workforce of over 7,000 and was able to produce 550,000 vehicles annually. (Courtesy of Shacklett's Photography.)

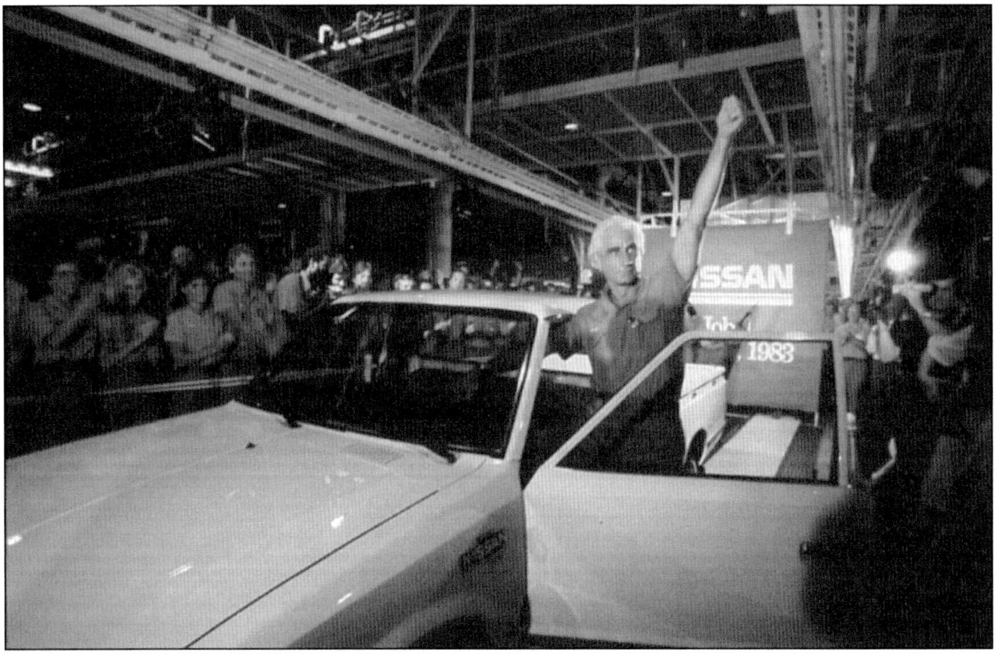

Marvin Runyon, then president and chief executive officer of Nissan Motor Manufacturing Corp. USA, and Nissan employees celebrate the start of vehicle production in Smyrna in June 1983. (Courtesy of Nissan North America, Smyrna.)

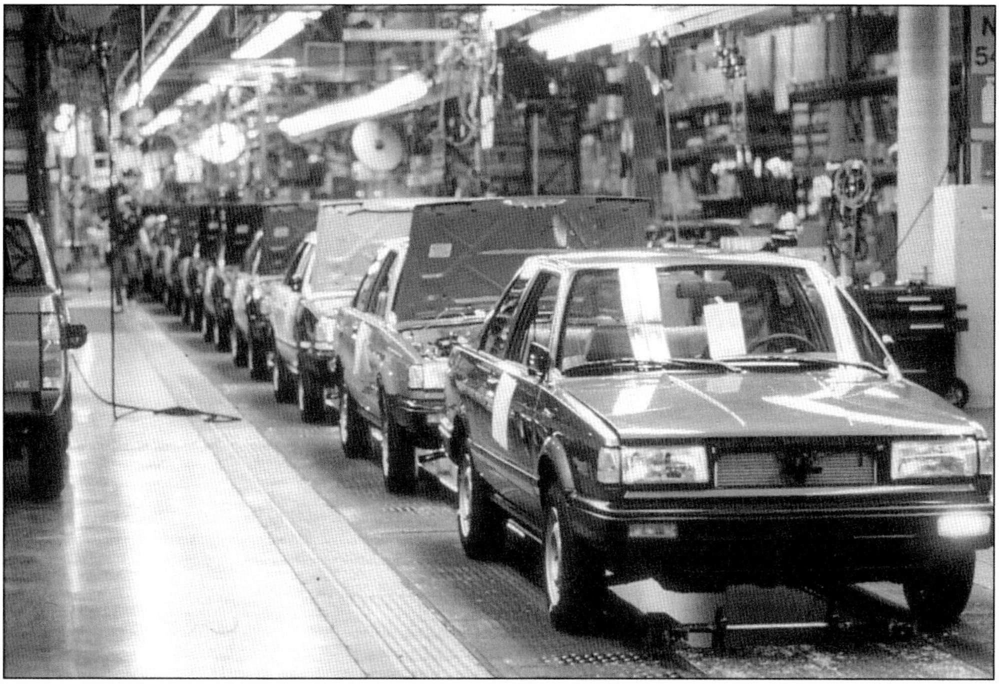

The Nissan plant in Smyrna became well known for Sentra production and also built the Altima, Maxima, Pathfinder, Infinity, and Rogue. In 2013, production of Nissan's first mass-produced, all-electric car, the LEAF, began. (Courtesy of Shacklett's Photography.)

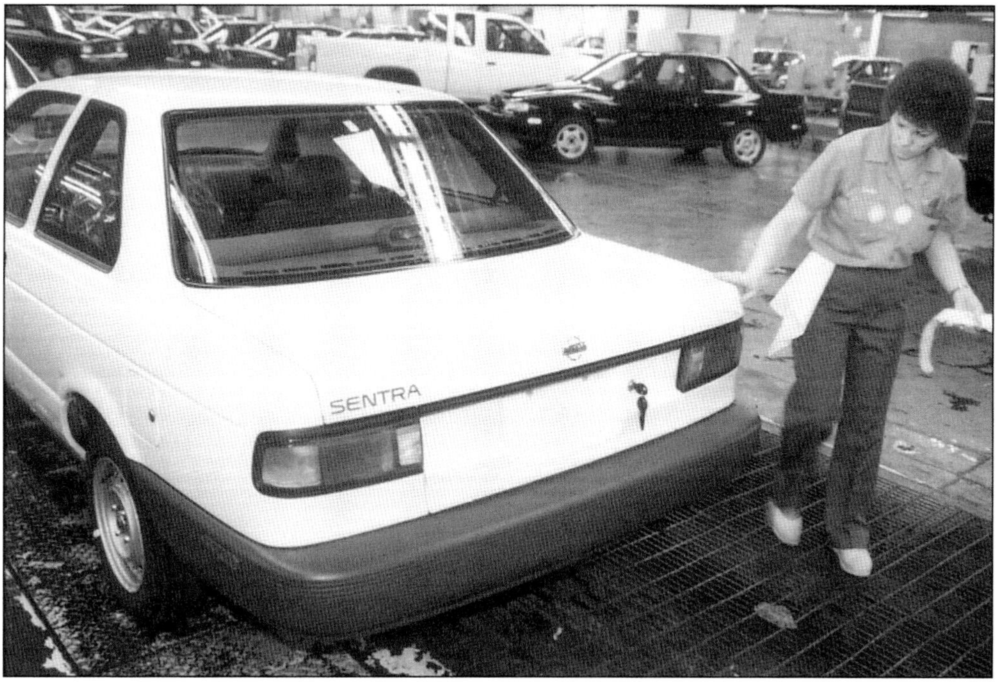

An employee works on the Nissan Sentra in a late-1980s photograph. Production of this car began in March 1985, the first passenger car produced in the United States by Nissan. (Courtesy of Shacklett's Photography.)

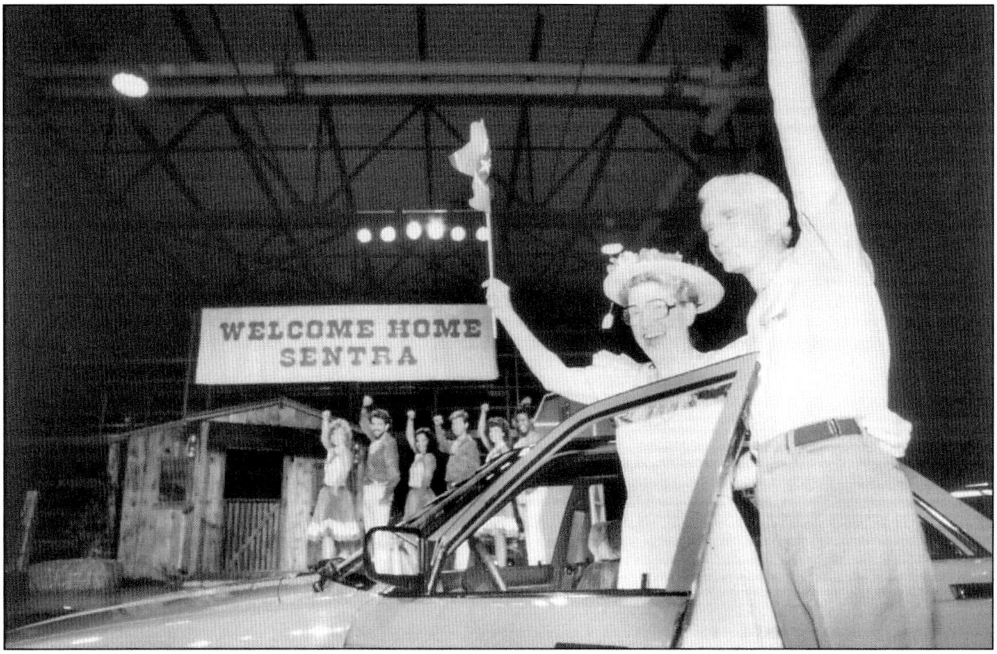

Nissan Motor Manufacturing Corp. USA president and chief executive officer Marvin Runyon poses with Minnie Pearl during Tennessee Homecoming in 1986. This statewide event was organized by Gov. Lamar Alexander; Pearl served as an ambassador for the campaign. (Courtesy of Shacklett's Photography.)

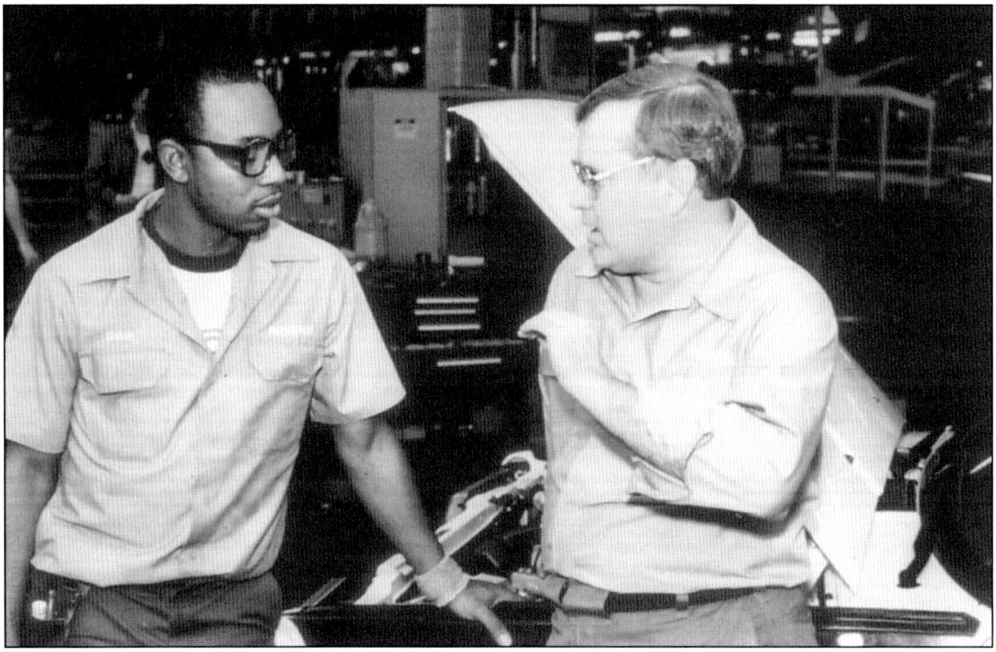

Jerry Benefield (right), chief executive officer and president of Nissan in 1987, is pictured with a supervisor. Benefield succeeded Runyon as president and chief executive officer when Runyon was appointed by Pres. Ronald Reagan to head the Tennessee Valley Authority. Both men had worked for Ford Motor Company prior to working for Nissan. (Courtesy of Shacklett's Photography.)

Three

School Days

Several one-room schools dotted the early Smyrna landscape, though few photographs of the structures or their pupils remain. Smyrna schools were operated by county boards of education by 1910. Florence School, Walnut Grove School, Cedar Grove School, Peru School, and Rock Springs were a few of the well-known teaching centers in the early part of the 1900s. Later schools included John Colemon Elementary, Thurman Francis Arts Academy, Rock Springs Middle, Smyrna Primary, and Smyrna High School.

Smyrna High School began in 1893 and was located where the present Smyrna Elementary School stands. It was modeled after the Webb School at Bell Buckle, Tennessee, a private school that was initially for boys only. In the early 1900s, a facility was built that included several classrooms, a music room, and a library. A new building was constructed in 1920 and was known as Smyrna "Rock School." The building had two wings, one for the upper grades and one for the lower grades, and an auditorium in the middle. In 1959, the younger students remained at the school while the older students moved to the new Smyrna High School on Hazelwood Drive. Rock School burned in 1976, and a new elementary school was built elsewhere.

In 1927, a Rosenwald School was built for African American students. It stood on Old Nashville Highway at an area known as the Hilltop community. Booker T. Washington joined efforts with philanthropist Julius Rosenwald to construct schools in rural areas of the South. Eventually, the pair would build over 5,000 schools. The Smyrna Rosenwald School had four rooms, one of which was a kitchen. By 1959, enrollment was at 185 students. A new Rosenwald School was built in 1960 with six classrooms, a principal's office, a teachers' lounge, a restroom, and a combination auditorium/cafeteria. By 1962, at least 237 students called this their school. It lasted only seven years before it was consolidated into another school during integration.

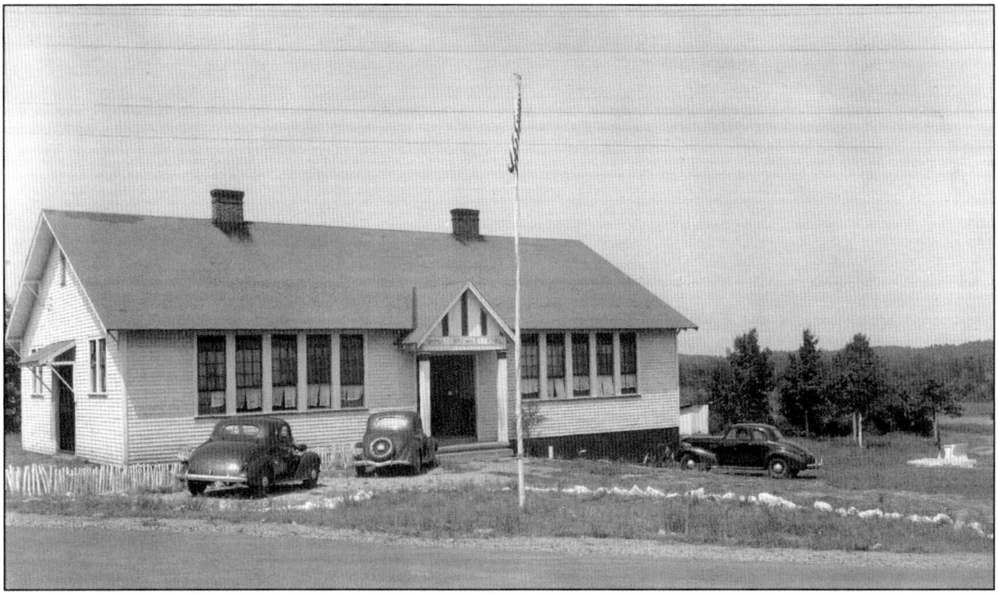

Julius Rosenwald began donating money for African American education in the first half of the 20th century. The Smyrna Rosenwald School was built in 1927 and had four rooms, including a kitchen. By 1959, enrollment reached 185 students from the surrounding community. The school is shown here in the 1940s, during which time it had 97 students and three teachers. This building stood until 1960, when a new school was built on a different site. (Courtesy of the Rutherford County Archives.)

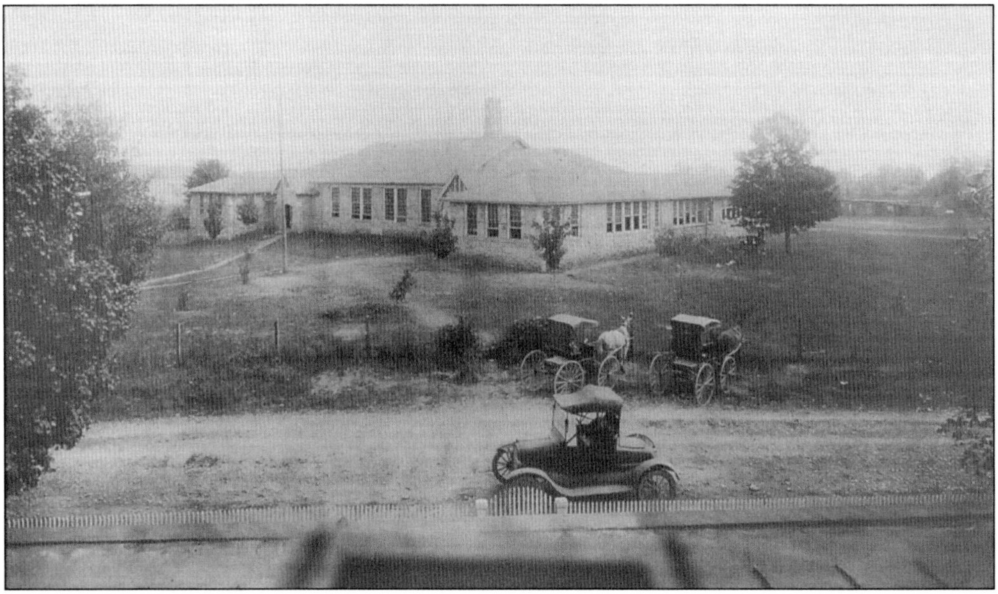

Smyrna residents sent their children to this school, known as Rock School. The building had an auditorium between two wings: the west wing contained four elementary classrooms, while the east wing contained six high school classrooms. A gymnasium was constructed in the 1920s, and the school was remodeled by the Works Progress Administration (WPA) in the 1930s. It burned in 1976, and the town decided to build its replacement elsewhere. (Courtesy of Rutherford County Archives.)

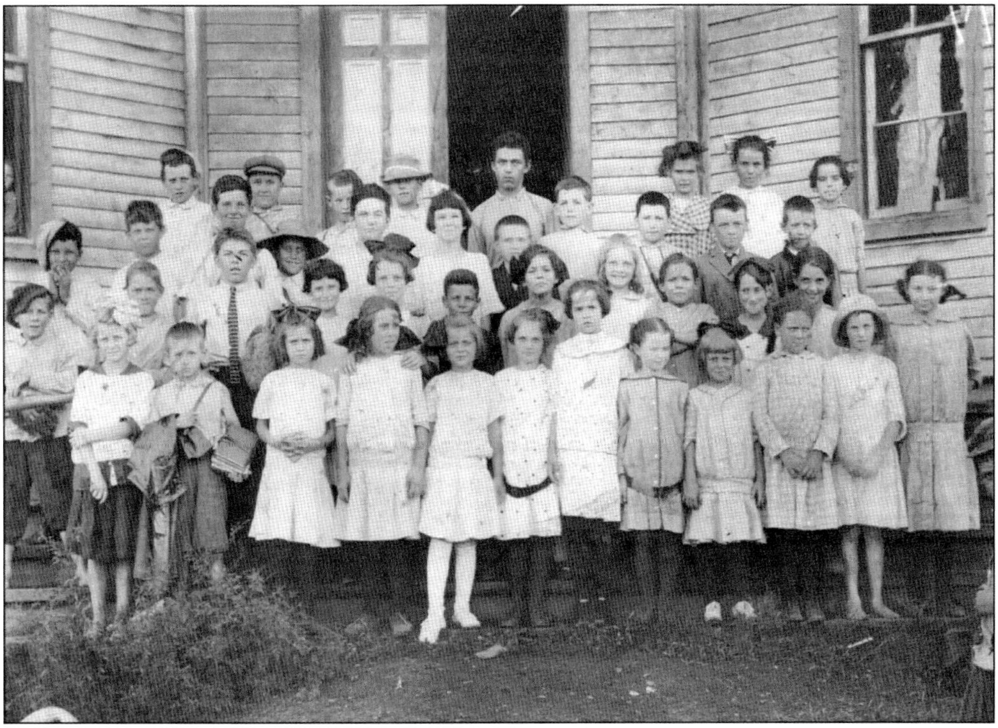

Both elementary and high school students attended Smyrna School until another building was constructed in 1920. This 1913 photograph shows the younger students in front of the school. Only a year earlier, the curriculum had introduced music, and a library had been added. (Courtesy of Smyrna Public Library.)

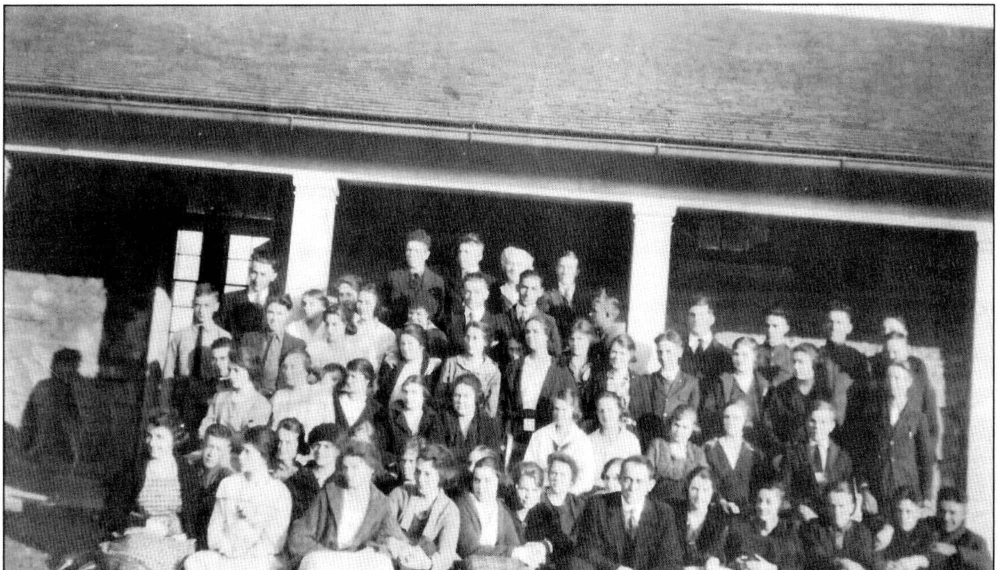

Smyrna High School students pose for a photograph in front of their school in 1920. This was the newly constructed Rock School, built after many local citizens donated $60,000 at the urging of Dr. J.S. Lowry, a prominent physician and leader in Smyrna. (Courtesy Smyrna Public Library.)

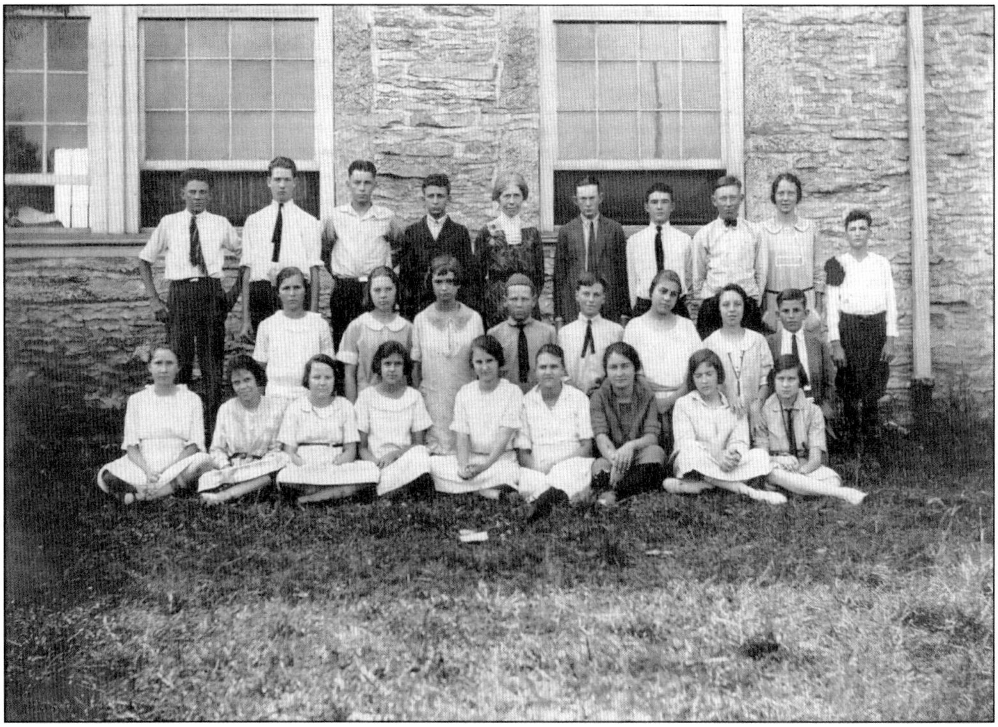

The seventh and eighth graders of Smyrna High School pose in front of the building in 1922. The school had four elementary classrooms and six high school classrooms, along with a music room, a library, and rooms for science experiments, home economics, and agriculture. (Courtesy of Smyrna Public Library.)

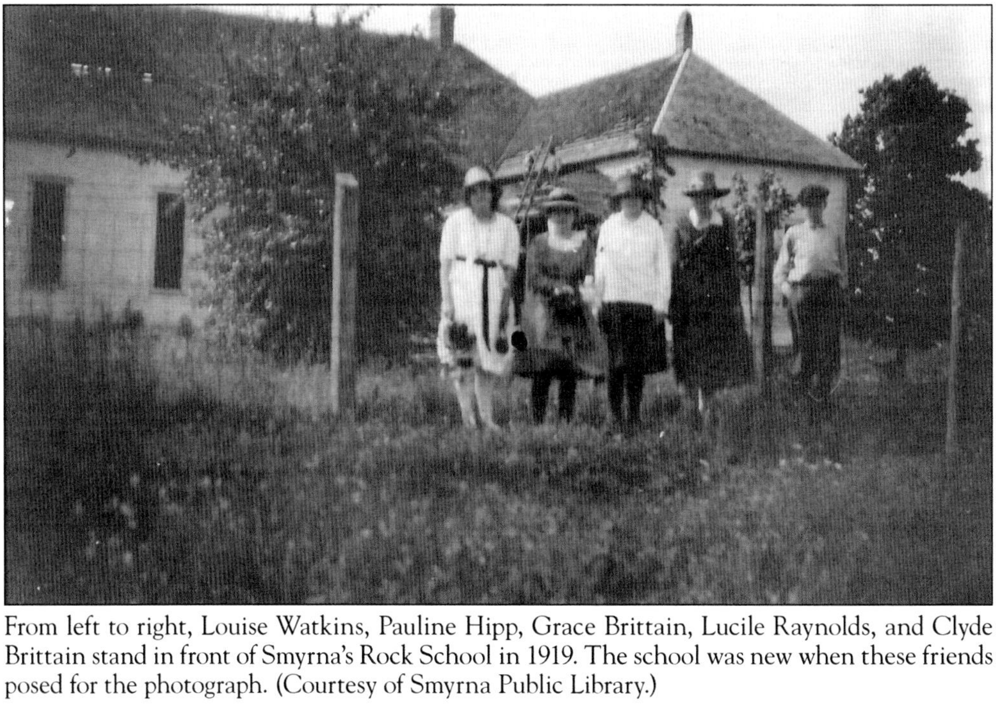

From left to right, Louise Watkins, Pauline Hipp, Grace Brittain, Lucile Raynolds, and Clyde Brittain stand in front of Smyrna's Rock School in 1919. The school was new when these friends posed for the photograph. (Courtesy of Smyrna Public Library.)

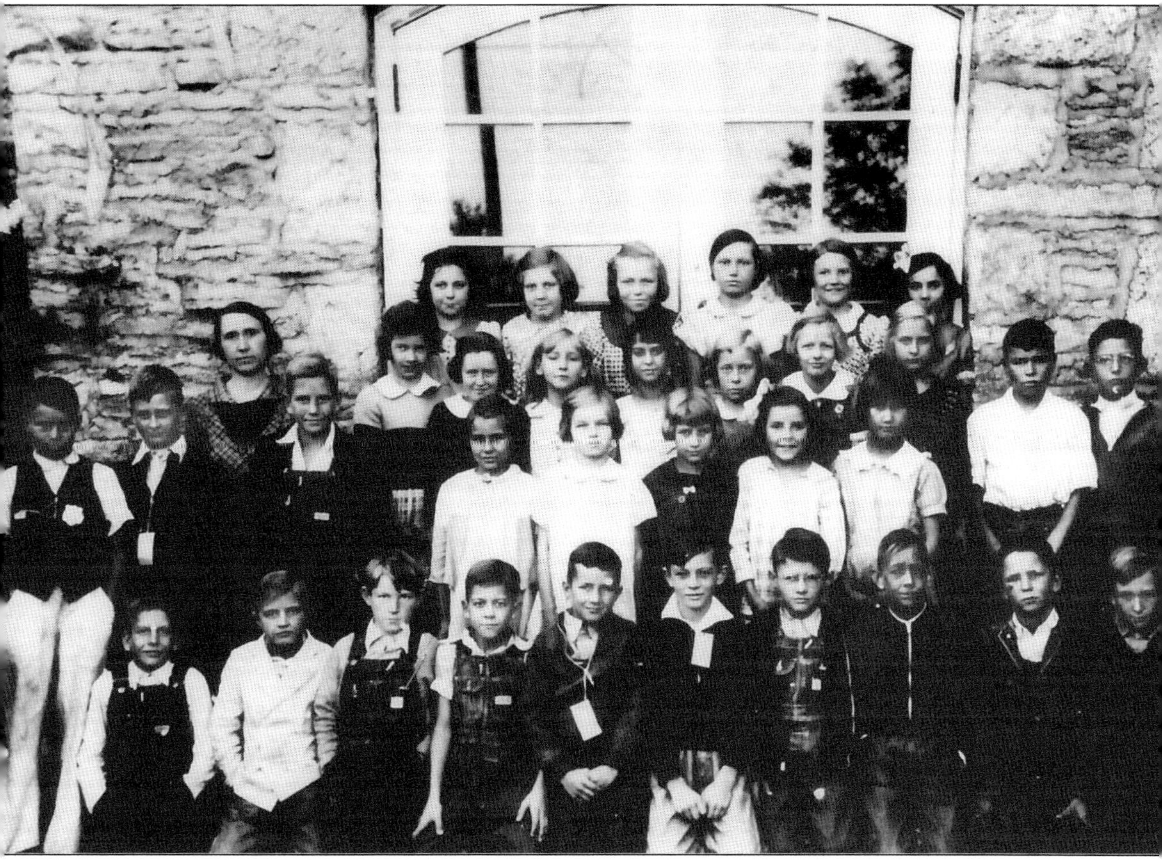

The fourth-grade class of the Smyrna Rock School poses for a photograph in 1935. They are led by teacher Ruby Goodman (third row, far left). (Courtesy of Smyrna Public Library.)

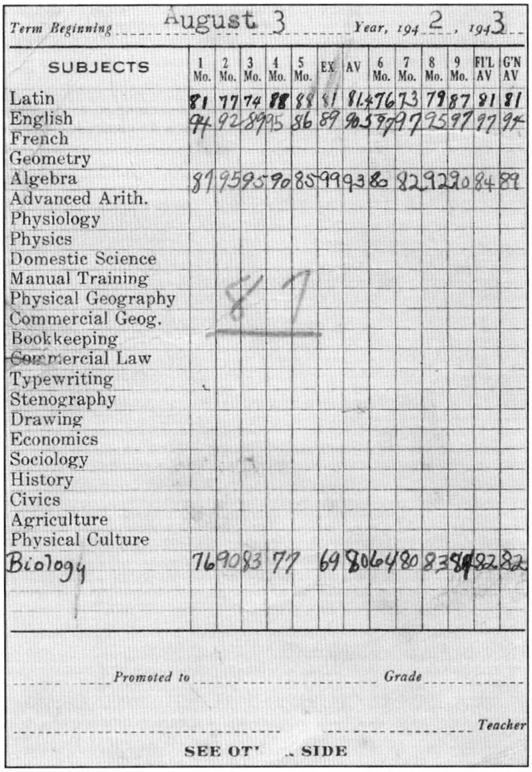

Term Beginning August 3 Year, 1942, 1943

SUBJECTS	1 Mo.	2 Mo.	3 Mo.	4 Mo.	5 Mo.	EX	AV	6 Mo.	7 Mo.	8 Mo.	9 Mo.	FI'L AV	G'N AV
Latin	81	77	74	88	88	81	81.4	76	73	79	87	81	81
English	94	92	89	95	86	89	90.5	97	97	95	97	97	94
French													
Geometry													
Algebra	87	95	95	90	85	99	93	86	82	92	90	84	89
Advanced Arith.													
Physiology													
Physics													
Domestic Science													
Manual Training													
Physical Geography													
Commercial Geog.													
Bookkeeping													
Commercial Law													
Typewriting													
Stenography													
Drawing													
Economics													
Sociology													
History													
Civics													
Agriculture													
Physical Culture													
Biology	76	90	83	77		69	80	64	80	83	84	82	82

87

Promoted to ______ Grade ______

______ Teacher

SEE OT' .. SIDE

This example of a Smyrna High School report card in 1943 shows a student's classes and grades. Teachers filled out the grades of their students monthly and tracked progress closely. This student received high marks in Latin, Algebra, Biology, and English during her high school years. (Courtesy of Smyrna Public Library.)

Smyrna High School graduated 19 students in 1949. Dora Thompson, pictured to the right of the school's name, sponsored many groups and clubs throughout her years there. (Courtesy of Smyrna Public Library.)

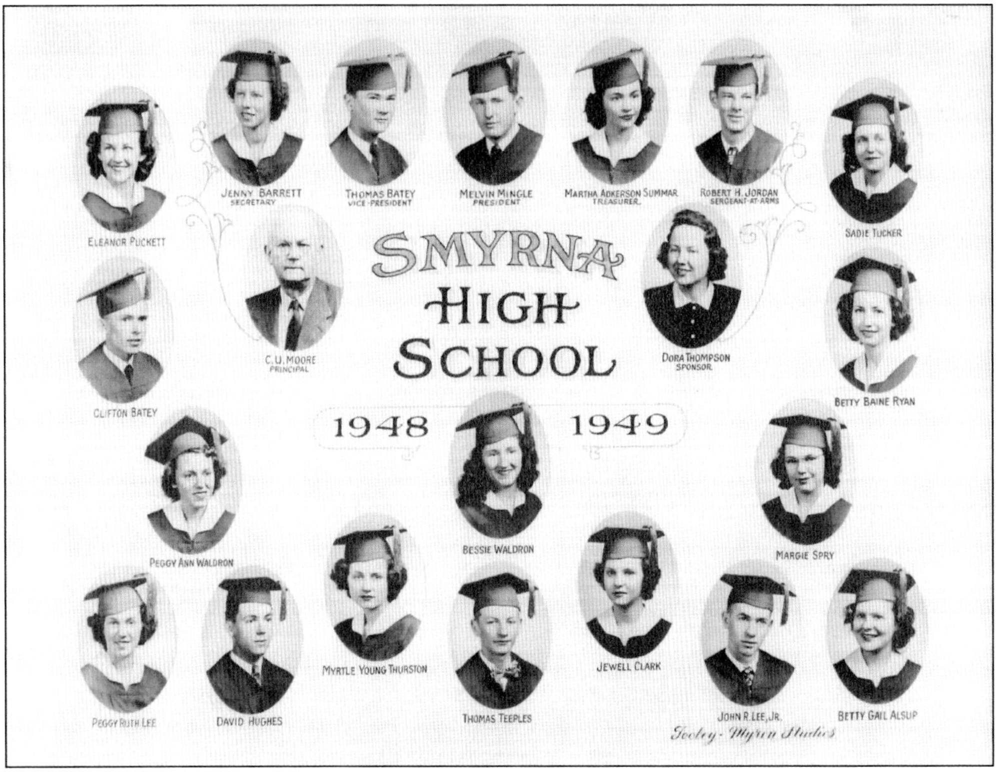

In the mid-1920s, basketball became popular in Smyrna. Here, the 1945 Smyrna High School girls' team poses in the school gymnasium. (Courtesy of Smyrna Public Library.)

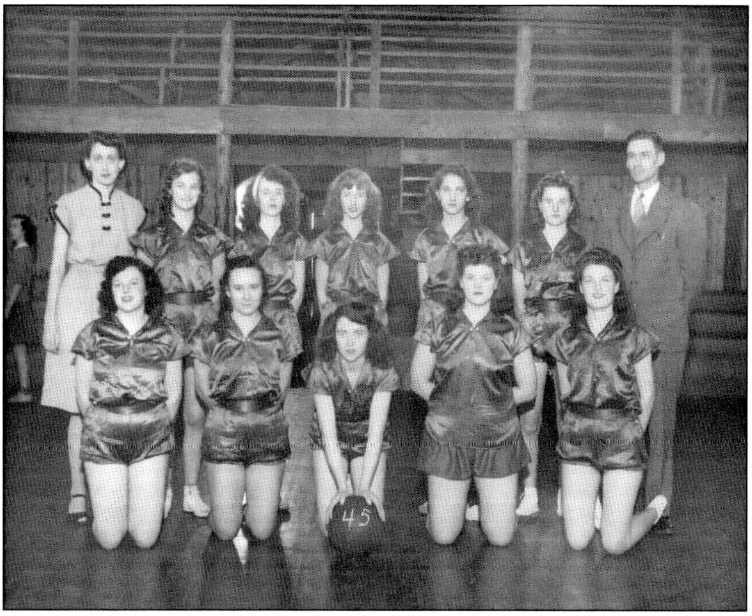

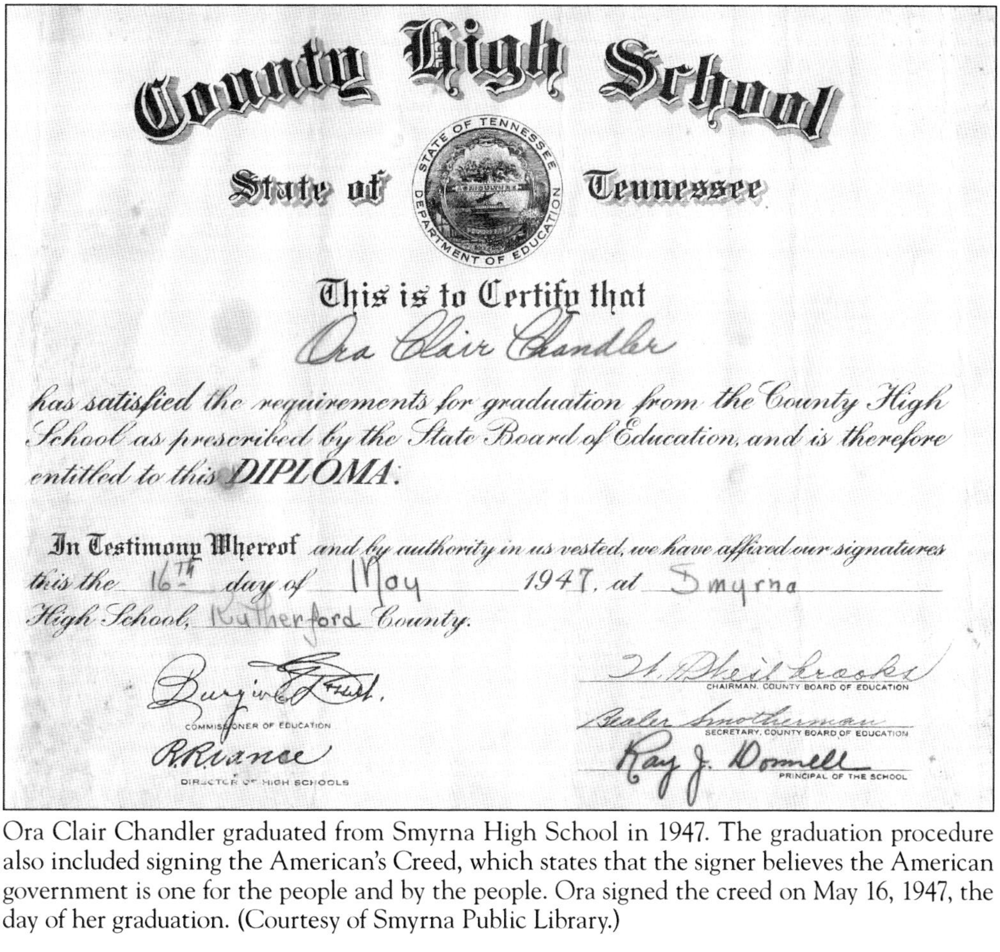

County High School

State of Tennessee

STATE OF TENNESSEE DEPARTMENT OF EDUCATION

This is to Certify that

Ora Clair Chandler

has satisfied the requirements for graduation from the County High School as prescribed by the State Board of Education, and is therefore entitled to this DIPLOMA.

In Testimony Whereof and by authority in us vested, we have affixed our signatures this the 16th day of May 1947, at Smyrna High School, Rutherford County.

COMMISSIONER OF EDUCATION

DIRECTOR OF HIGH SCHOOLS

CHAIRMAN, COUNTY BOARD OF EDUCATION

Bealer Smotherman

SECRETARY, COUNTY BOARD OF EDUCATION

Ray J. Donnell

PRINCIPAL OF THE SCHOOL

Ora Clair Chandler graduated from Smyrna High School in 1947. The graduation procedure also included signing the American's Creed, which states that the signer believes the American government is one for the people and by the people. Ora signed the creed on May 16, 1947, the day of her graduation. (Courtesy of Smyrna Public Library.)

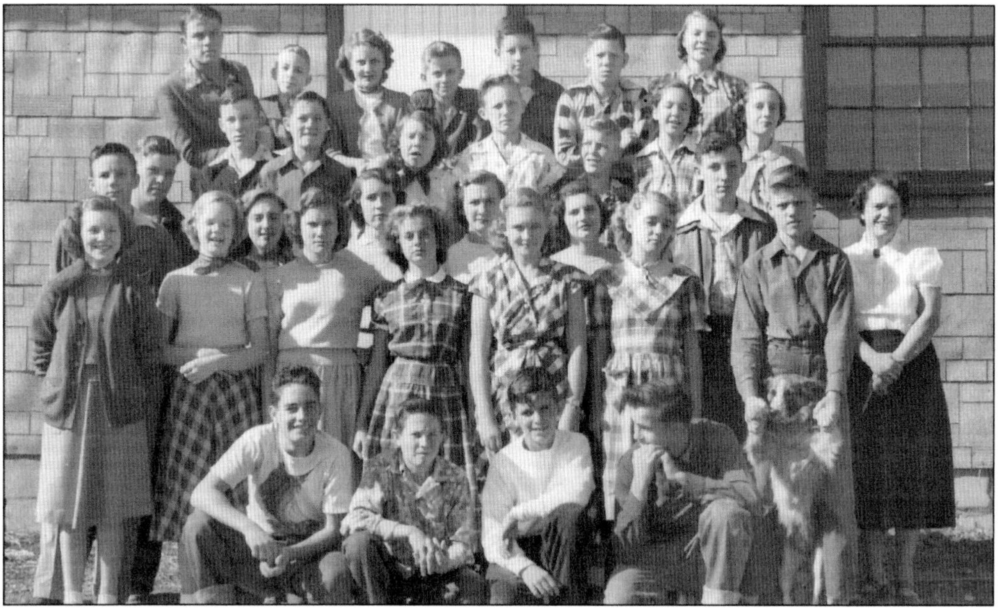

The eighth-grade class of Smyrna High School poses for this photograph in the late 1940s. With the new Air Force base in town, enrollment increased, and the school had to add classrooms. Barracks were converted and used as additional classrooms and cafeteria. (Courtesy of Robert "Bud" Raikes.)

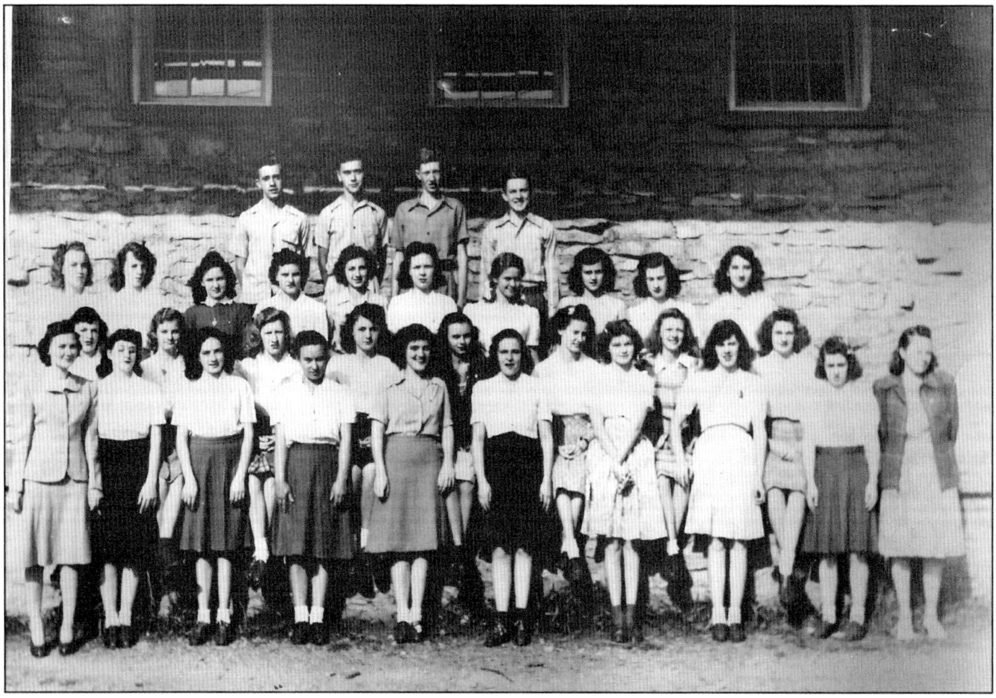

The Smyrna High School Beta Club poses in front of the school in the late 1940s. Member Katherine Walkup remembered the community-service aspect of the group and continued to serve several organizations throughout her life. (Courtesy of Smyrna Public Library.)

Margaret Cox works on the yearbook during her junior year of high school in the 1940s. The ring of her boyfriend, Robert "Bud" Raikes, hangs from her neck. (Courtesy of Robert "Bud" Raikes.)

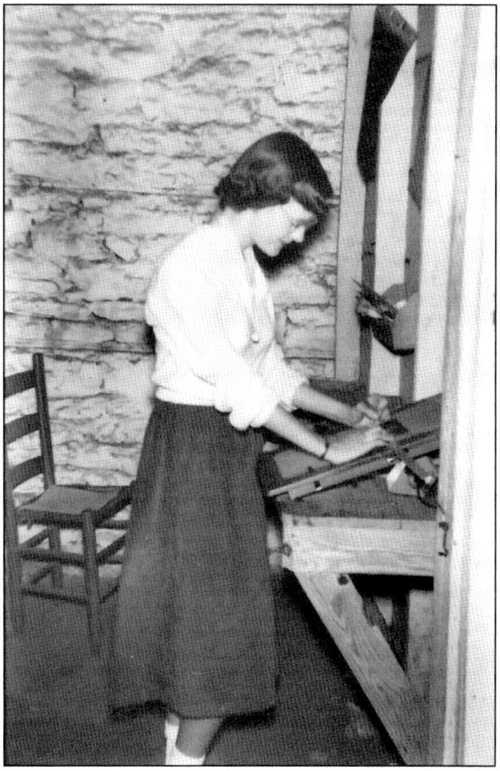

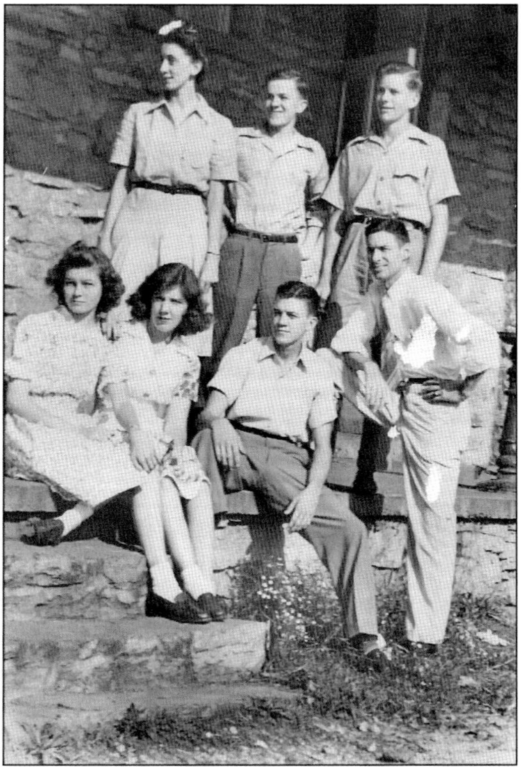

The officers of the Beta Club in the late 1940s pose for the camera with club sponsor Elba McCann (upper left) and school principal Ray Donnell (lower right). Beta Club members had high grades and were committed to leading through serving others. (Courtesy of Smyrna Public Library.)

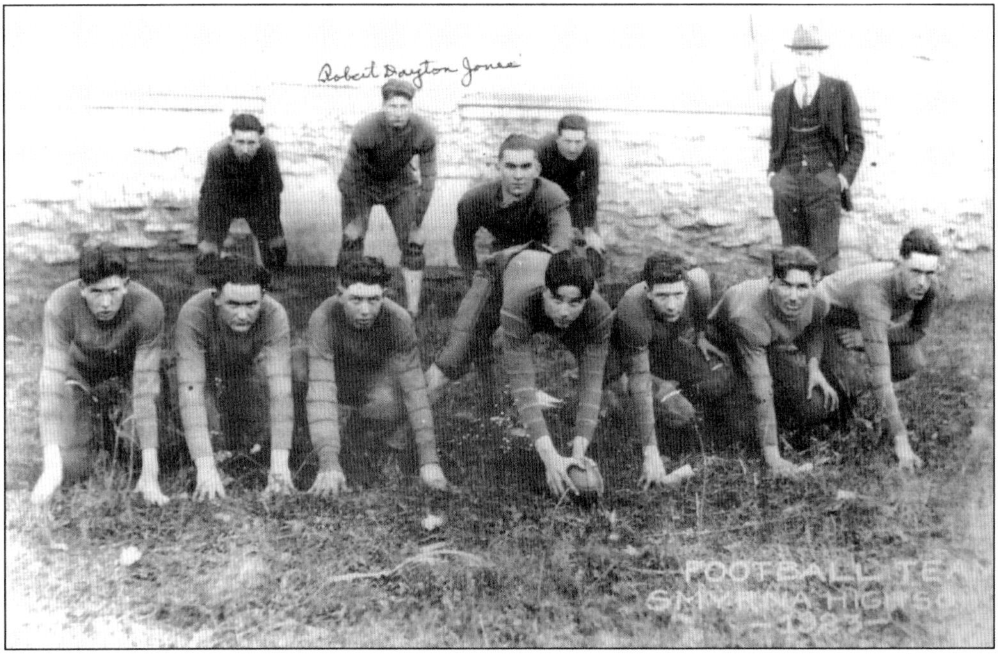

The Smyrna High School football team poses for a photograph in 1923. During the early 1920s, baseball was more popular than football. Coach John Tucker stands in the back right. J.B. McAdoo crouches in the middle, and Robert Dayton Jones stands behind him on the left. (Courtesy of Toby Francis.)

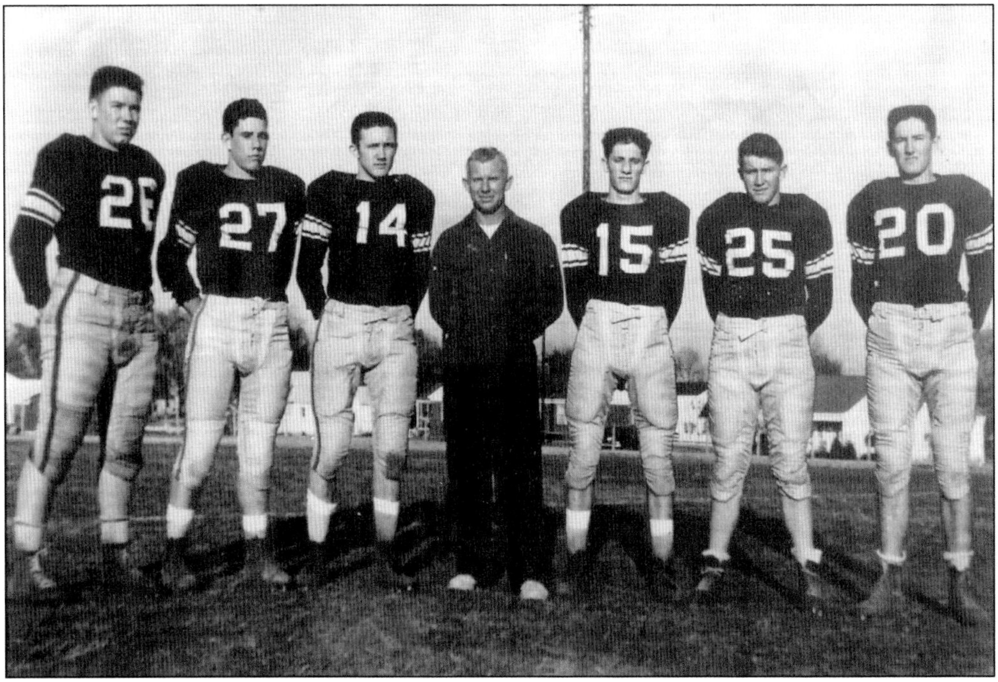

A few seniors from the Smyrna football team pose for this photograph in the mid-1950s. From left to right are John Mitchell, Dan Edwards, Boyd Coleman Jr., coach Dean Holland, Robert "Bud" Raikes, Homer Wisdom, and Cecil Lee. (Courtesy of Toby Francis.)

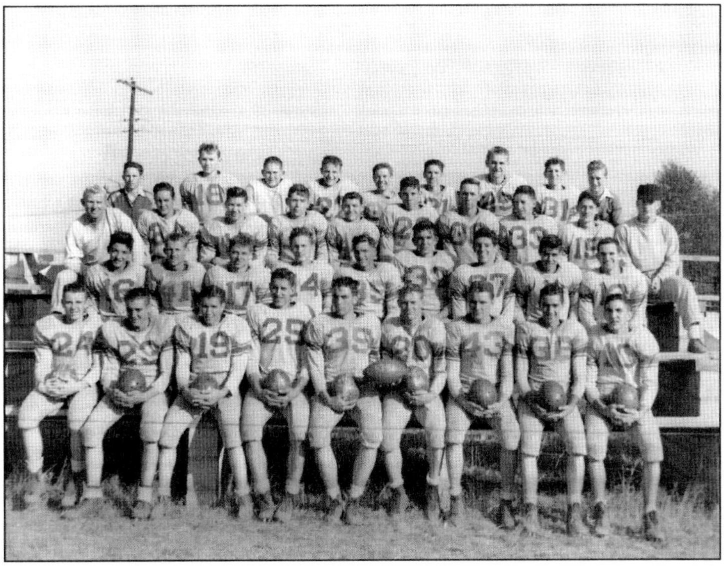

The 1953 Smyrna High School football team breaks from practice to take this photograph. The squad was led by coach Jimmy Joe Jackson (third row, far right). To the left of Jackson is Robert "Bud" Raikes, later a coach and principal of Smyrna High School. (Courtesy of Robert "Bud" Raikes.)

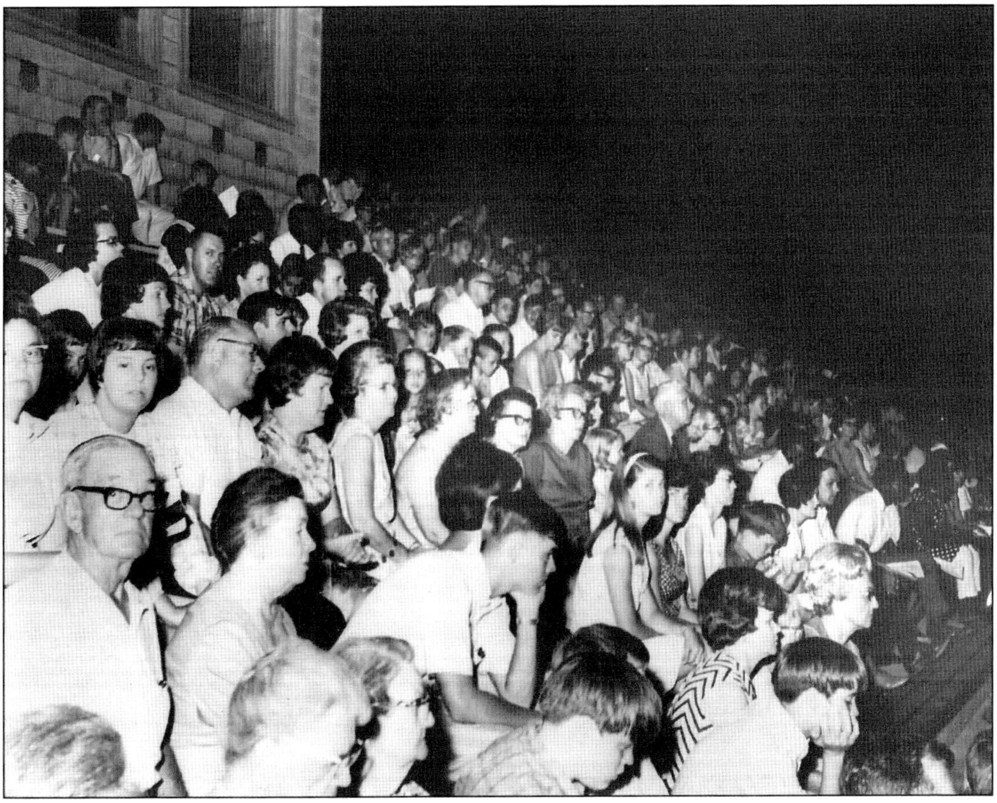

The town came out to support Smyrna High School students in July 1969. Approximately 1,500 people attended a program called "Smyrna Happening," a discussion between several Smyrna High School students and the adults in the community on their difference of views. A few well-known dignitaries also participated, including Olympic medalist Ralph Boston and one-time Chicago Bears quarterback Bill Wade. (Courtesy of Smyrna Public Library.)

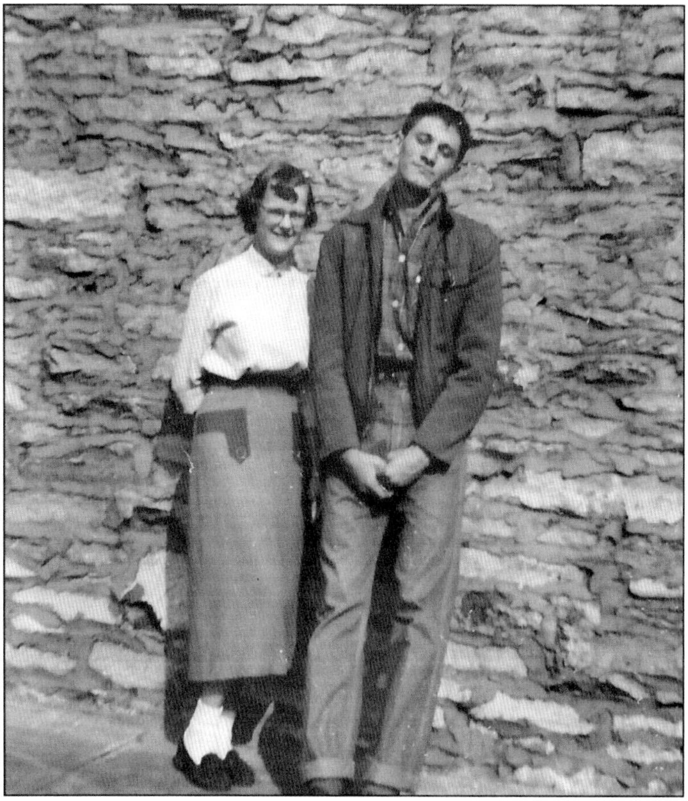

Margaret Cox and Robert "Bud" Raikes, ages 16 and 18, respectively, pose after Robert's football practice in 1955. Raikes later became the coach of the Smyrna High School football team, and the couple started a tradition of inviting the team over for a cookout during the season. (Courtesy of Robert "Bud" Raikes.)

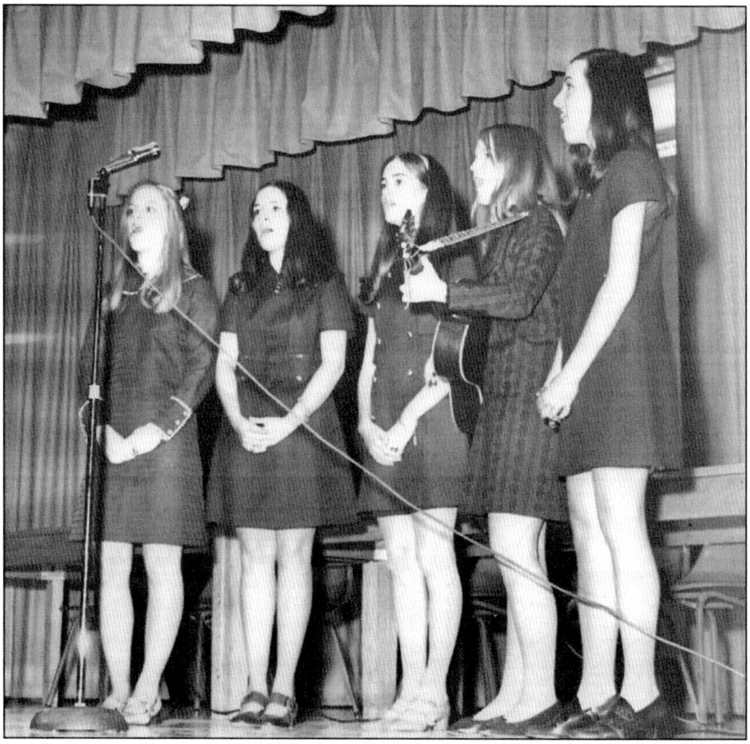

A group of girls performs at the school in 1964. Smyrna High School did not have a band until the mid-1960s. In November 1964, the Rutherford County School Board voted to give Rutherford County principals a pay raise. They also sought $177,630 from the county court to add new classrooms, a library, and to enlarge the kitchen at La Vergne High School. (Courtesy of Smyrna Public Library.)

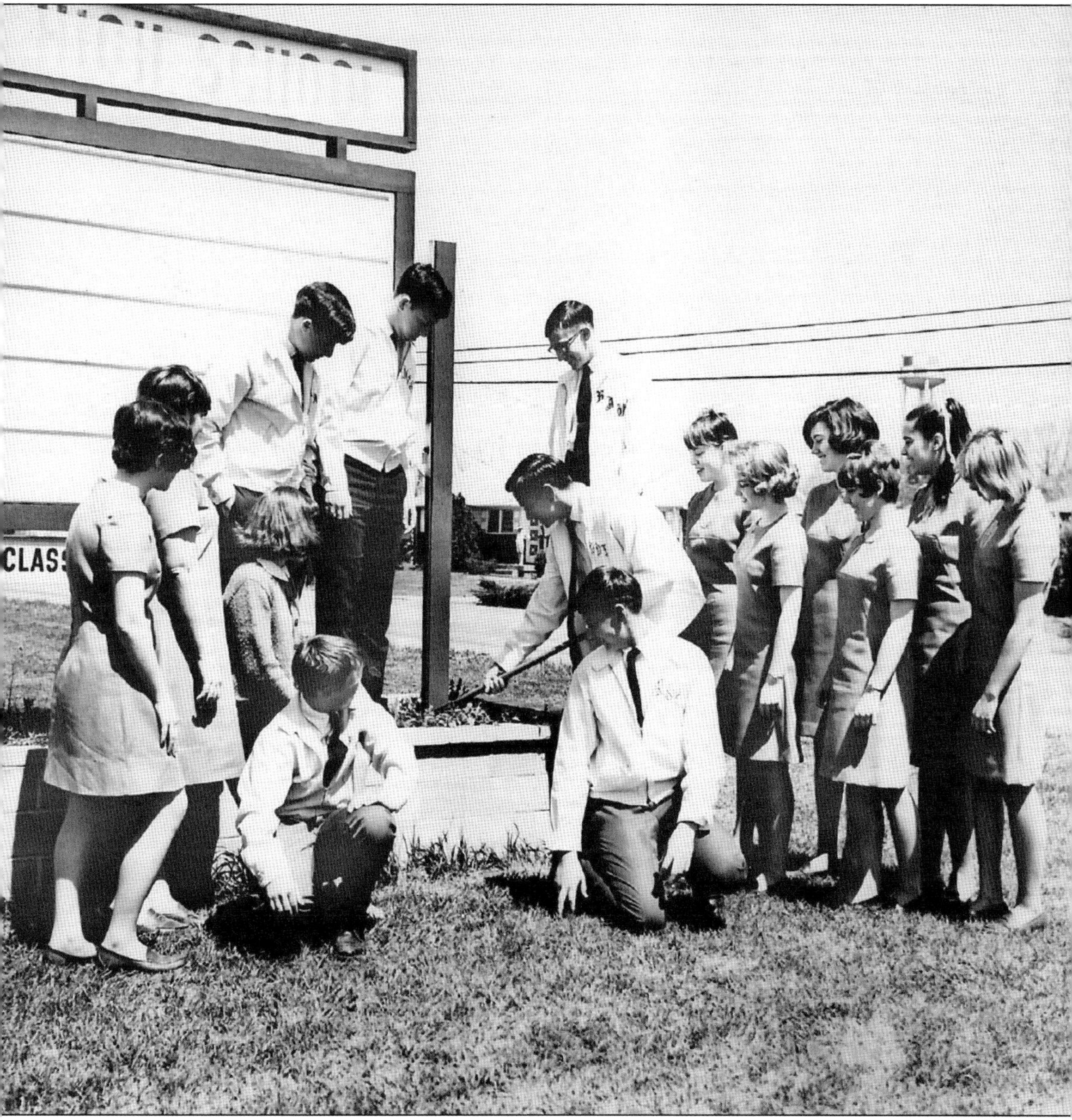

Members of the Smyrna Senior 4-H Club maintain the school sign and plant flowers as they pose for this April 1968 photograph. The group also picked up trash on the streets throughout Smyrna as part of their community-service project. Helping in various capacities around the school, it began in 1902 as a service club to develop leadership and citizenship skills through experiential learning. On March 24, 1965, in Nashville, 14 members of the club also performed at the 4-H Congress. (Courtesy of Smyrna Public Library.)

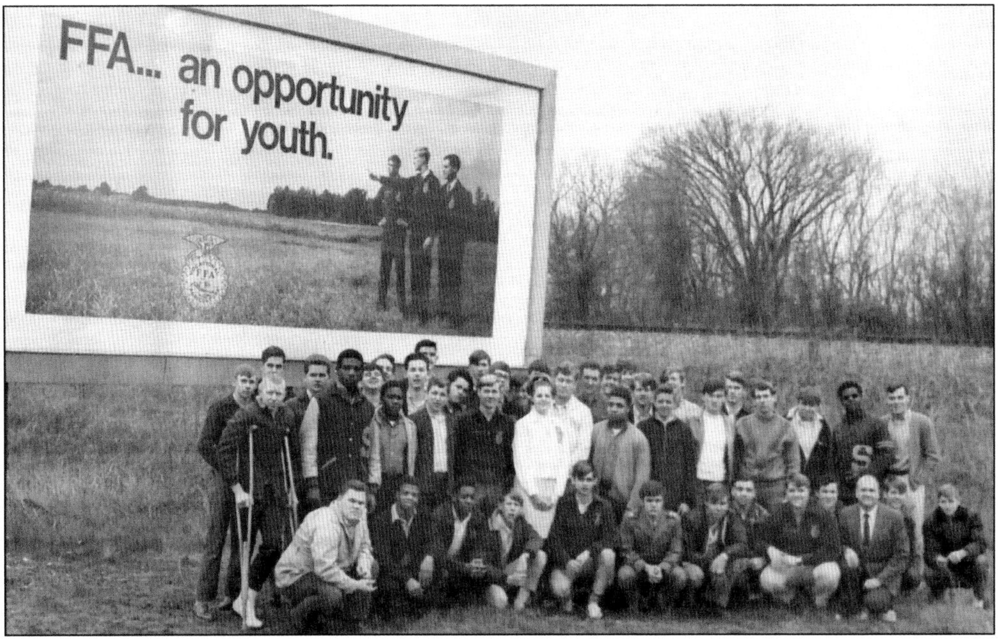

Smyrna Future Farmers of America students pose in front of an area billboard in March 1969. This photograph ran in the *Rutherford Courier* to celebrate Future Farmers of America Week. The Smyrna High School chapter studied vocational agriculture. John H. Buckner (first row, far right) was the chapter advisor. (Courtesy of Smyrna Public Library.)

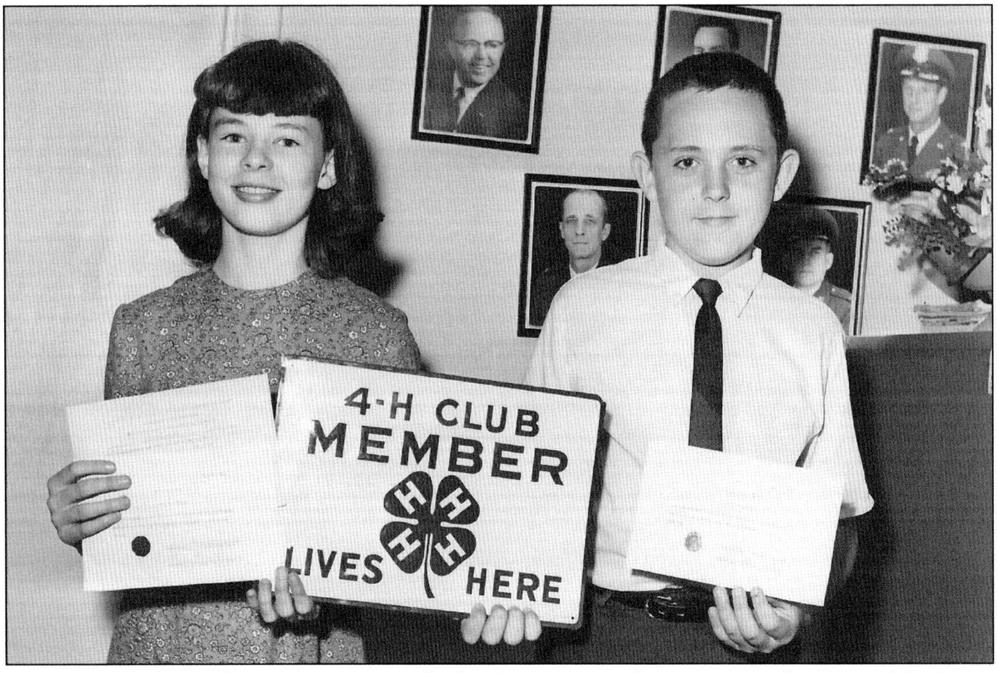

Merilyn Dobson and Marvin Stem smile for the camera after winning the 4-H Club Camp Scholarship in May 1968. The scholarship provided money from the Smyrna Home Demonstration Club and was awarded to students with the understanding that they would uphold the club's areas of focus: head, heart, hands, and health. (Courtesy of Smyrna Public Library.)

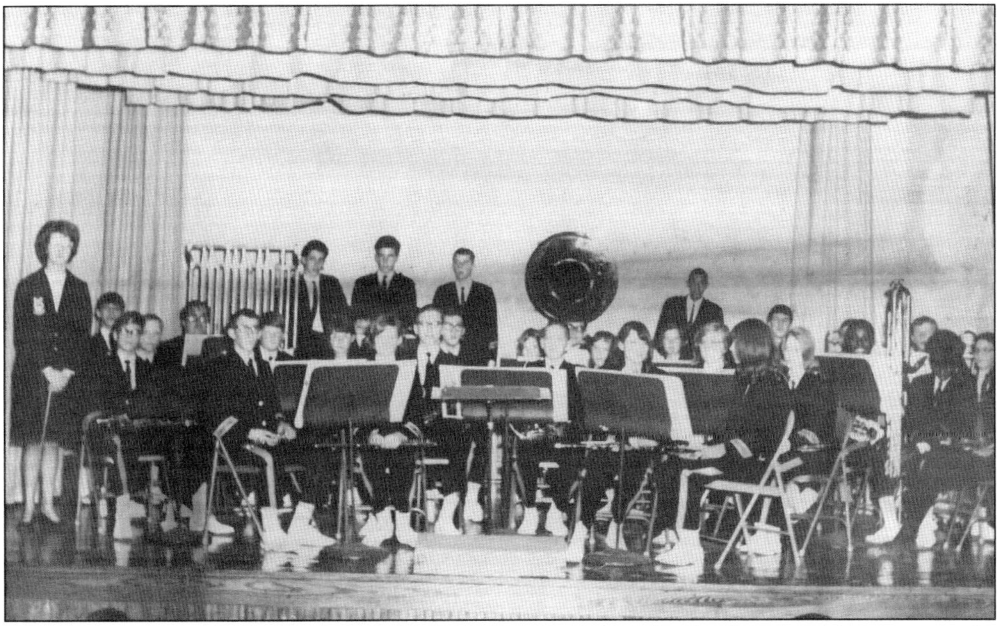

The Smyrna High School band performs here in 1969 at the school. The school first organized a band in 1957 under Joe D. Van Sickle with 30 members. By 1962, it was 60 members strong, and in 1962 the band gave its first marching performance and competed in the annual band festival in Clarksville. (Courtesy of Smyrna Public Library.)

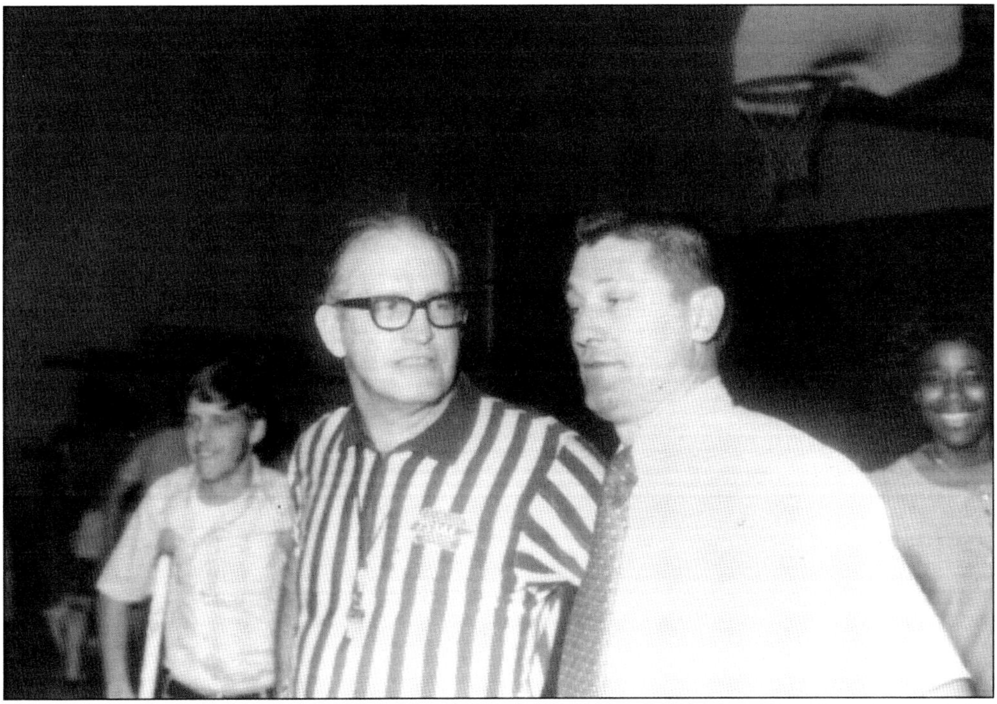

Wrestling coach Jack Black Hayes (left) talks with new principal Robert "Bud" Raikes in 1973. Bud had recently begun his position as principal. (Courtesy of Robert "Bud" Raikes.)

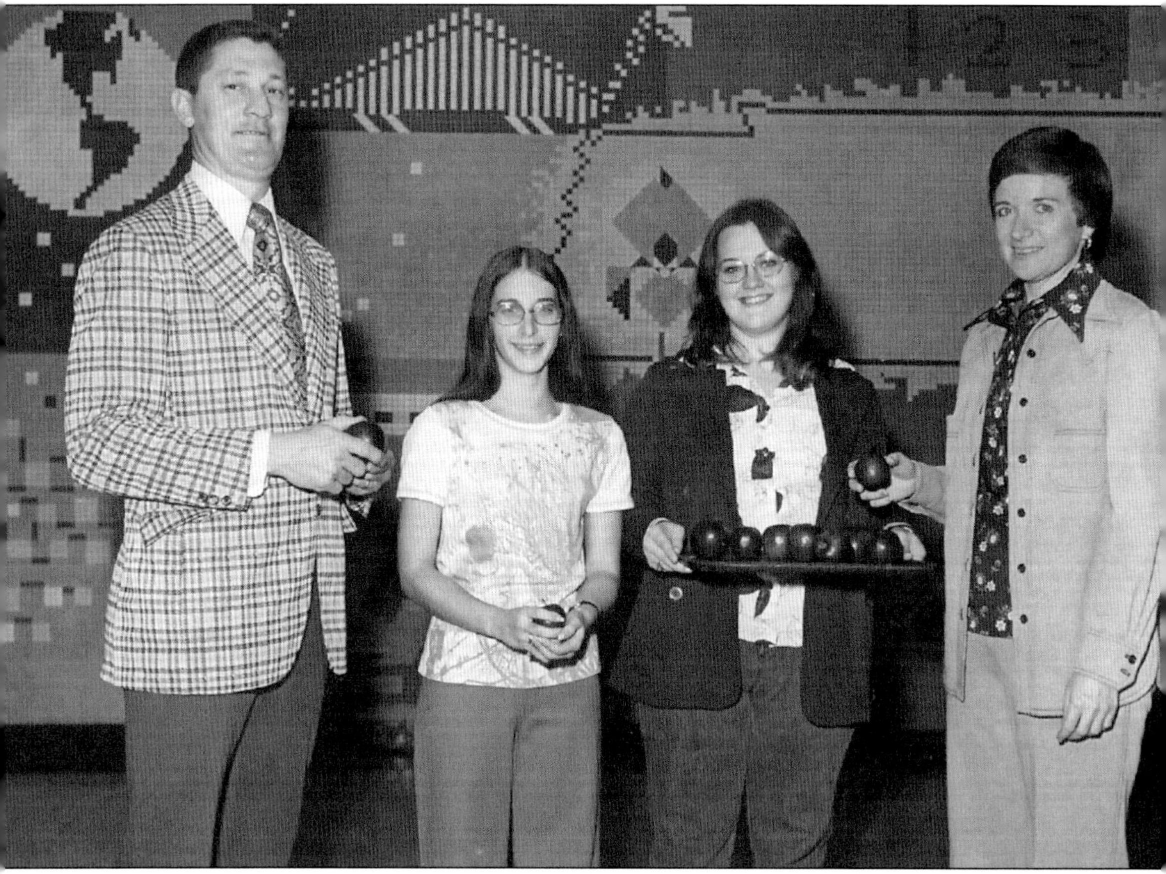

Students deliver apples to teacher Patricia Smithson and principal Robert "Bud" Raikes during Teacher Appreciation Week in 1975. The National Parent Teacher Association did not institute an annual Teacher Appreciation Week until 1985. (Courtesy of Robert "Bud" Raikes.)

Four

The Air Force Comes to Town

National celebrities, local dignitaries, and everyday people have used the airfields of Smyrna/Rutherford County Airport. Before the airport authority utilized the airfields, thousands of young men were trained there to fight overseas in World War II and the Korean Conflict.

The State of Tennessee began purchasing land for the soon-to-come military base in the early 1940s. One large property came from the Gooch family. Their home, Goochland, was well known locally. Dr. Gooch purchased 1,600 acres in 1842 and built the large and stately home. In the 1940s, the military was looking for a site for long-range bomber training and needed several criteria met, including favorable weather conditions, good topography, access to rail, and expansion opportunities. Three other towns were in the running for the base: DeRidder, Louisiana; Jackson, Mississippi; and Greenville, South Carolina. After the bombing of Pearl Harbor, the Army Air Corps selected Smyrna as one of 14 installations for pilot training. Construction began immediately, and the site was ready for use by July 1942. When soldiers started their training in Smyrna, the base had two 300-foot-by-5,500-foot runways, hangars, fueling facilities, seven miles of underground drainage pipe, barracks, and a control tower. Near the end of construction, the military decided to use the Smyrna Army Airfield, as it was named, to train combat crews and air transport. Local airlines also used the base to train their pilots and crews. After the war, the air base was placed on the inactive list, but by September 1948 it was reactivated. In early 1950, it was renamed Sewart Air Force Base in honor of a local man, Maj. Allan J. Sewart Jr., who was killed while on a combat mission over the Solomon Islands in 1942.

The base saw action again in the 1950s with the Korean Conflict. The 9th Air Force's 314th Troop Carrier Wing, stationed in Smyrna, was activated to Korea. Support for Korean operations caused a large increase of troops into the base, with the addition of three new units. After Korea, they were activated to Vietnam before being relocated in 1966. In June 1970, the base was deactivated and split among the Metropolitan Nashville Airport Authority, Rutherford County, the US Army Corps of Engineers, and the Town of Smyrna. Today, the Smyrna/Rutherford County Airport Authority maintains much of the land once covered by the base.

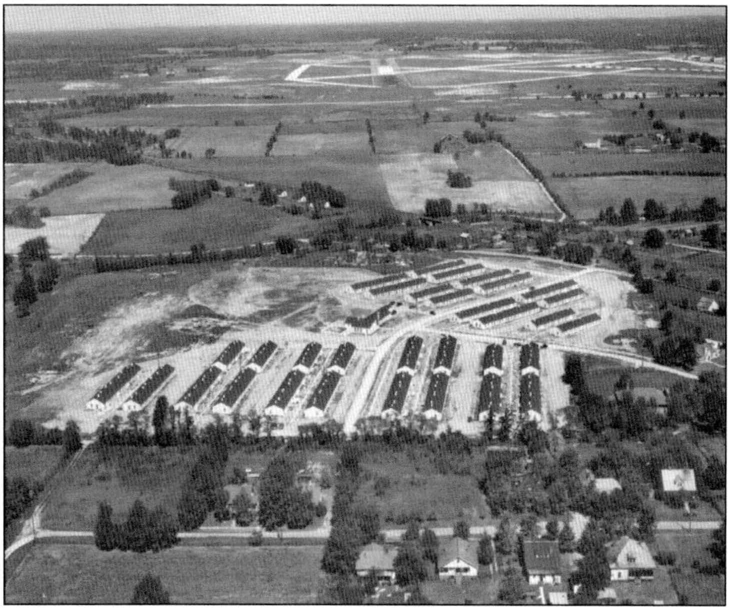

Meadowlawn Homes was built during World War II to house military families stationed at Smyrna Army Airfield. Because of Smyrna's favorable weather conditions, good topography, access to rail, and expansion capability, the US military chose the town for an army airfield in the early 1940s. (Courtesy of David Bucher.)

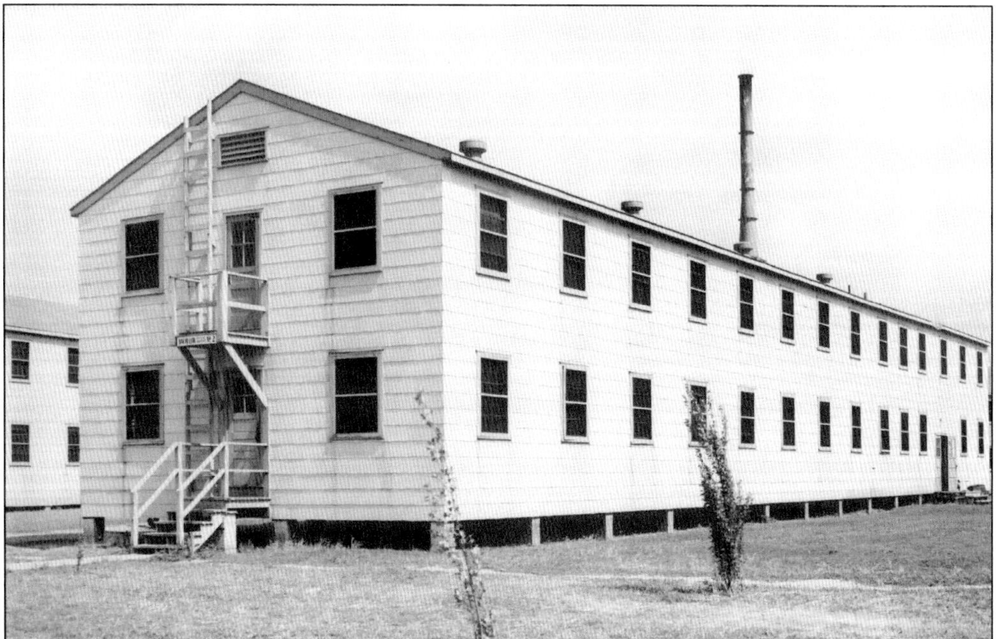

The World War II barracks at Smyrna Army Airfield were used until the based closed. Some still exist today as part of the Tennessee National Guard Complex, but they have been remodeled. (Courtesy of Rutherford County Archives.)

The Smyrna Army Airfield celebrated Army Air Forces Day on August 1, 1945. This program shows three B-24 bombers flying in formation. Smyrna Army Airfield was a training base for these planes during World War II. (Courtesy of Rutherford County Archives.)

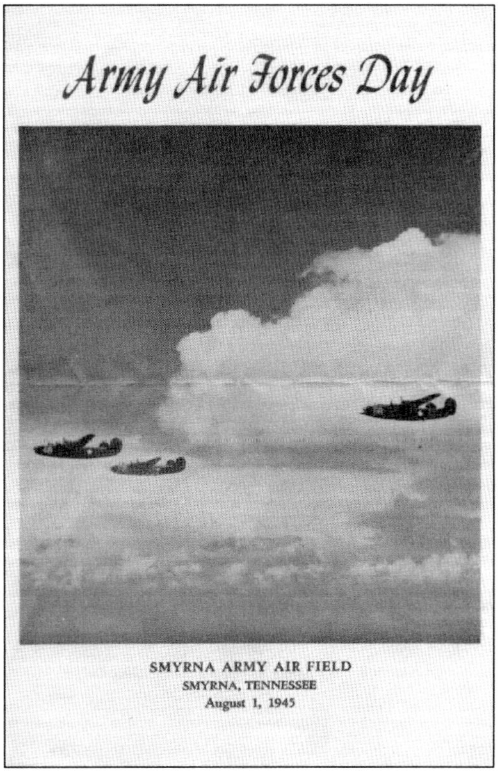

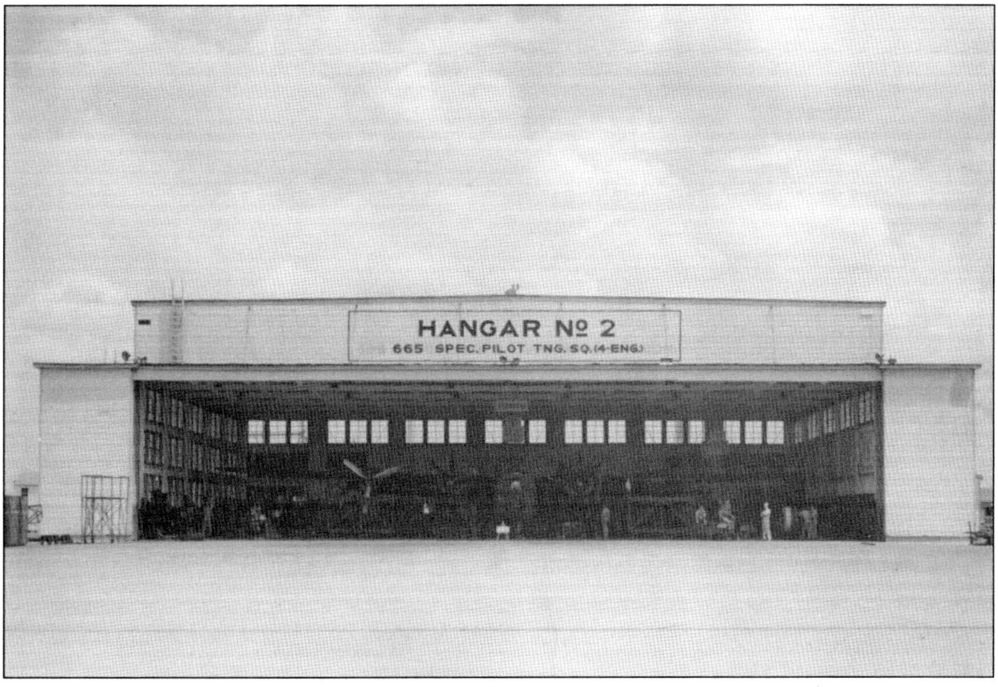

This photograph shows a B-24 undergoing maintenance in Hangar No. 2 at the Smyrna Army Airfield in the 1940s. The base was a training facility for various aircraft, including the B-17, B-24, C-82, C-119, and C-130. (Courtesy of Rutherford County Archives.)

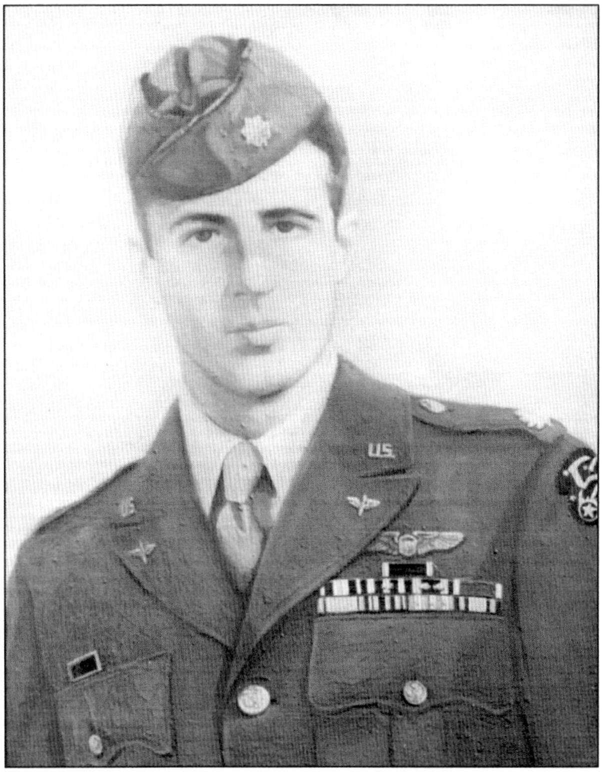

Maj. Allan J. Sewart Jr. lived in Nashville prior to his deployment during World War II. During the war, he received the Distinguished Service Cross. While flying on a combat mission over the Solomon Islands, he was killed on November 18, 1942. Smyrna Army Airfield was renamed in his honor and was officially dedicated in March 1950. (Courtesy of Smyrna Public Library.)

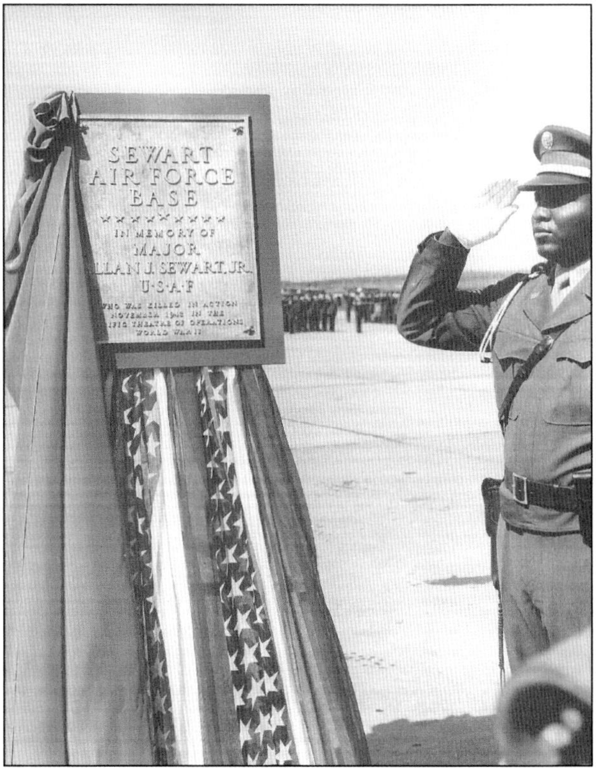

An air policeman stands next to a plaque dedicating the base to Alan Sewart in 1950 during the dedication ceremony. This took place after the integration of military services; the job of air policeman would not previously have been filled by an African American except in an all-black unit. (Courtesy of David Bucher.)

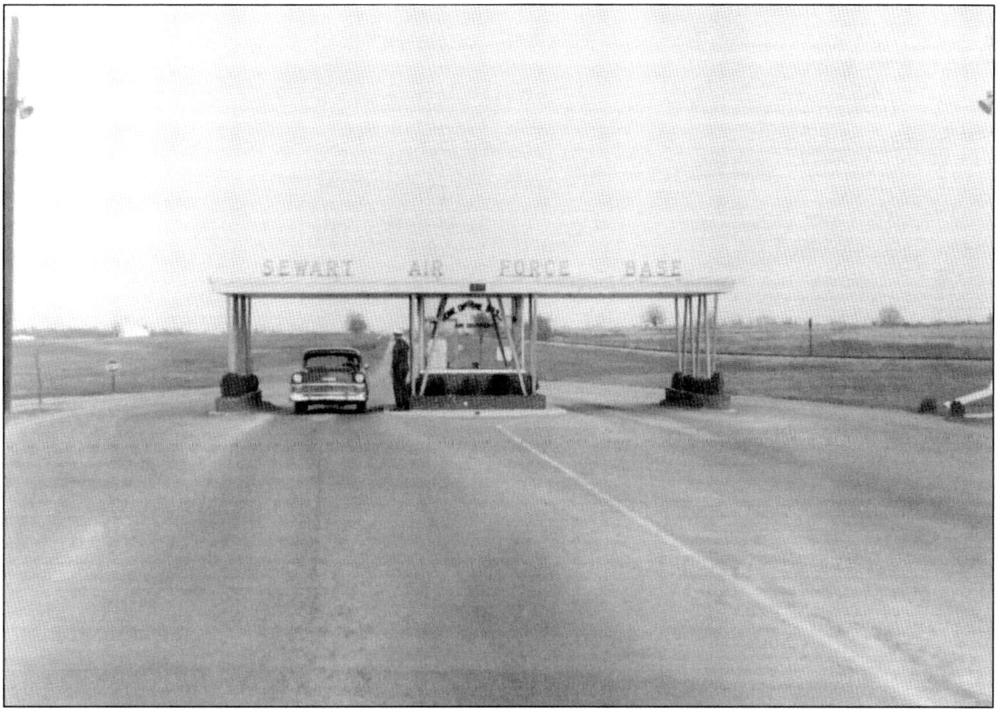

This 1950s photograph shows the main gate to Sewart Air Force Base, located near where the Smyrna Town Centre is today. (Courtesy of David Bucher.)

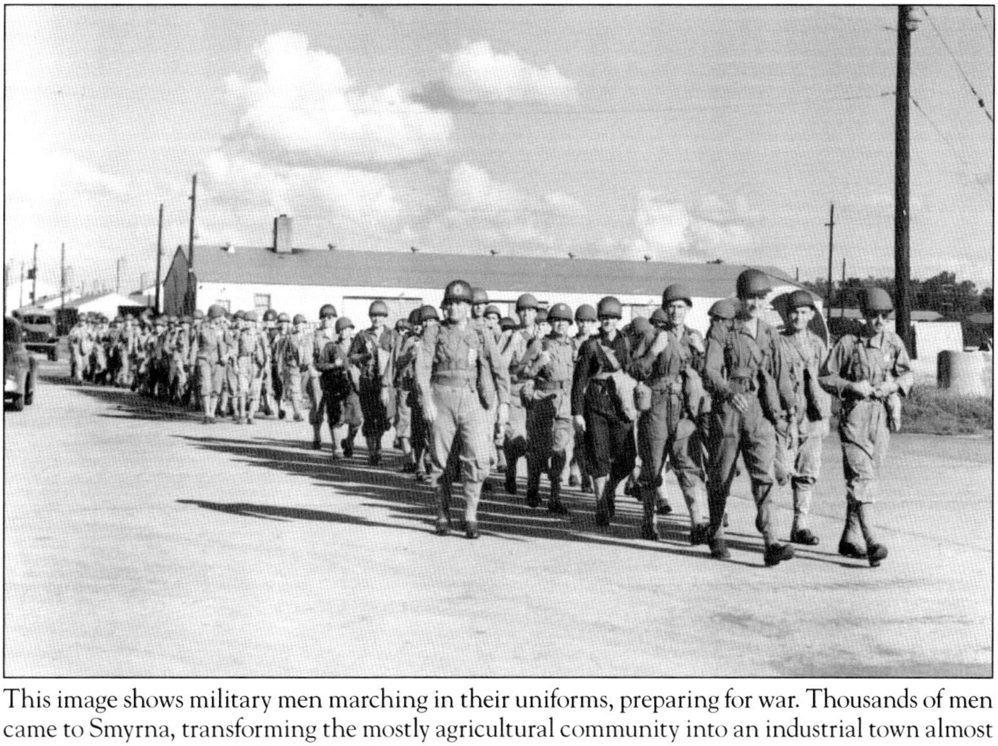

This image shows military men marching in their uniforms, preparing for war. Thousands of men came to Smyrna, transforming the mostly agricultural community into an industrial town almost overnight. (Courtesy of David Bucher.)

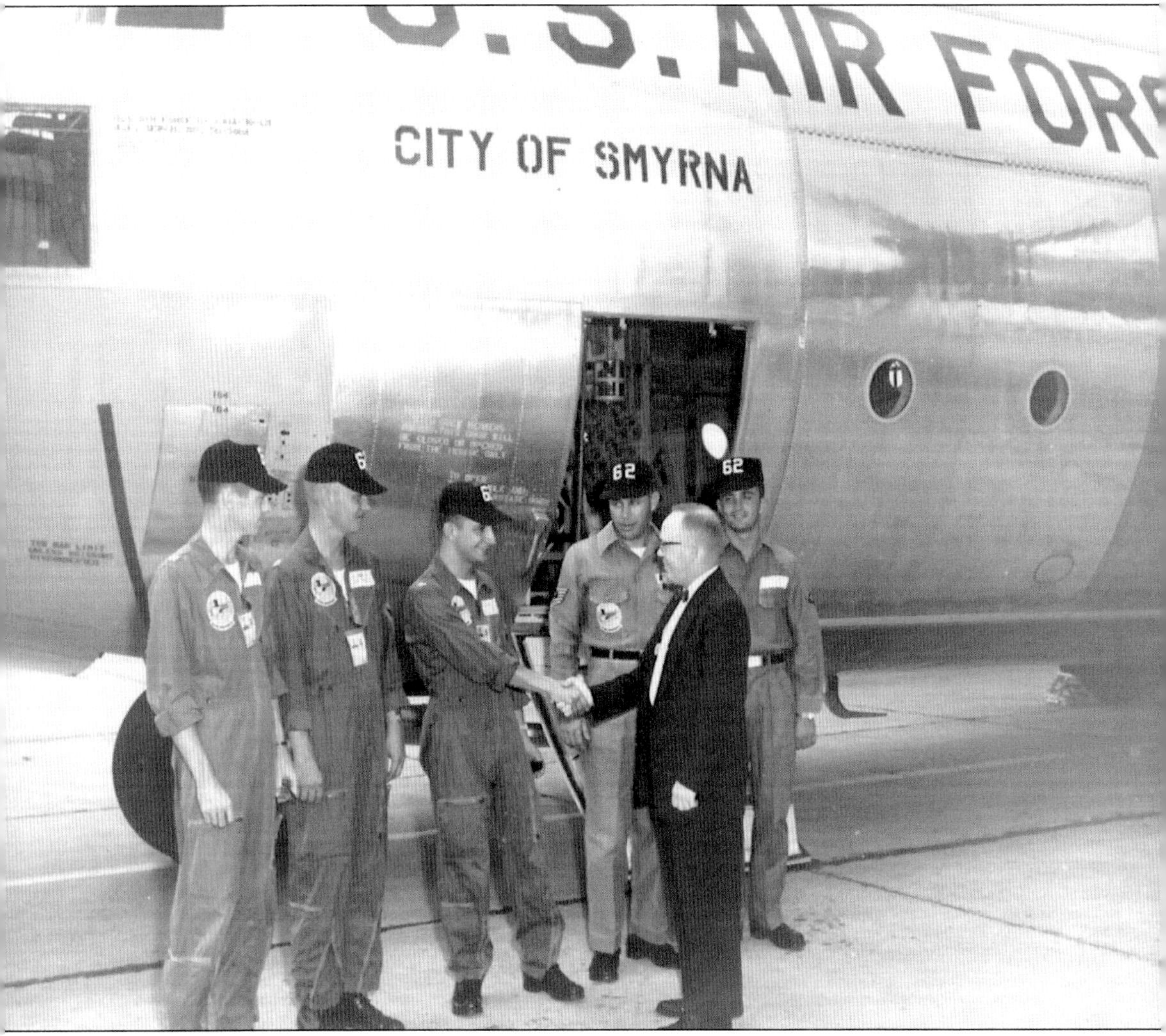

Mayor Sam Ridley greets the crew of the C-130A aircraft *Town of Smyrna* in the late 1950s or early 1960s. (Courtesy of David Bucher.)

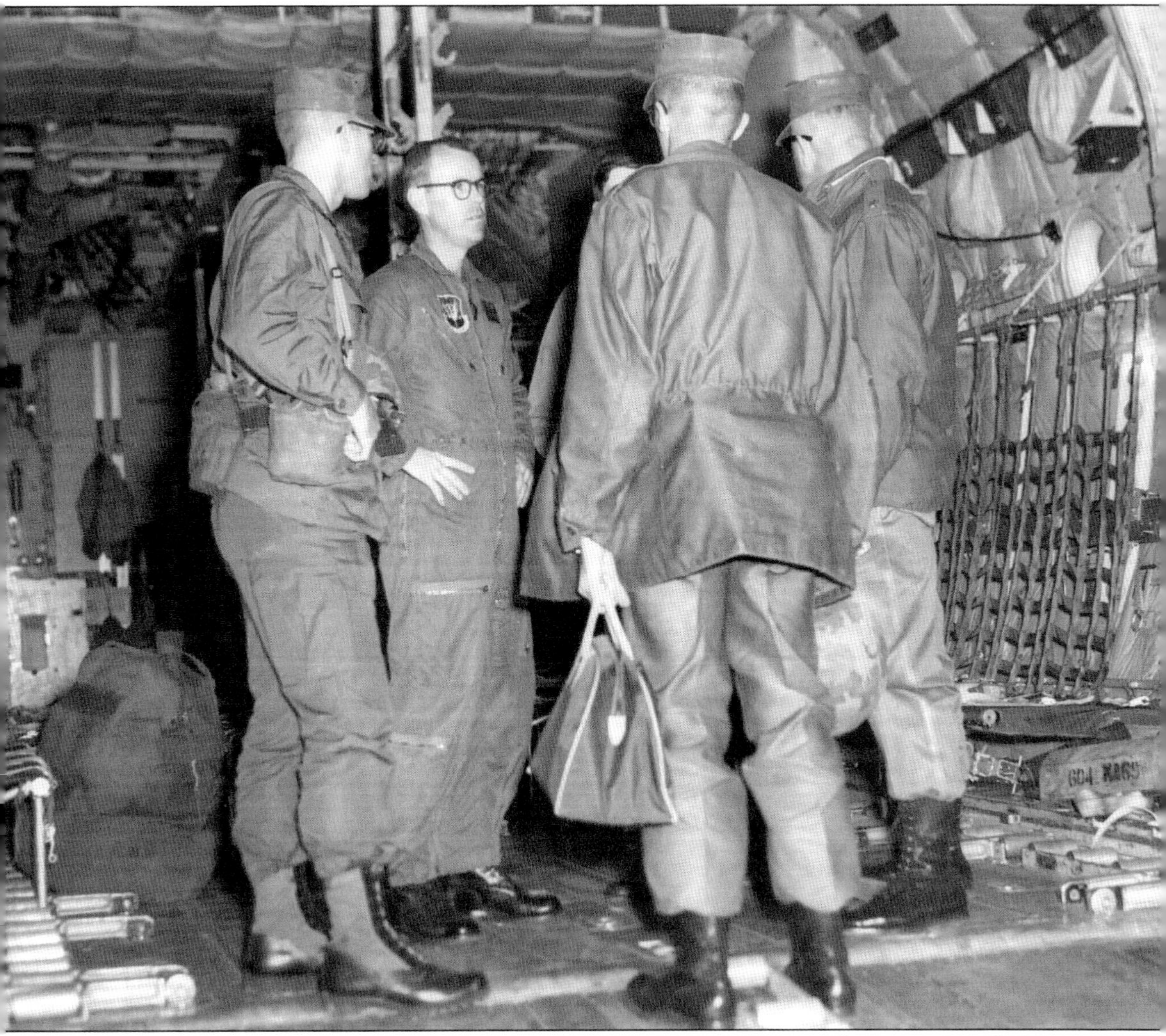

The men of Sewart Air Force Base prepared for war through practice on the same aircraft they would be using overseas. Most planes could hold only limited resources beyond those needed for the conflict. (Courtesy of David Bucher.)

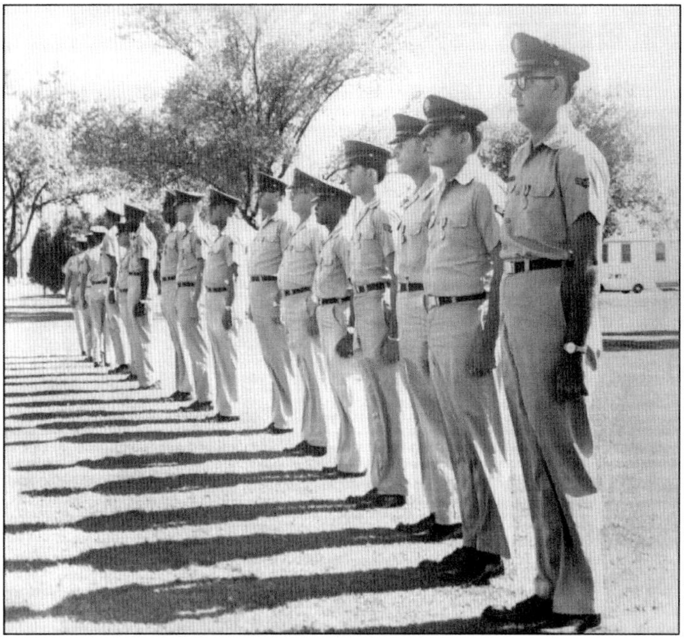

Men line up at attention before departing in this 1940s photograph. Thousands of men went through training at Sewart Air Force Base. (Courtesy of David Bucher.)

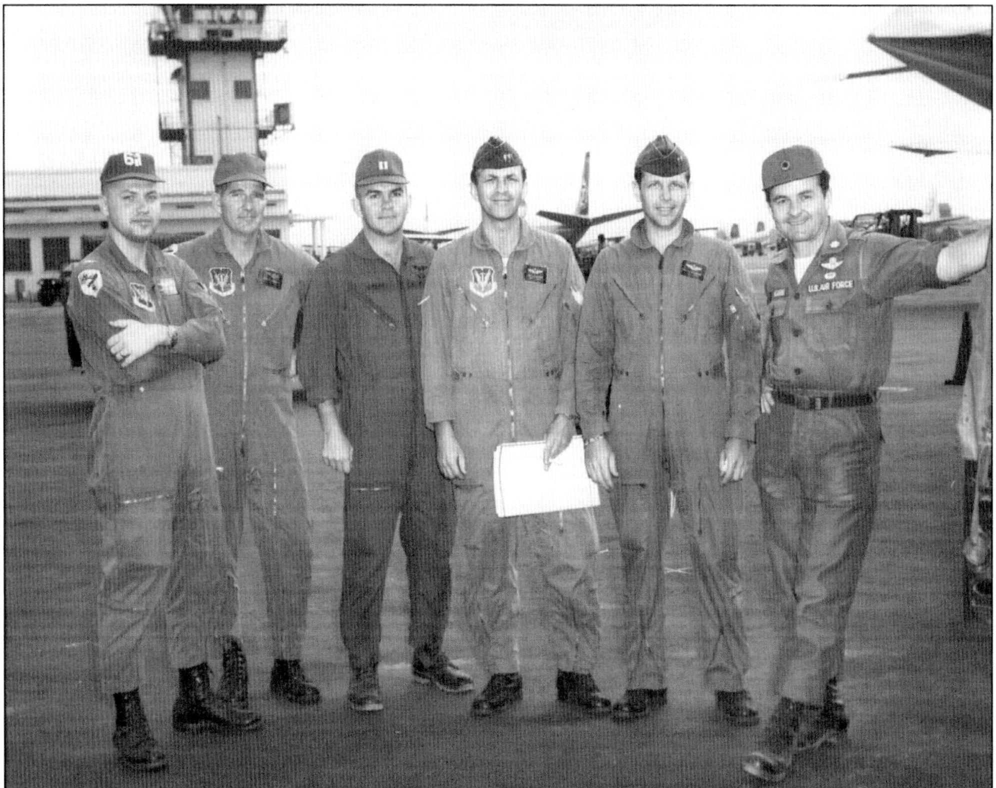

Training was vigorous at the air force base. One of the drills was to run several miles while wearing heavy packs. These men are taking a break from training for a photo op in the 1950s. (Courtesy of David Bucher.)

Several nearby journalists took their turn in military planes for photo ops. This 1950s image shows a photographer capturing three planes in flight. (Courtesy of David Bucher.)

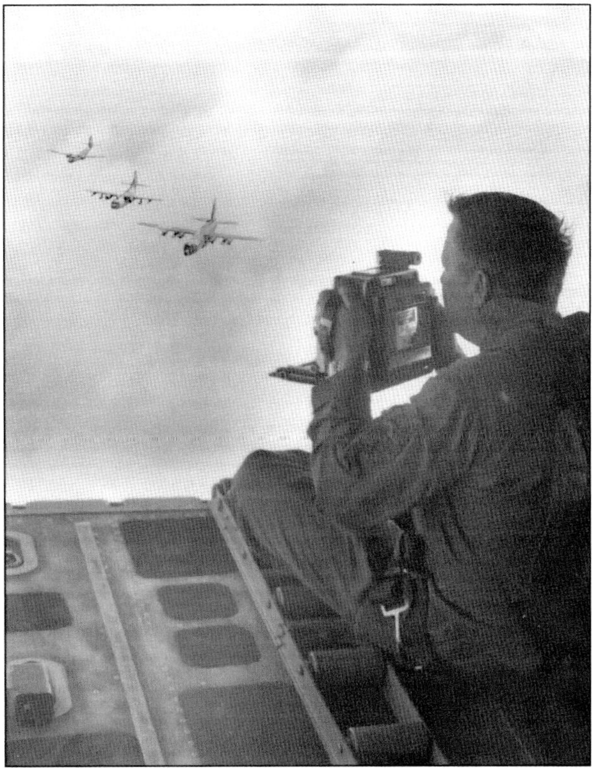

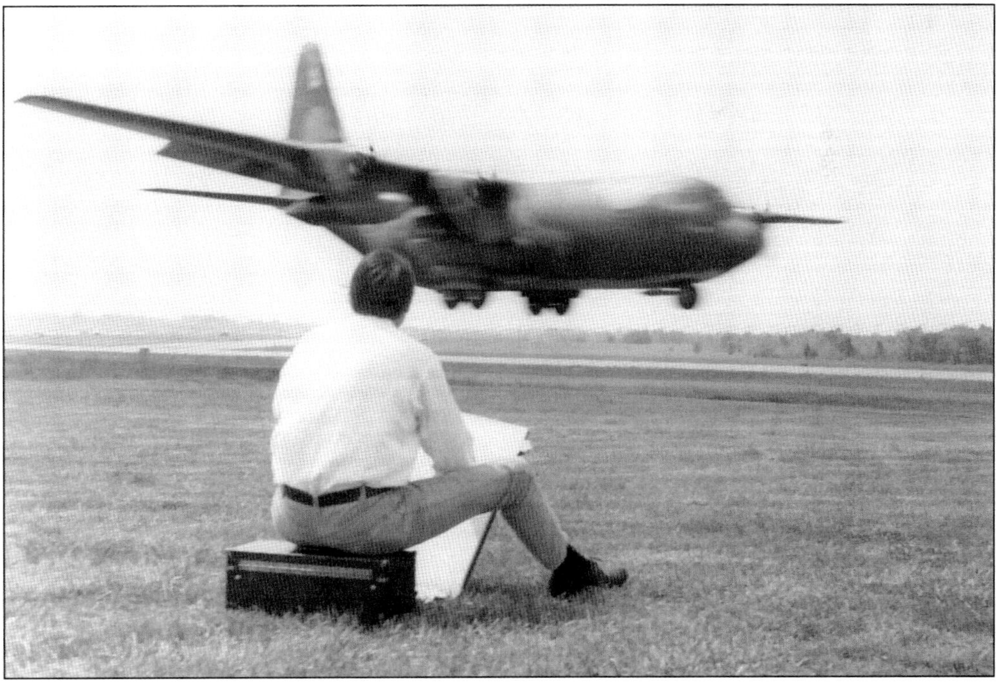

A man watches the landing gear on a C-130 in the late 1960s. The plane was developed in the mid-1950s as a cargo-transport aircraft and was originally built by Lockheed. (Courtesy of David Bucher.)

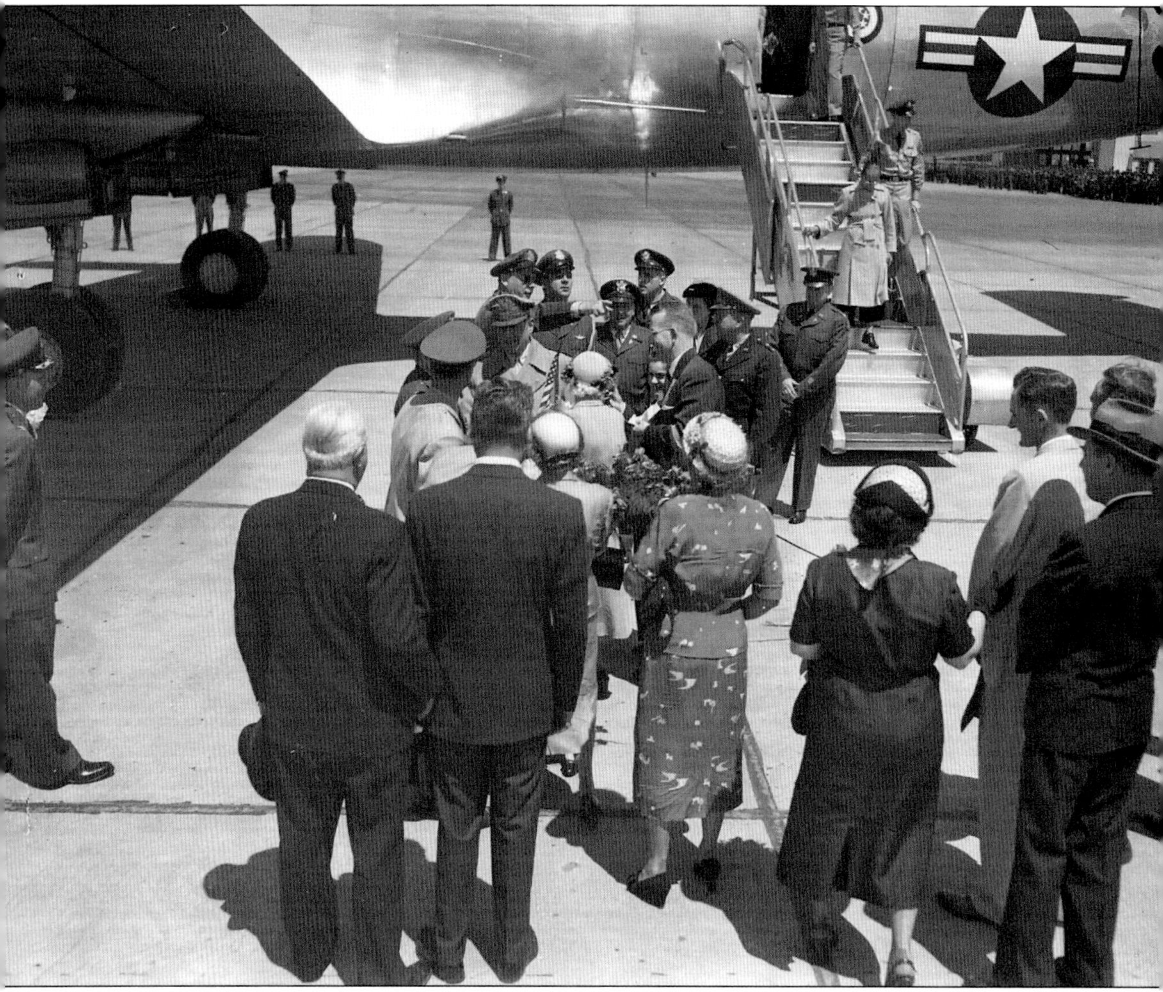

Gen. Douglas and Jean MacArthur exit their plane at Sewart Air Force Base in 1951. After leaving Smyrna, the family traveled to nearby Murfreesboro, where a parade and several other events were held in their honor. (Courtesy of David Bucher.)

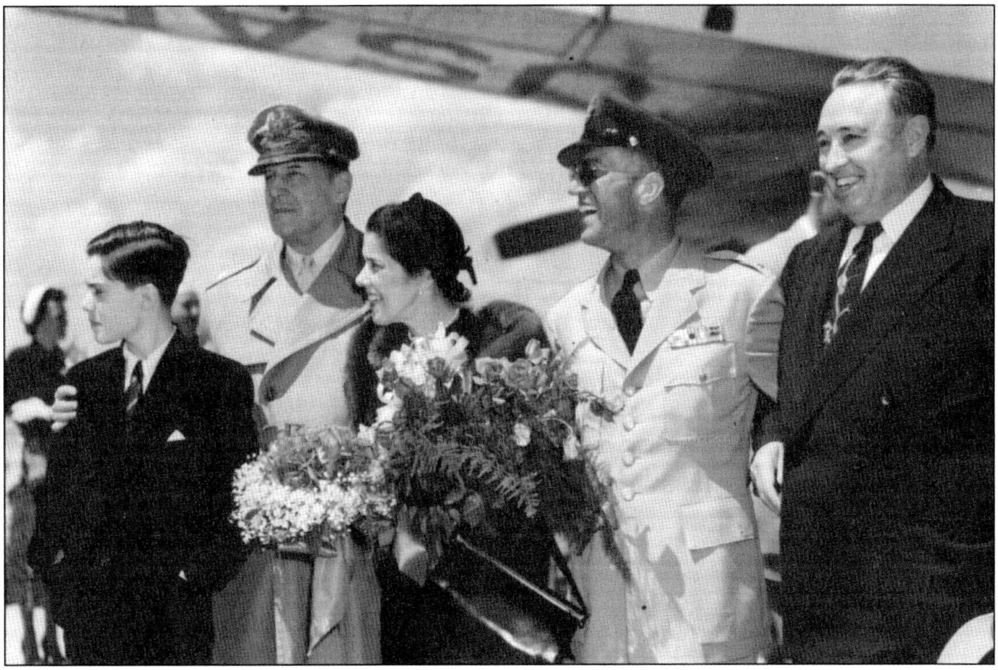

Jean Faircloth MacArthur (center) was born in Nashville but at age eight moved to Murfreesboro to live with her grandparents. Her grandfather fought for the Confederate army during the Civil War. Jean attended college in Nashville but graduated from Soule College in Murfreesboro. She met Douglas MacArthur (second from left) in 1935, and they married two years later. They are pictured here with their son Arthur IV (far left). (Courtesy of David Bucher.)

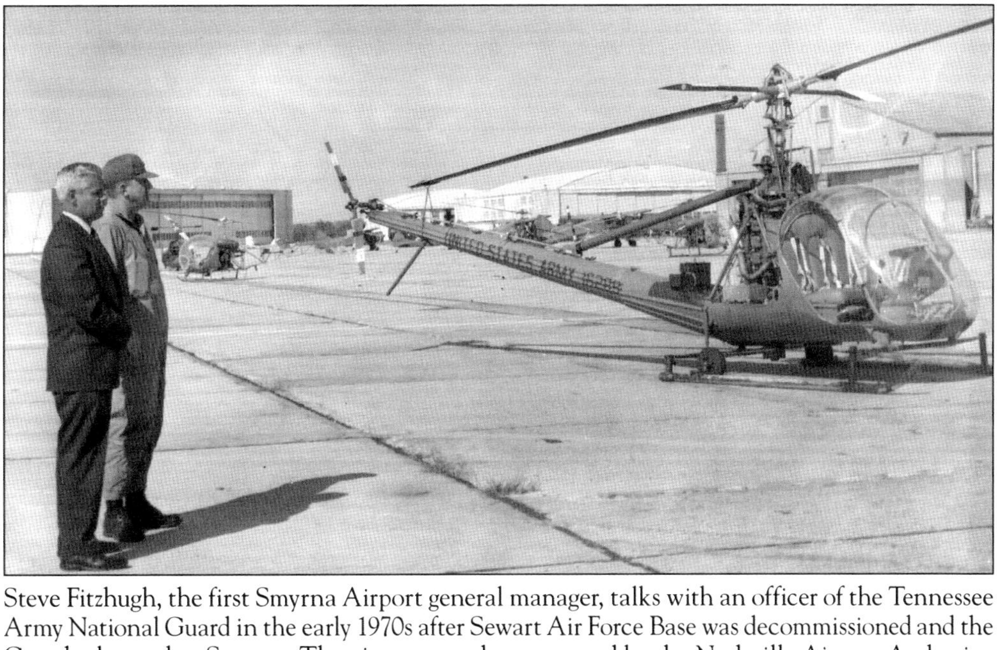

Steve Fitzhugh, the first Smyrna Airport general manager, talks with an officer of the Tennessee Army National Guard in the early 1970s after Sewart Air Force Base was decommissioned and the Guard relocated to Smyrna. The airport was then operated by the Nashville Airport Authority. Fitzhugh Boulevard, located on the Smyrna Airport property, is named after Fitzhugh; during the time of the air force base, this street was called A Street. (Courtesy of David Bucher.)

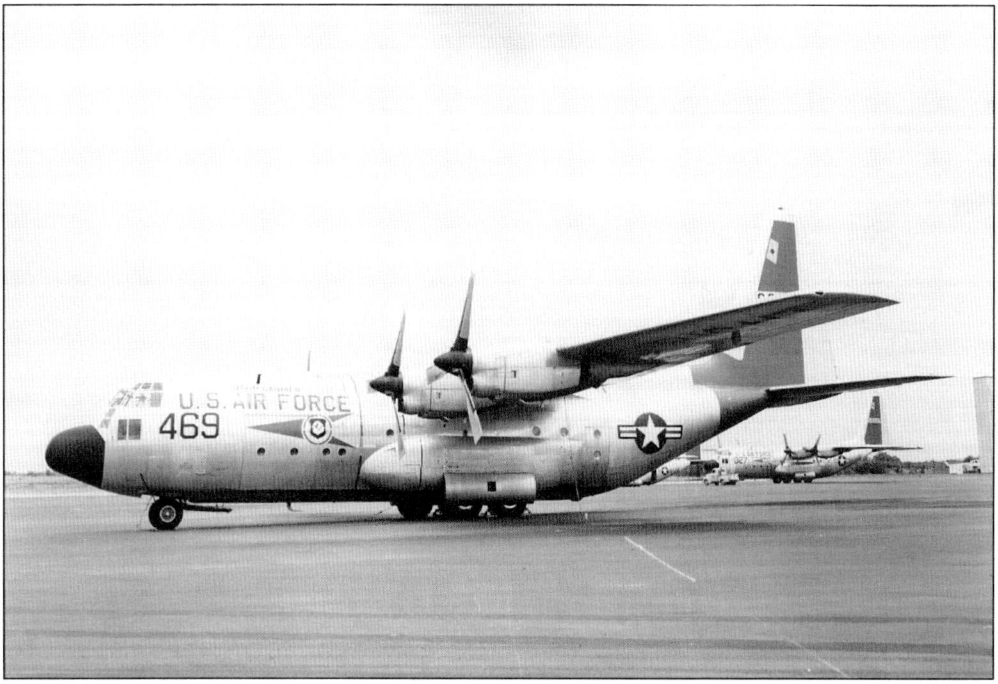

The air force base used C-130 Hercules planes, such as this one, for training purposes in the 1950s and 1960s. The plane was similar to its larger, four-engine predecessor, the C-123, which was originally designed to provide transport and serve as a glider. (Courtesy of Shacklett's Photography.)

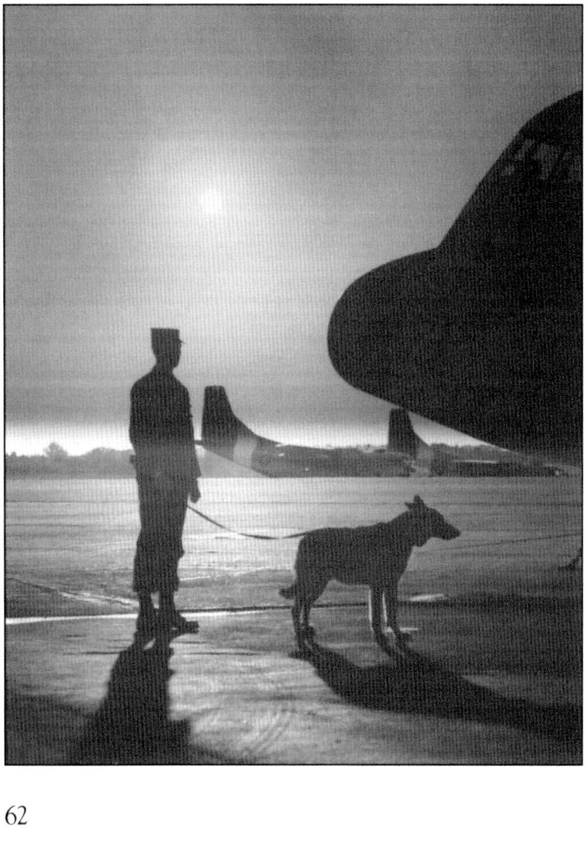

An Air Force serviceman patrols an aircraft with his canine partner in the early 1960s. The aircraft in the background is a C-123, and in the foreground is a C-130. (Courtesy of Rutherford County Archives.)

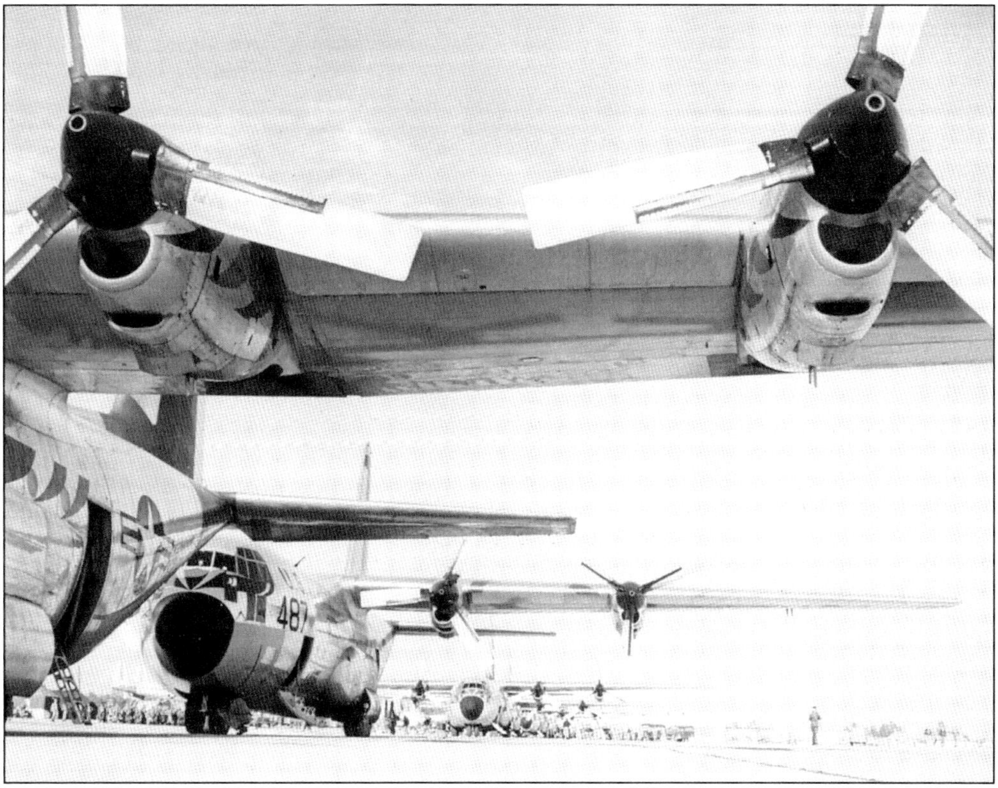

This c. 1955 photograph shows a line of C-130 aircraft at the tarmac of Sewart Air Force Base. At the time, the C-130 was the latest in technology and was able to use unprepared runways for both takeoff and landing. (Courtesy of Rutherford County Archives.)

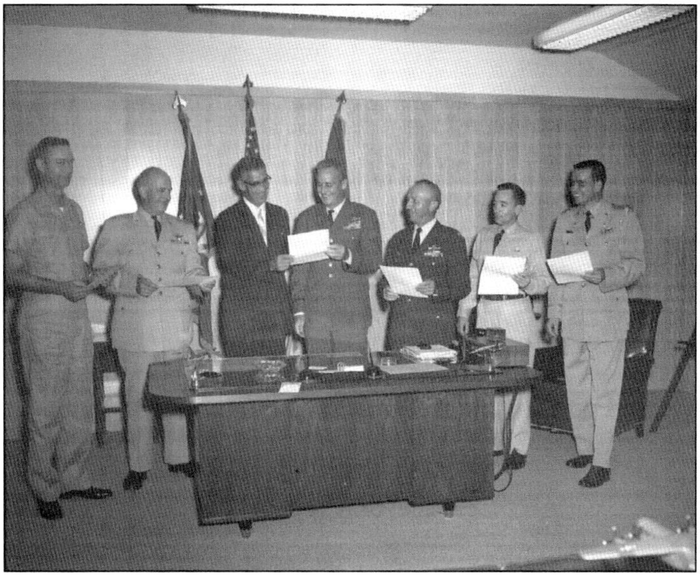

The men at Sewart Air Force Base had a lot to celebrate. Several high-ranking officials were awarded top honors during this ceremony in 1961. (Courtesy of Shacklett's Photography.)

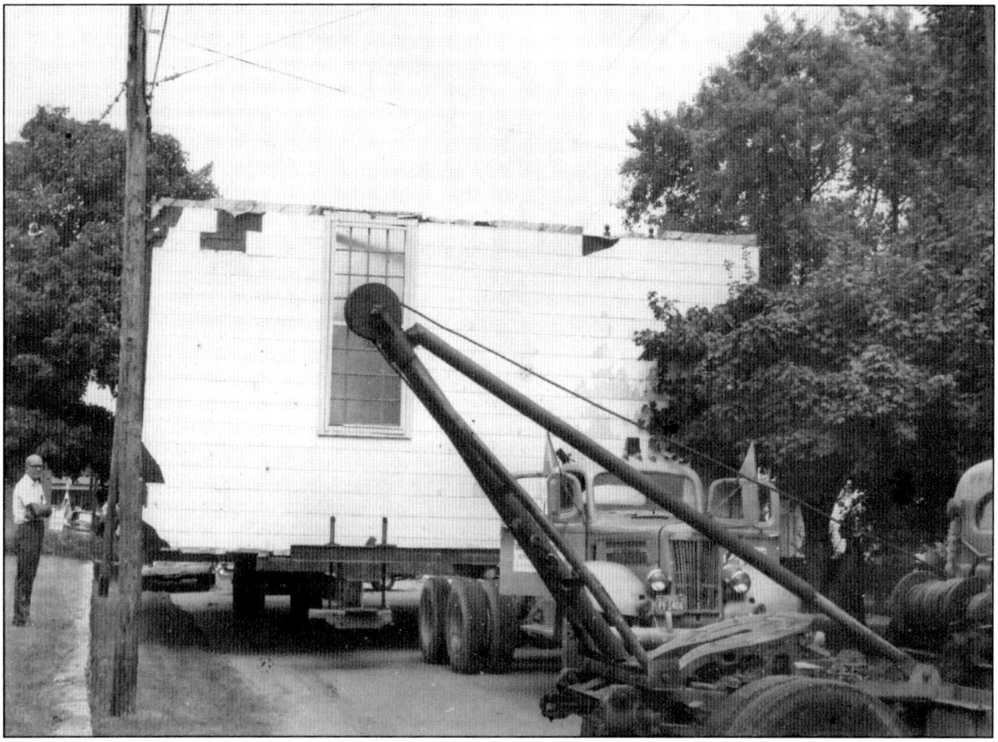

In 1970, the base was deactivated, and all remaining units were transferred to the Little Rock Air Force Base in Arkansas. The base property was divided among the Town of Smyrna, the Metro Nashville Airport Authority, Rutherford County, and the US Army Corps of Engineers. Here, the Catholic chapel from the base is being moved along Division Street to its new home near First Baptist Church. Frank Barnett, a local businessman, stands on the left, assisting with the loading of the structure. (Courtesy of David Bucher.)

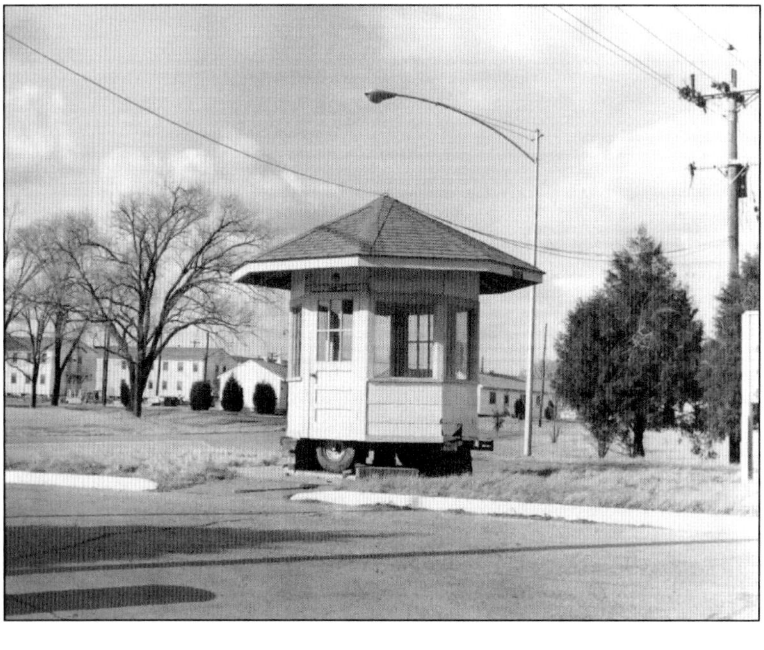

After the closing of Sewart Air Force Base, the guard shack was moved. It was originally at the back entrance of the base on Weakley Lane, between the base headquarters and the entrance to Wherry Housing. (Courtesy of David Bucher.)

Five

The Davis Family and Home

In the 1820s, Charles Davis moved his family from Mecklenburg County, Virginia, to Stewartsboro, Tennessee. His wife died shortly after their arrival, leaving Charles a single father of four. In 1841, Charles married Jane Simmons, who gave birth to Sam Davis the next year. Eventually, she would have nine children, with eight living to adulthood.

Sam served as a Coleman Scout in the Confederate army after fighting in Company I of the 1st Tennessee Infantry. One day, while bringing Union papers to his commander, Sam was captured near Pulaski, Tennessee. Gen. Grenville Dodge was so angered that Sam had paperwork from his desk, he considered Sam a spy rather than a scout. Sam was sentenced to hang, but his life would be spared if he told Dodge the name of his informant. Sam held steadfast and refused to tell. Later accounts recalled Sam's words in the moments before his death, "I would die a thousand deaths before I would betray a friend." Sam died on November 27, 1863. His story was picked up by the editor of *Confederate Veteran* magazine in the 1890s, and Sam Davis became a household name throughout the South.

Sam's family remained in the area, running businesses and working the land. When Sam's younger brother Oscar Davis died in 1927, the family decided to sell the house to the State of Tennessee, and by 1930 the state deeded the home to the Sam Davis Memorial Association for use as a historic house museum. Sam's niece Andromedia Davis Sinnott lived on the property and provided some of the first tours of the home. Throughout the years, hundreds of thousands of tourists have passed through Smyrna, learning about the Davis family and the sacrifice that young Sam Davis made.

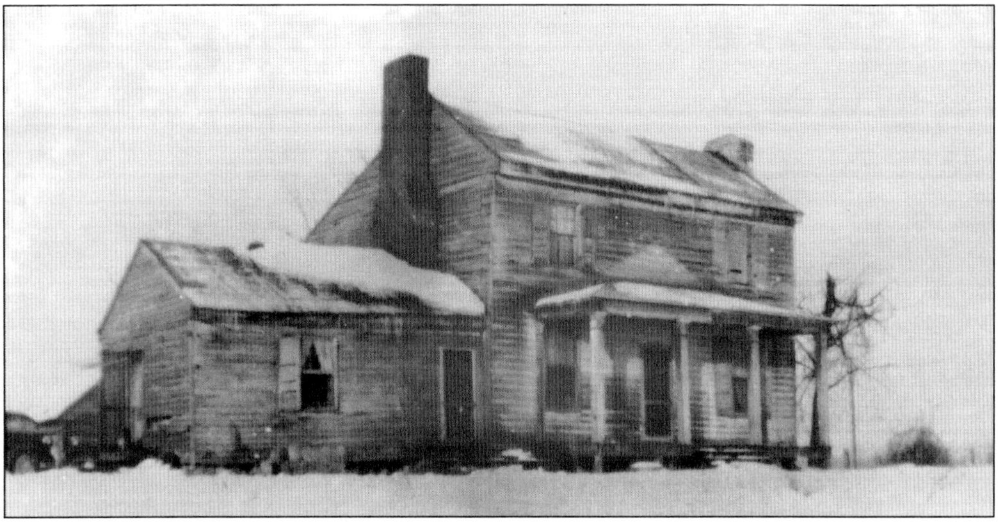

This 1960s photograph of the boyhood home of Sam Davis shows the structure with weatherboard covering original late-1800s logs. The Davises lived here prior to moving to the Sam Davis Home. (Courtesy of Smyrna Public Library.)

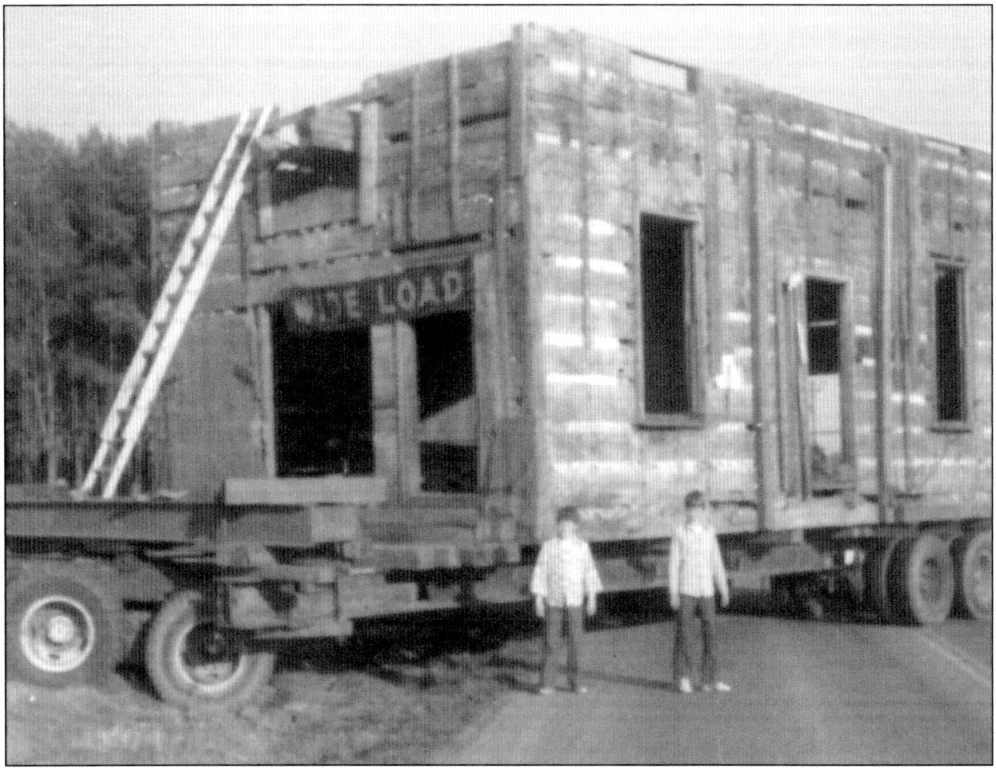

The Sam Davis Memorial Association acquired Davis's boyhood home and moved the structure from its original location on Almaville Road to the Sam Davis Home property in 1974. The kitchen was removed and the chimneys deconstructed for the trip. (Courtesy of Sam Davis Memorial Association.)

Two women and a man stand in front of the Sam Davis Home in the late 1800s or early 1900s. Their identities are unknown, but it is likely that they are Davis family members or friends. (Courtesy of Sam Davis Memorial Association.)

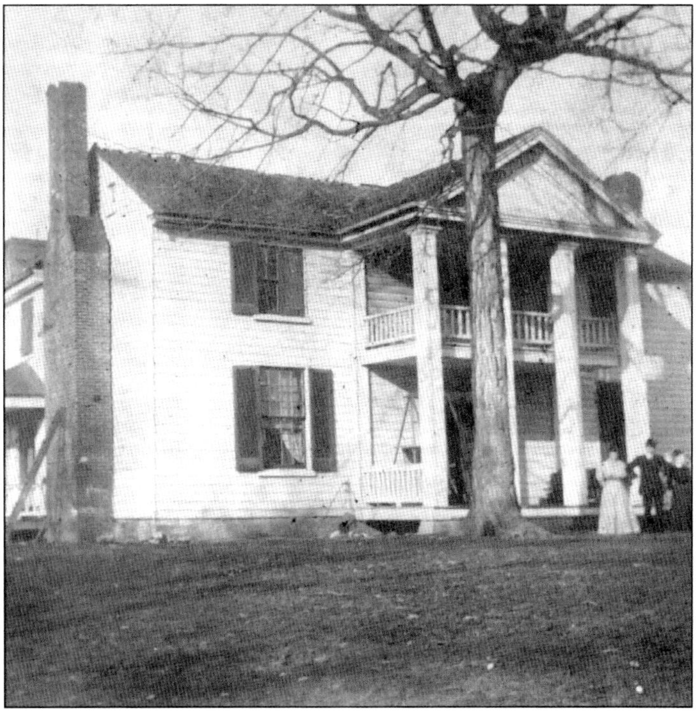

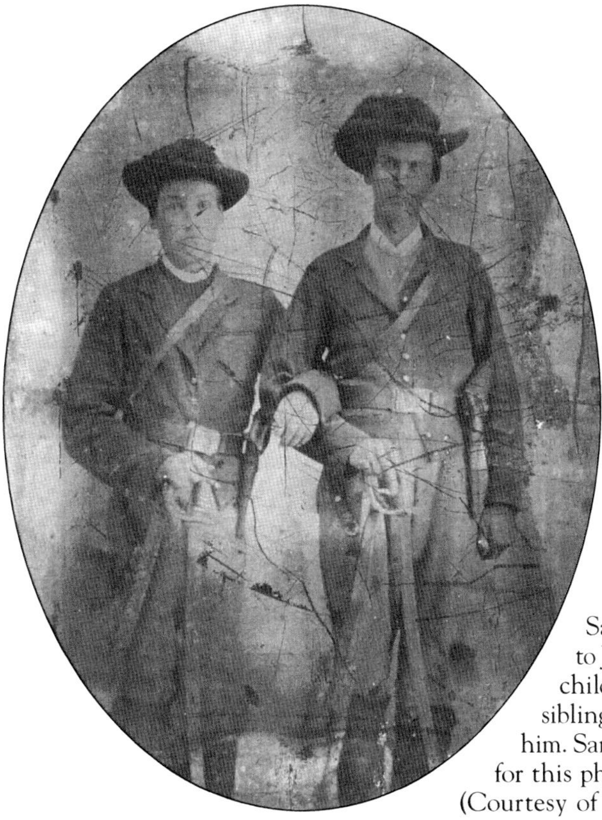

Sam Davis was born on October 6, 1843, to Jane and Charles Davis and was the first child of the couple. He had four older half siblings, one of whom is pictured here with him. Sam (left) and his half brother John posed for this photograph after the Civil War began. (Courtesy of Sam Davis Memorial Association.)

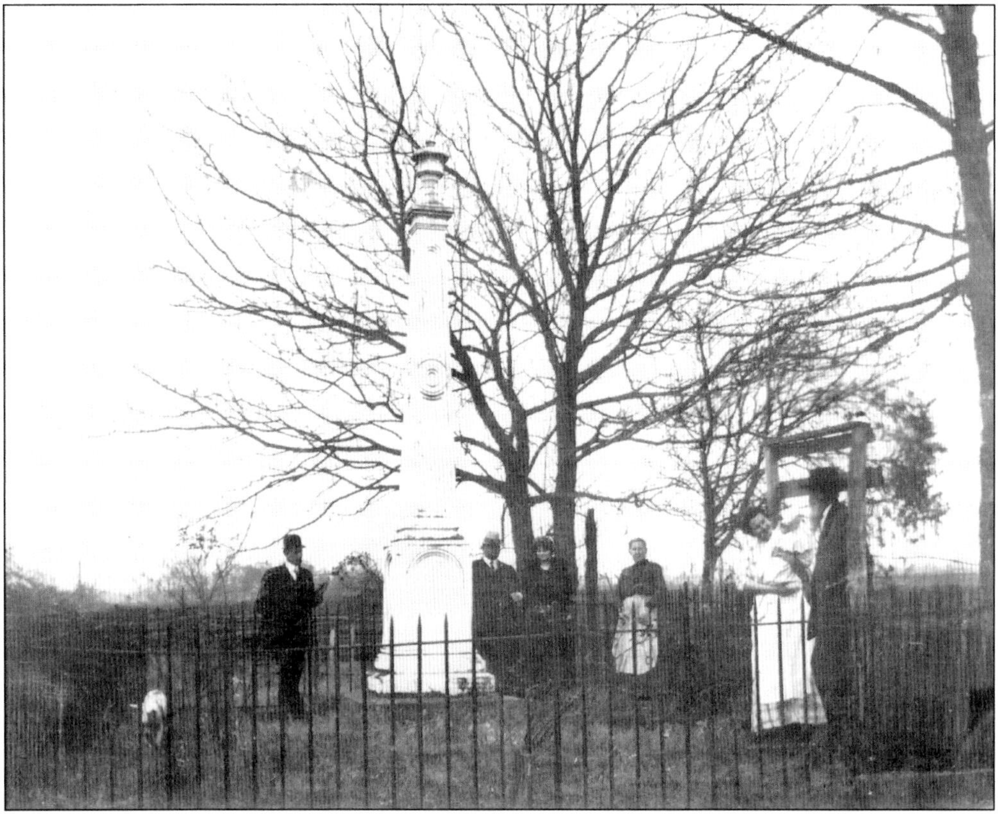

Sam Davis was hanged on November 27, 1863, in Pulaski, Tennessee. He was initially buried across the creek from his family home but was later moved to the family garden near the house. In 1866, the Coleman Scouts raised enough money to pay for this marble monument to honor him. In this late-1800s or early-1900s photograph, the family gathers at the monument. (Courtesy of Sam Davis Memorial Association.)

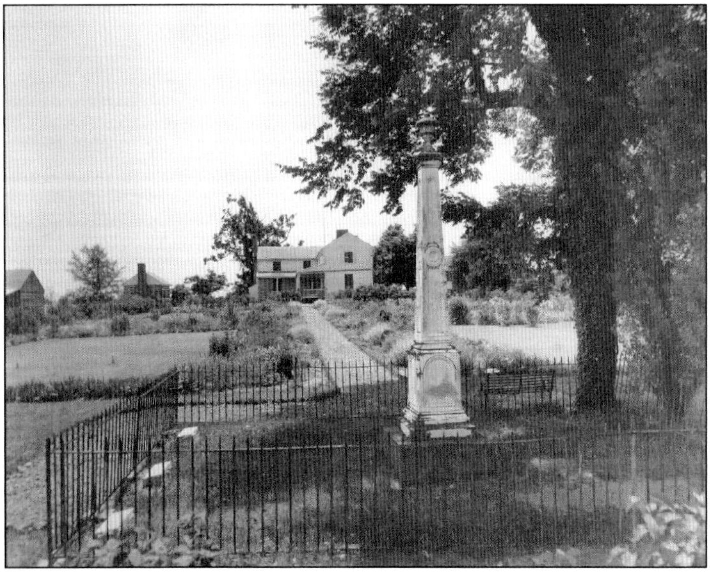

The Davis cemetery, shown here in the early 1940s, now includes Sam; his parents, Jane and Charles Davis; his sister Andromedia; his brother Oscar; Oscar's wife, Ida; and his grandmother Elizabeth Collier Simmons. (Courtesy of Sam Davis Memorial Association.)

Charles Davis was from Mecklenburg County, Virginia, and came to Middle Tennessee in the early 1800s. He established a farm in the area, and it grew rapidly. By 1860, Charles had over 800 acres. (Courtesy of Sam Davis Memorial Association.)

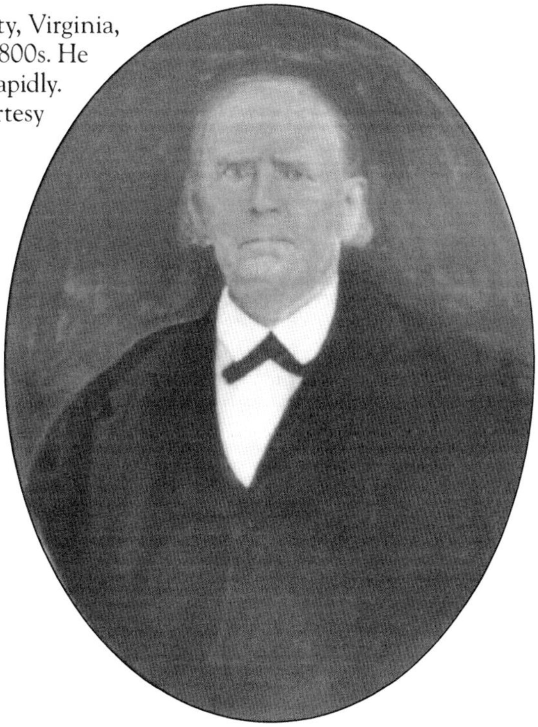

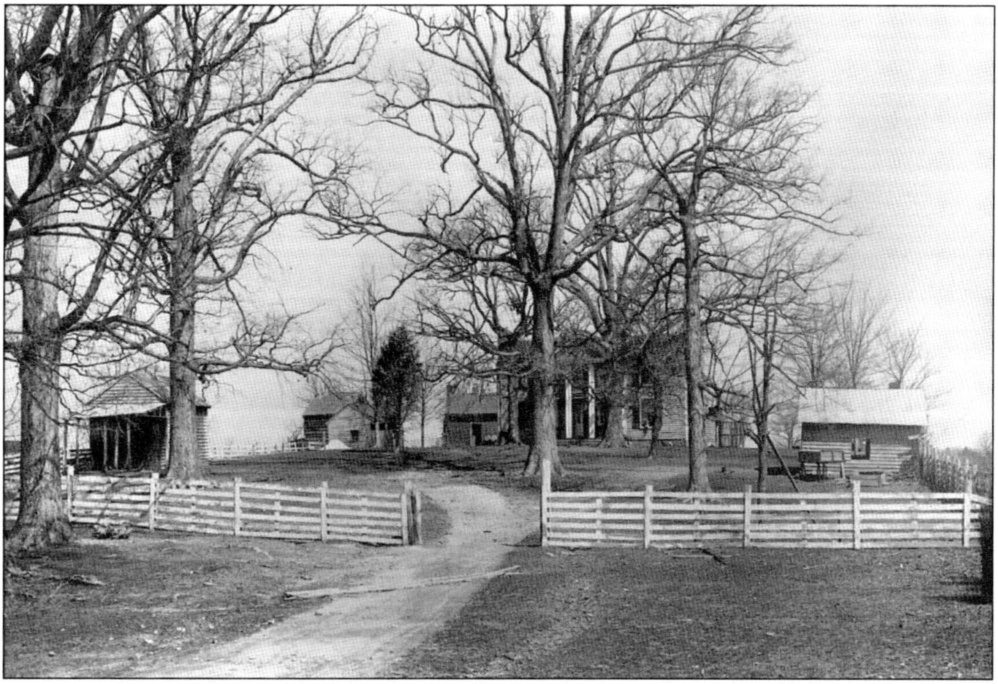

This photograph was taken in the early 1900s when the Davises still resided in the house. The two structures in the foreground are no longer standing. The building on the right was a garage used from around 1900 until 1927. An archeological investigation found a large number of vehicle-associated artifacts, both horse-drawn and motorized. (Courtesy of Sam Davis Memorial Association.)

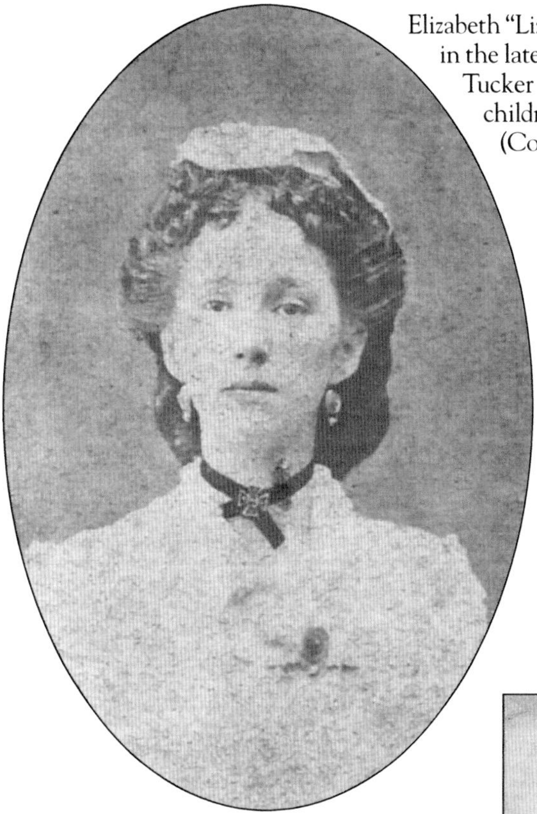

Elizabeth "Lizzie" Davis Tucker, Sam's sister, is pictured here in the late 1800s. She was born in 1854 and married Lee Tucker on October 11, 1871. The couple had seven children and lived within a mile of her parents' house. (Courtesy of Sam Davis Memorial Association.)

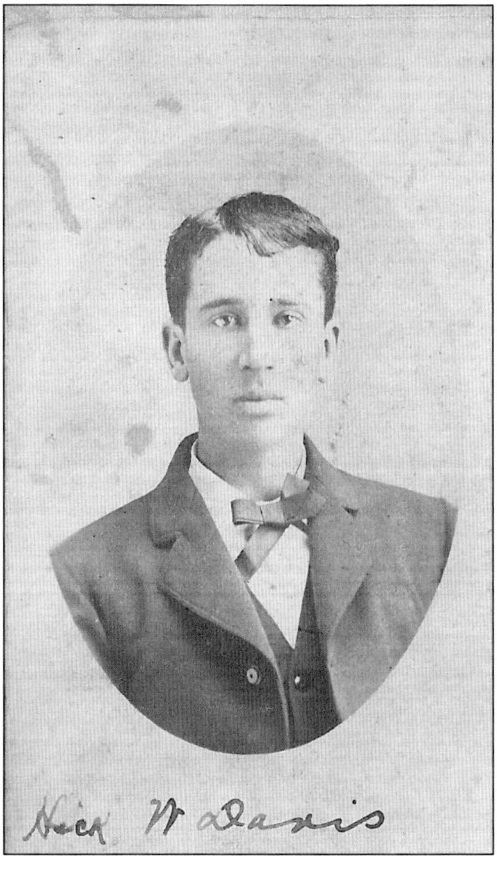

Born in 1861, Hickman Weakley Davis was only a baby when Sam left to join the military. This photograph from the late 1800s or early 1900s shows him as a young man. In 1886, he married Elizabeth Everett Cannon, and they had a daughter, Emma Cannon, the next year. (Courtesy of Sam Davis Memorial Association.)

Charles Louis Davis Jr. was born on June 19, 1859, and was only a toddler when Sam was killed. He and his wife, Mary Hollis, had two children, Andromedia Davis and Charles L. Davis III. (Courtesy of Sam Davis Memorial Association.)

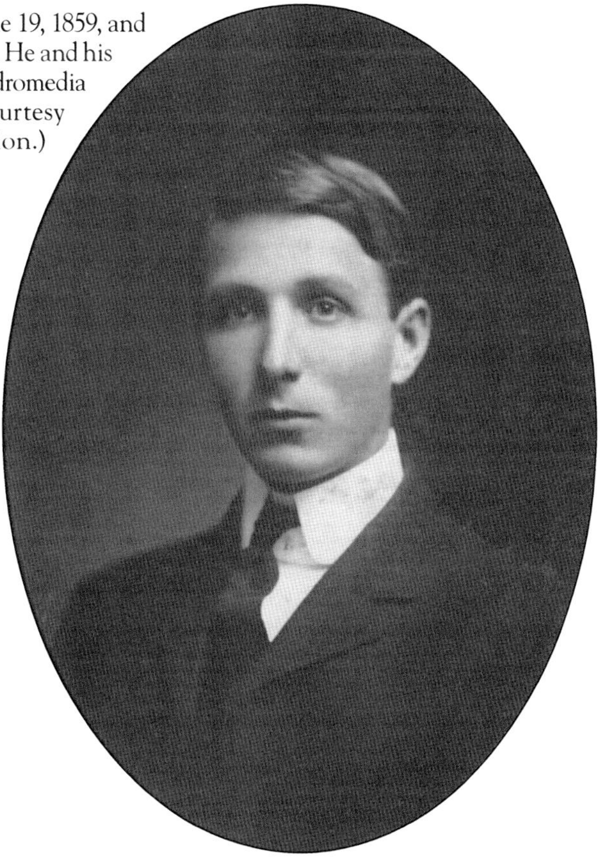

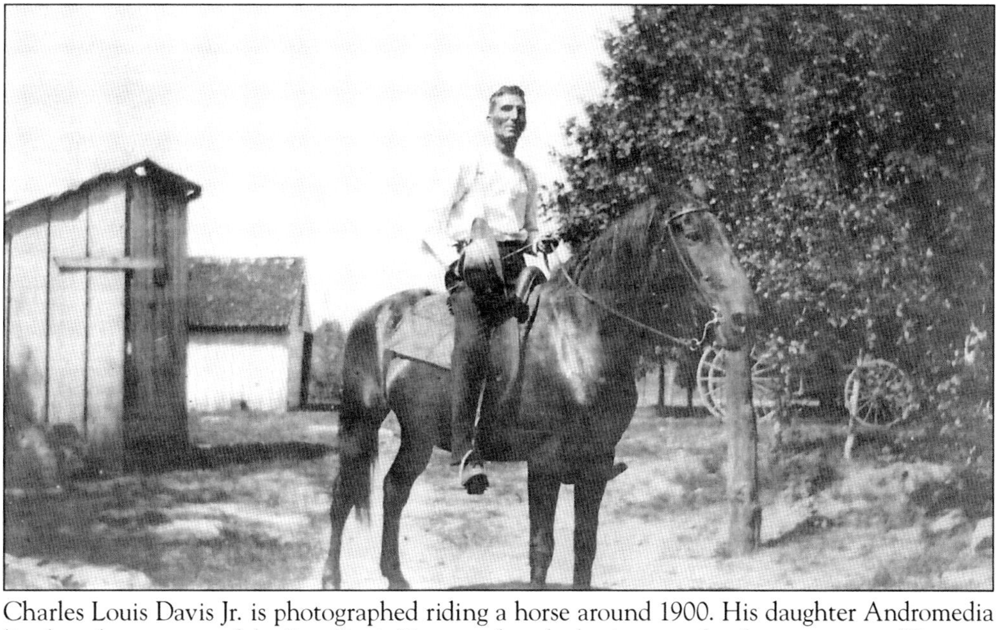

Charles Louis Davis Jr. is photographed riding a horse around 1900. His daughter Andromedia lived on the property of the Sam Davis Home and worked as its caretaker for many years. (Courtesy of Sam Davis Memorial Association.)

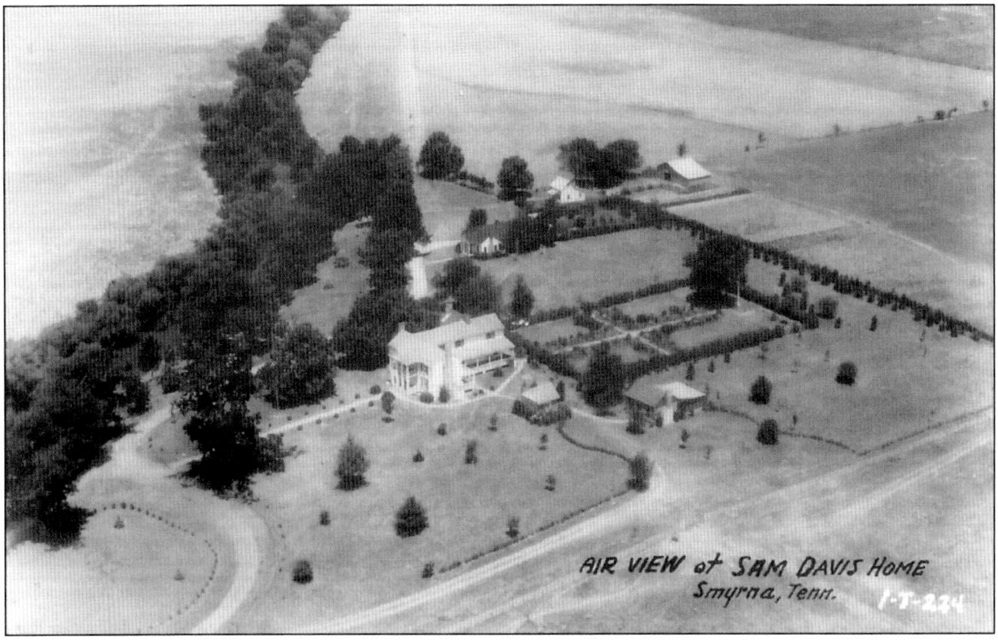

This 1940s aerial view of the Sam Davis property provides a unique look at the main house and surrounding area. The trees on the left follow Stewart's Creek, and most of the land surrounding the house was still being used for farming. Noticeably missing from the photograph are the enslaved workers quarters later purchased by the Sam Davis Memorial Association (SDMA) and placed near the dirt road close to the bottom of the image. (Courtesy of Chuck Clark.)

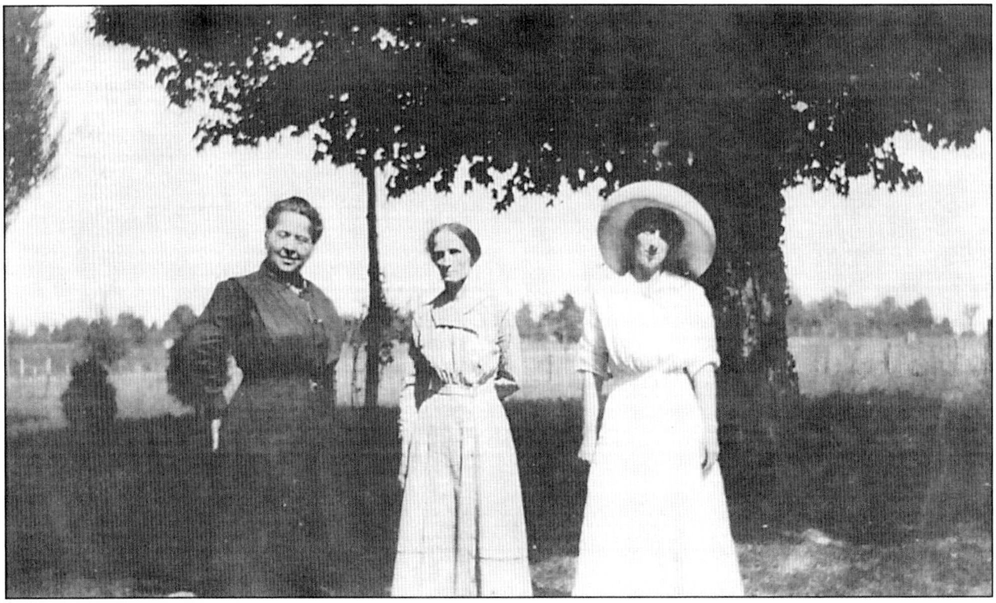

Aunts Fannie Davis Winstead (left) and Mary Davis (center) stand to the left of their niece Andromedia Davis Sinnott around 1900. Mary, the first child of Charles Davis and his first wife, Margaret Saunders, was born in 1829. She died at 74 years old in 1903. (Courtesy of Sam Davis Memorial Association.)

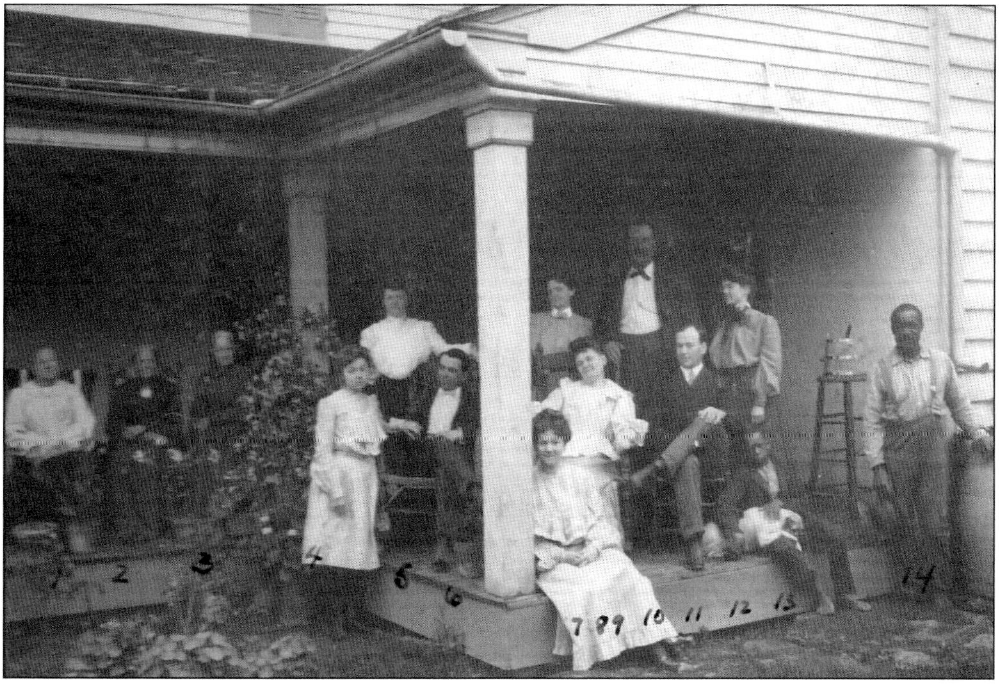

A few of Hickman Davis's friends gather around a Smyrna-area house in the early 1900s. Davis is labeled "10." He owned a farm as well as a livery stable that he operated with Silas Tucker in the 1910s. (Courtesy of Sam Davis Memorial Association.)

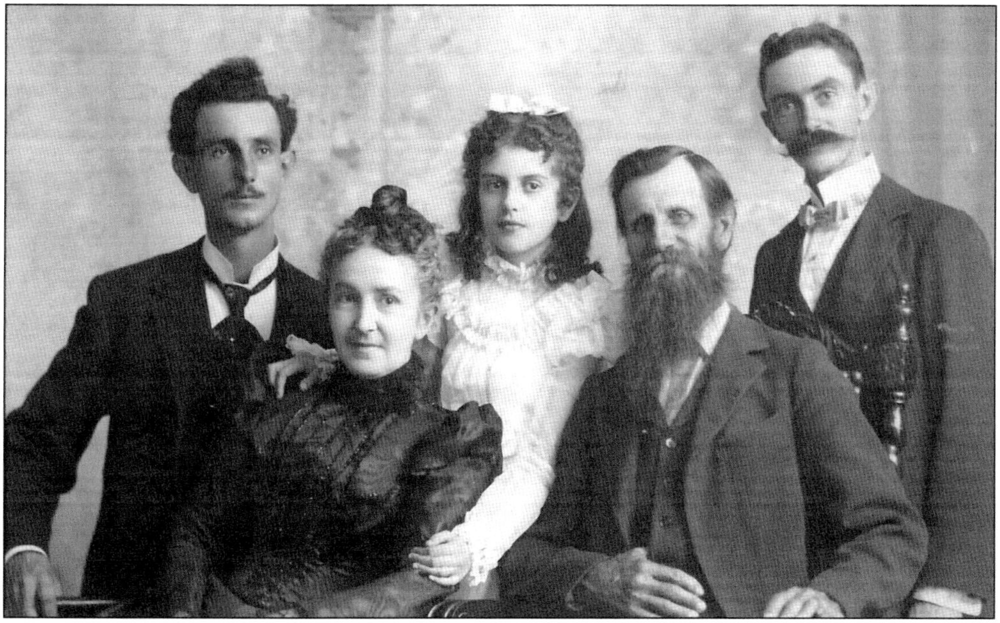
Sam's sister Andromedia Davis (second from left) is seen with her family around 1896. With her are husband Samuel H. Matthews, daughter Frances "Fannie," and sons Lewis and Samuel. The photograph was taken in Nashville by Calvert Bros. & Taylor. The Calvert brothers, Ebenezer and Peter, immigrated to America from England and began their photography company in 1889. In 1896, S.A. Taylor joined the business. (Courtesy of Sam Davis Memorial Association.)

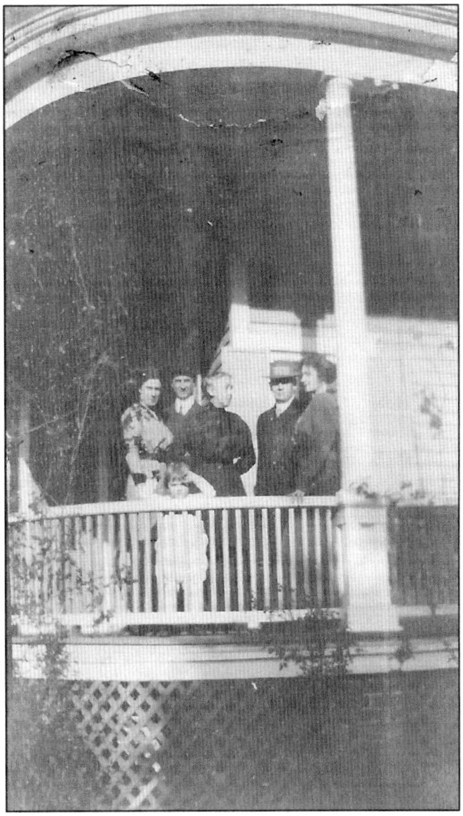

Andromedia Davis (center), her daughter Frances "Fannie" (left), granddaughter Frances S. Boyles (in front of Fannie), and others pose for this photograph around 1913. Andromedia named her daughter in honor of her sister. (Courtesy of Sam Davis Memorial Association.)

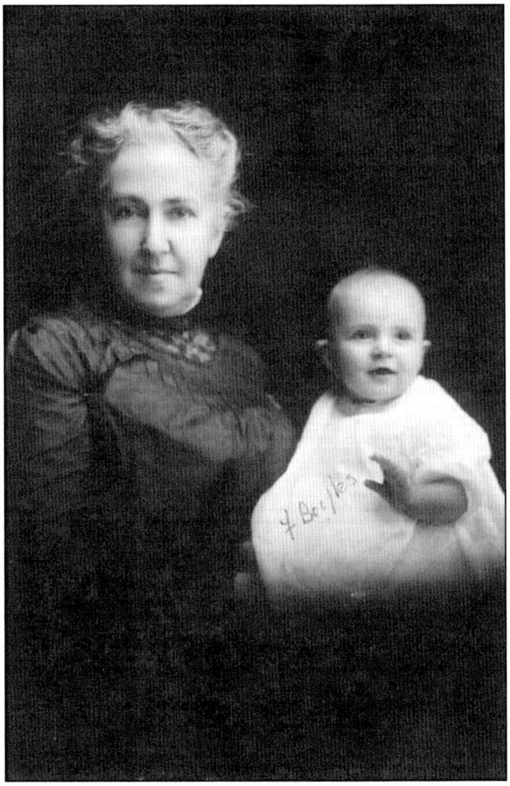

Andromedia Davis sits with her granddaughter Frances S. around 1910. Andromedia lived with her daughter and her family after the death of her husband, Samuel Matthews, in 1904. She remained with them in Texas until her death in 1938. (Courtesy of Sam Davis Memorial Association.)

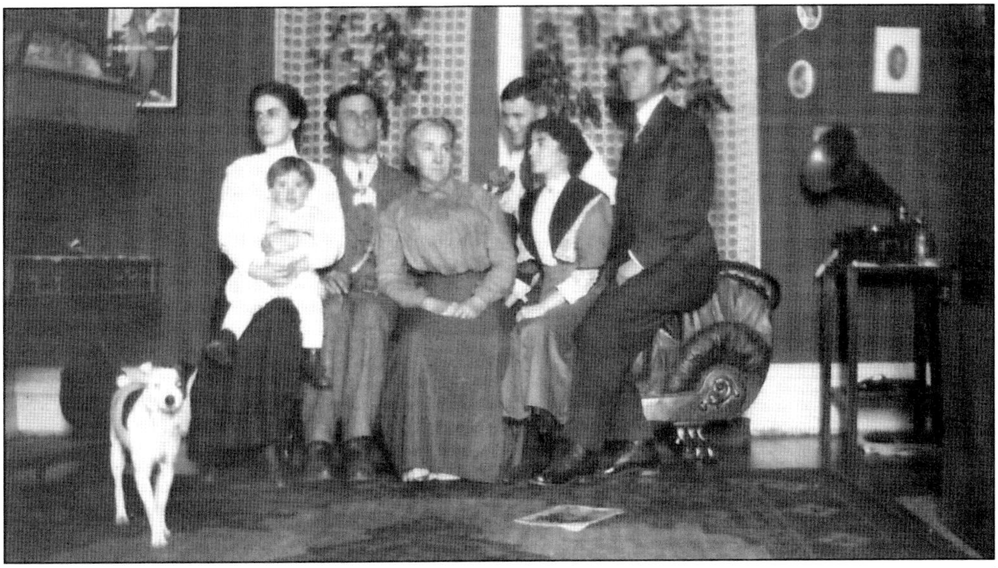

Andromedia Davis is surrounded by her family in this photograph taken during the winter of 1912. Andromedia's daughter Frances went to the Smyrna Fitting School, as did Frances's cousin Andromedia "Media" Davis Sinnott. (Courtesy of Sam Davis Memorial Association.)

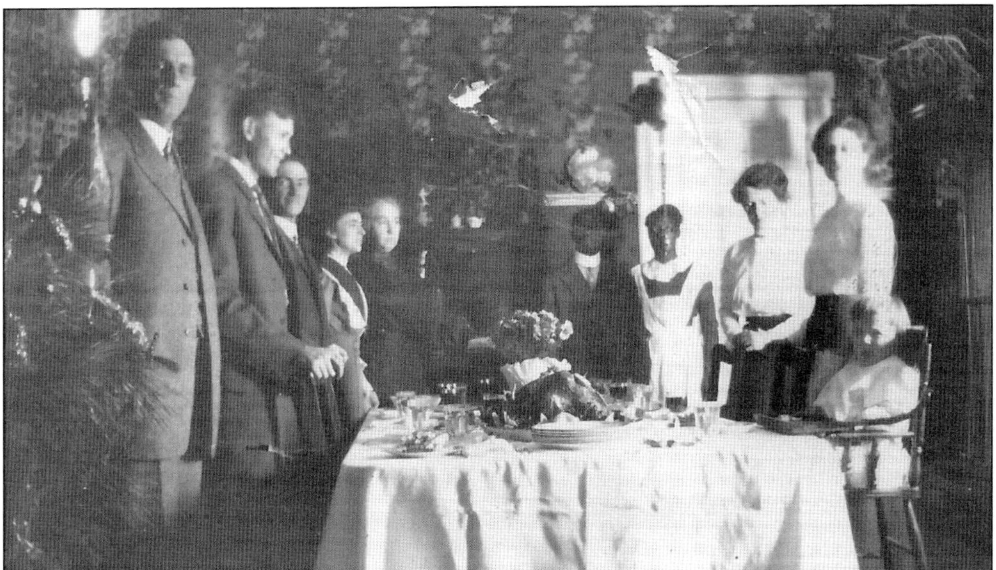

Sam's sister Andromedia is shown here with her family on Christmas Day in 1912. Andromedia is at the head of the table on the left, and the child on the far right is Frances S., her beloved granddaughter. (Courtesy of Sam Davis Memorial Association.)

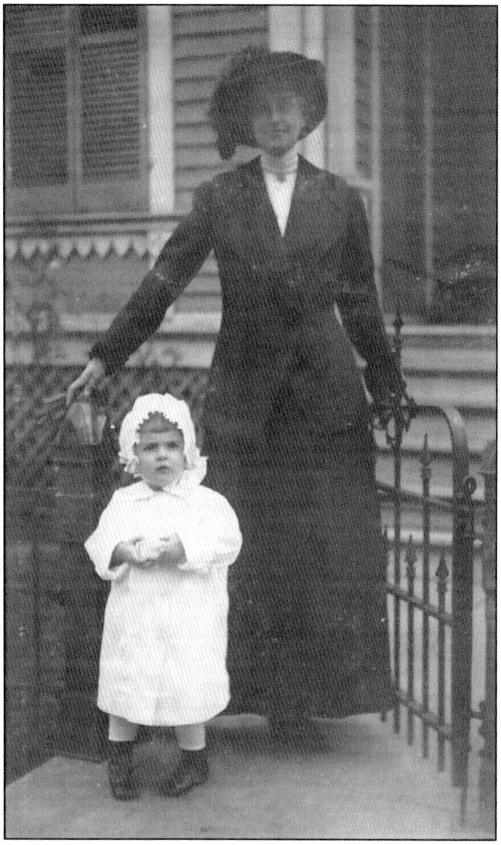

Frances stands with her daughter Fannie Boyles outside of a home in November 1912. Fannie grew up with several cousins, including Andromedia "Media" Sinnott, daughter of her uncle Charles L. Davis Jr. (Courtesy of Sam Davis Memorial Association.)

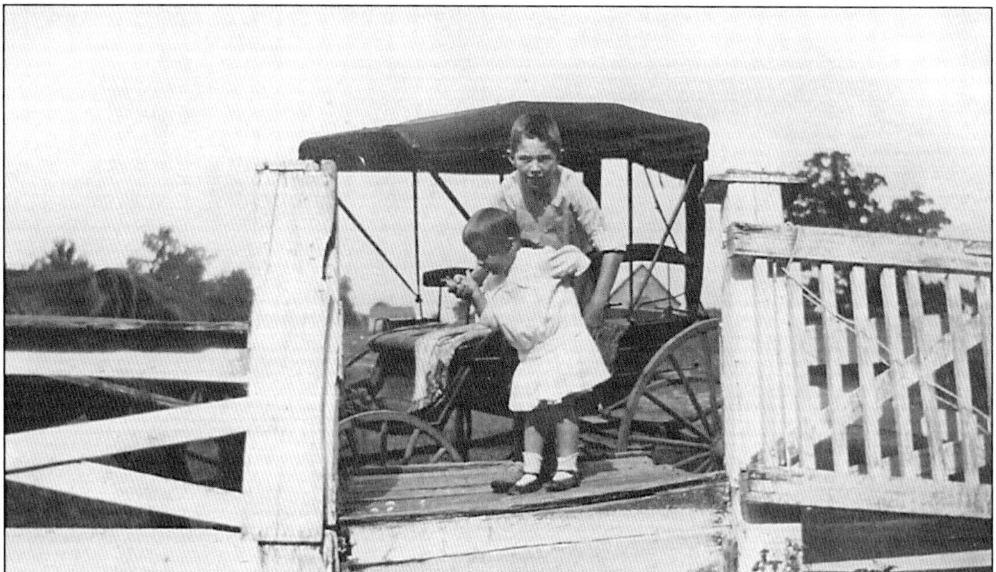

Frances S. Boyles and an older boy unload a buggy around 1912. The photograph is believed to have been taken at her aunt Fannie's house in Smyrna. By 1920, the family was living in Houston, Texas. (Courtesy of Sam Davis Memorial Association.)

An unidentified man holds Frances S. in August 1913 at her aunt Elizabeth "Lizzie" Davis's property. Fannie was the granddaughter of Andromedia Davis and Samuel Matthews. (Courtesy of Sam Davis Memorial Association.)

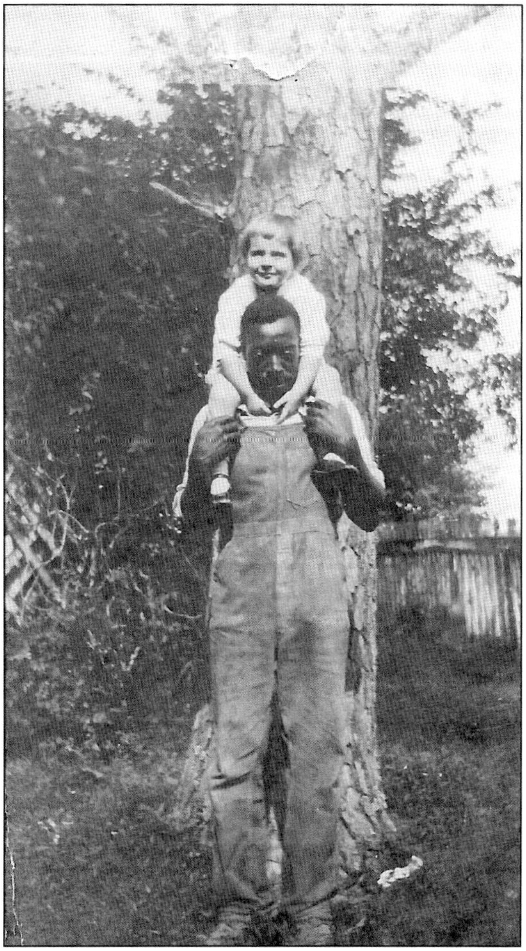

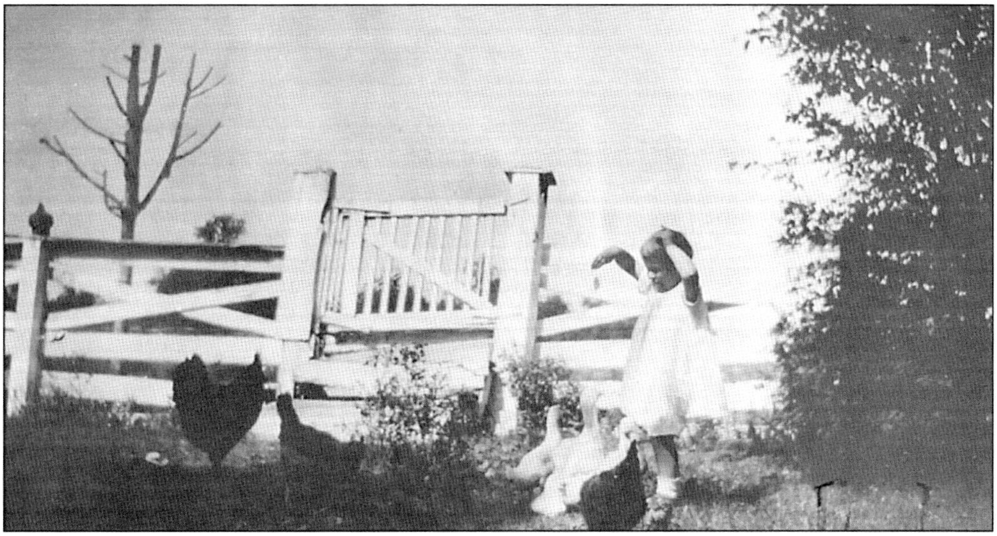

Frances S. plays among the chickens in this c. 1912 photograph. Fannie loved visiting her aunts' houses and playing with the animals on the property. (Courtesy of Sam Davis Memorial Association.)

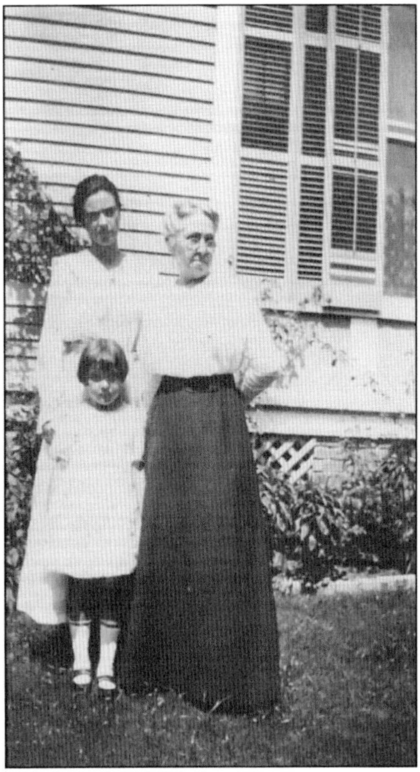

Andromedia stands with her daughter Frances B. and granddaughter Frances S. in this c. 1913 photograph. Andromedia conducted interviews with the press and others that asked her about her family and her brother Sam Davis. (Courtesy of Sam Davis Memorial Association.)

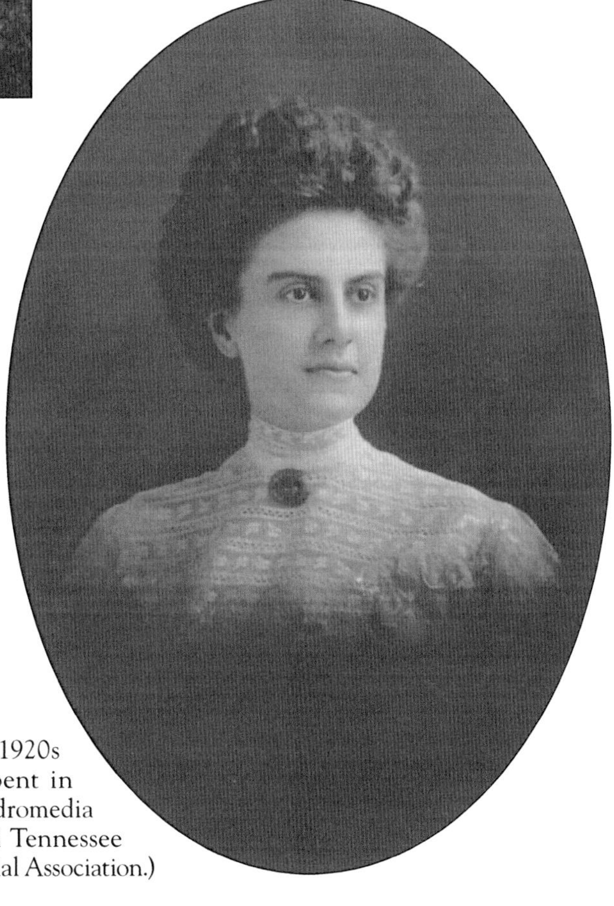

Frances S. Boyles poses for this 1920s photograph. Her early life was spent in Texas, where her grandmother Andromedia lived with her family. They visited Tennessee often. (Courtesy of Sam Davis Memorial Association.)

Andromedia "Media" Davis Sinnott, daughter of Charles Davis Jr., spent several years as the caretaker for the Sam Davis Home after it became a historic site. She lived on the property and is shown here in the 1920s. (Courtesy of Sam Davis Memorial Association.)

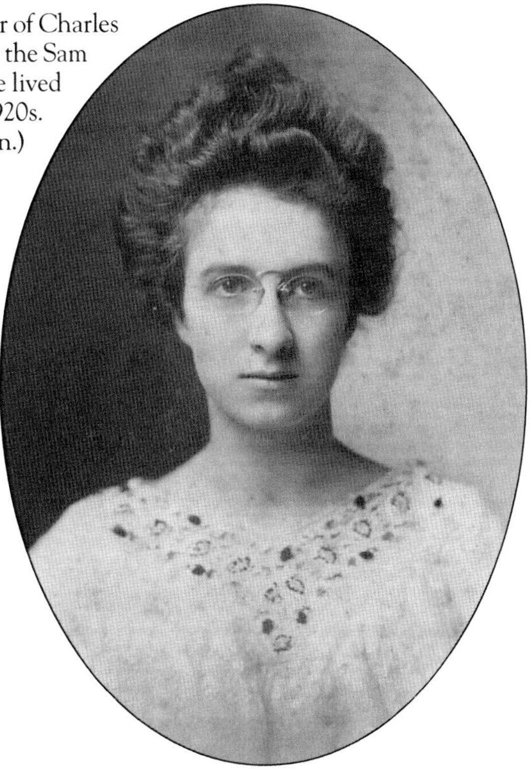

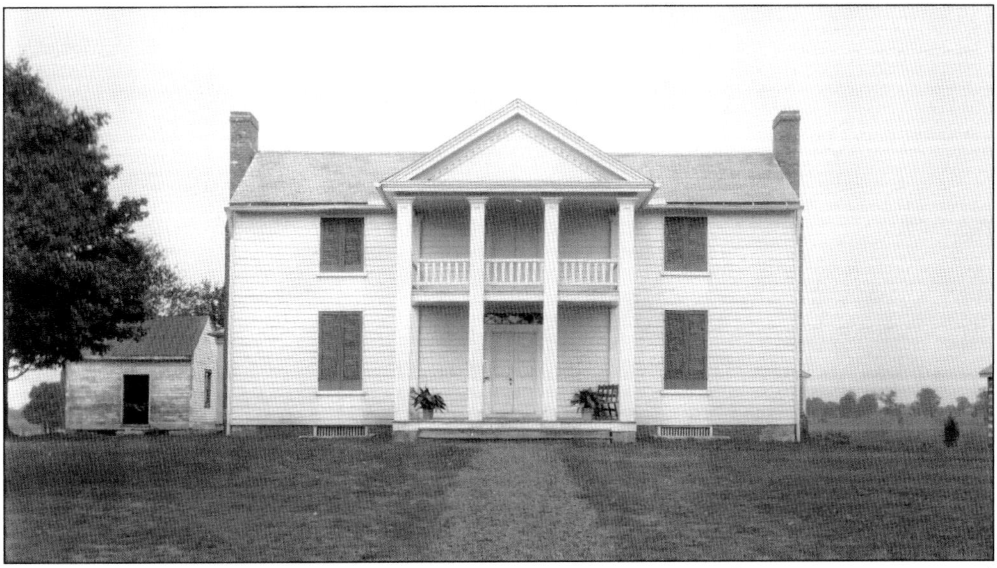

This photograph of the Sam Davis Home was taken shortly after the Sam Davis Memorial Association took over the historic site in 1930. The white structure to the left of the house is the original kitchen and is reported to have been the residence of Uncle Charlie, a former enslaved worker to the Davises. An archeological dig found several arrowheads beneath another building occupied by him, showing his interest in the past. The building to the right of the house is the original overseer's cabin. The overseer made $550 in 1860. (Courtesy of Sam Davis Memorial Association.)

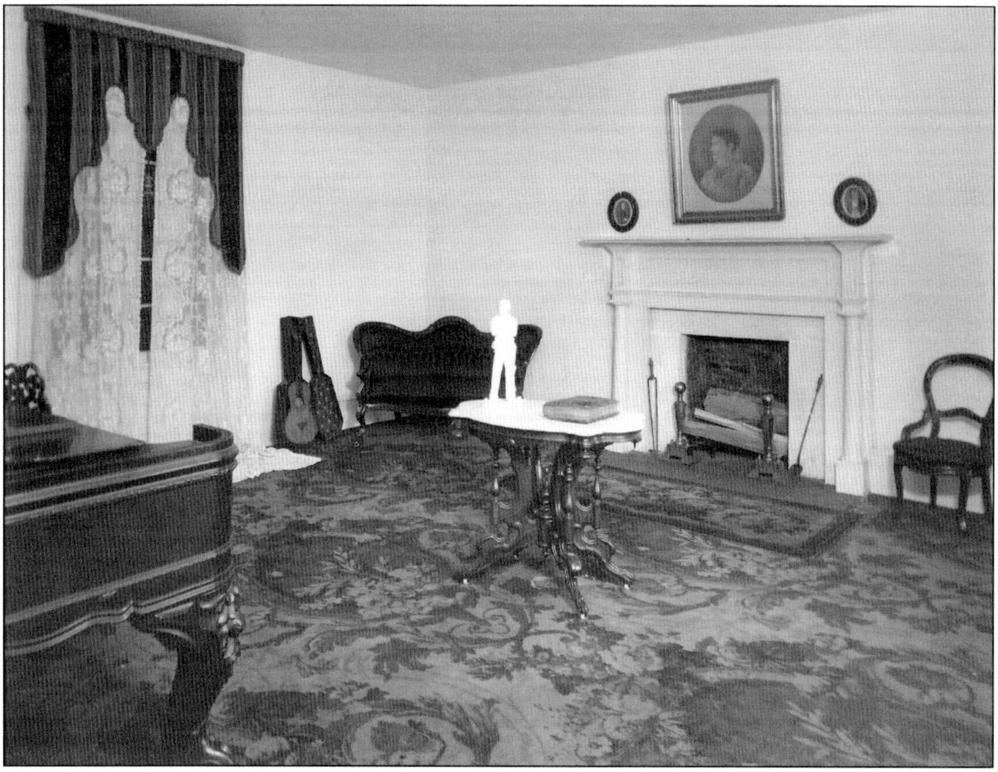

The formal parlor was the room to which the family took guests for entertaining. The Brussels carpet seen here is one of the original pieces in the house, as are the horsehair couch and chair (with a matching set). These were purchased by the family in the 1870s and are shown in this 1940s photograph. (Courtesy of Sam Davis Memorial Association.)

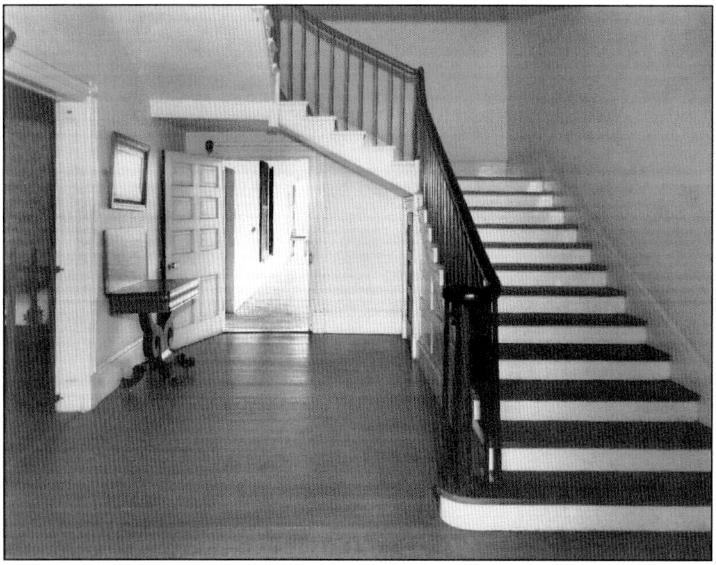

This 1940s view of the front hallway shows the house prior to the 1968 renovations. The SDMA board and staff added period-correct reproduction wallpaper to the front hallway and updated the wallpaper in the informal parlor and many other rooms. (Courtesy of Sam Davis Memorial Association.)

Six

Personalities

Smyrna is nothing without its people. Those in charge and the everyday residents make Smyrna a wonderful place to live. The late 1700s and early 1800s saw an influx of immigration to the area. Homesteaders and farmers lived throughout the hills, but it was not until the 1850s that Smyrna began to boom when the Nashville & Chattanooga Railroad created a stop in the area. Situated firmly in Middle Tennessee, Smyrna residents sided mostly with the Southern cause of the Confederacy, though some residents were thought to be favorable toward the Union, including Dr. John Kennedy. Sam Davis is known now for his loyalty to a friend, whom he gave his life for, and to the South. Another famous citizen from that time was large landowner Col. J.S. Gooch, who commanded the 20th Tennessee Regiment in the Army of Tennessee. Family names, including Coleman, Gracy, Haber, King, Lowry, Moore, Victory, and Weakley, all trace their roots back to the early days of Smyrna. The town was made up of the same families for generations, and it was not until the Air Force and industry came to the area that Smyrna grew rapidly.

Thurman Francis is another well-known name in town. Francis was the commissioner of fire and police for Smyrna in the 1970s and owned Bi-Rite Supermarket.

Many Smyrna residents recognize the name Ridley. Brothers Knox and Sam Ridley served as mayors for Smyrna from the 1940s through the 1980s, with Knox taking office in 1987 and his brother serving in the same position in the years preceding that. The pair opened several successful businesses in town, including Klassic Kleaners, Ridley Chevrolet, Smyrna Insurance Agency, and Sam Davis Development Corporation. They developed the first residential subdivision in Smyrna and later created similar subdivisions in Murfreesboro. Sam was a major proponent of the Air Force Base coming to Smyrna and worked tirelessly to make it happen. He also drove the first Nissan vehicle, a Datsun truck, off the line.

After the introduction of the Nissan North America manufacturing plant, people began moving to the area, and the population more than doubled.

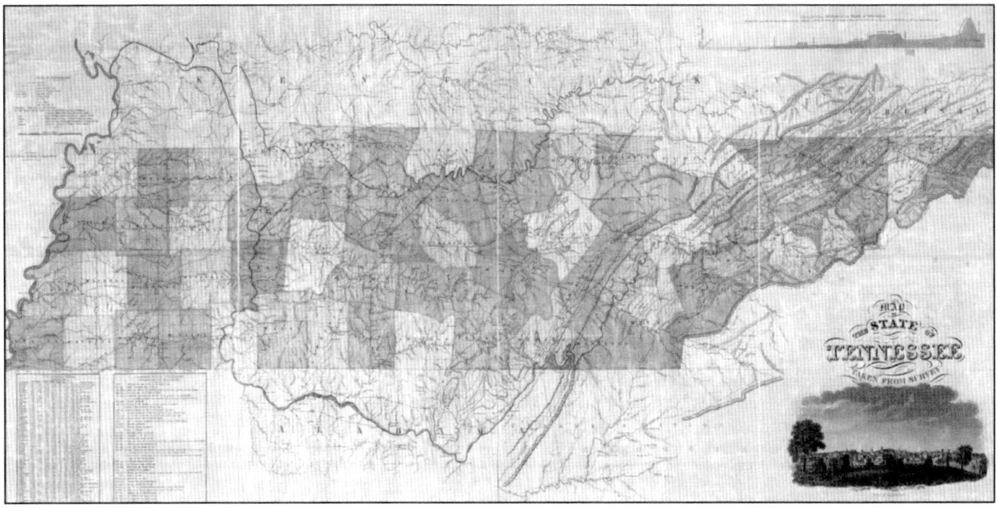

The Trail of Tears passed through Jefferson and part of Smyrna in October and November 1838. Matthew Rhea created this map, which was used by officials leading approximately 4,000 native people to the newly created Indian Territory. Instead of following the main routes, which passed toll roads, this group traveled on what is now Old Jefferson Pike to Sam Ridley Parkway, where they turned north near present-day Smyrna Airport. (Courtesy of Pat Cummins.)

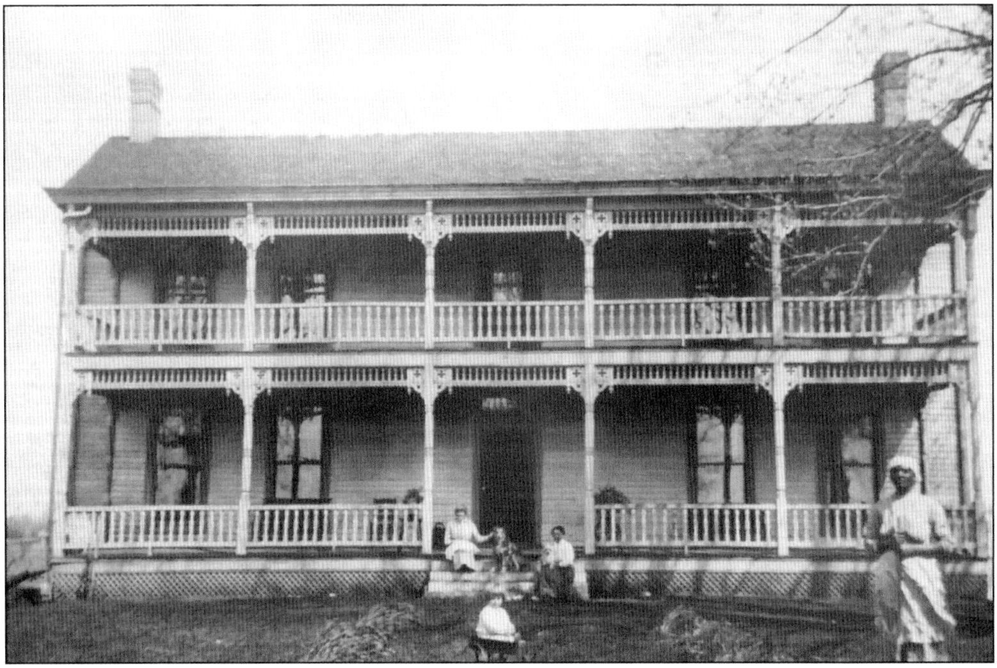

Built in the early 1830s for John McGregor and his wife, Milbry Donelson, this house was not completed before their deaths. John was a soldier during the Creek War and the War of 1812. Milbry was the daughter of early Nashville settler William Donelson. They both died of cholera within seven months of each other in 1835 and 1836, leaving behind six children, the youngest two months old. (Courtesy of Rutherford County Archives.)

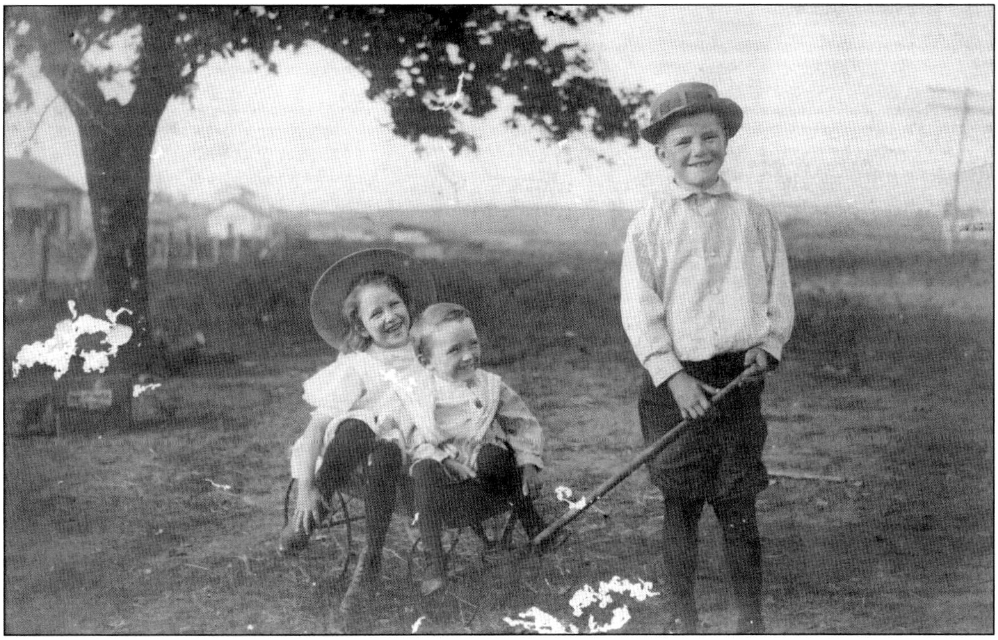

This c. 1909 postcard showing Margaret (left), Kelly (center), and Emmett Weakley was sent to Margaret Weakley, care of Robert Weakley, in Smyrna. The Weakley family was prominent in the area. Col. Robert Weakley owned land near Stones River in the late 1700s. (Courtesy of Rutherford County Archives.)

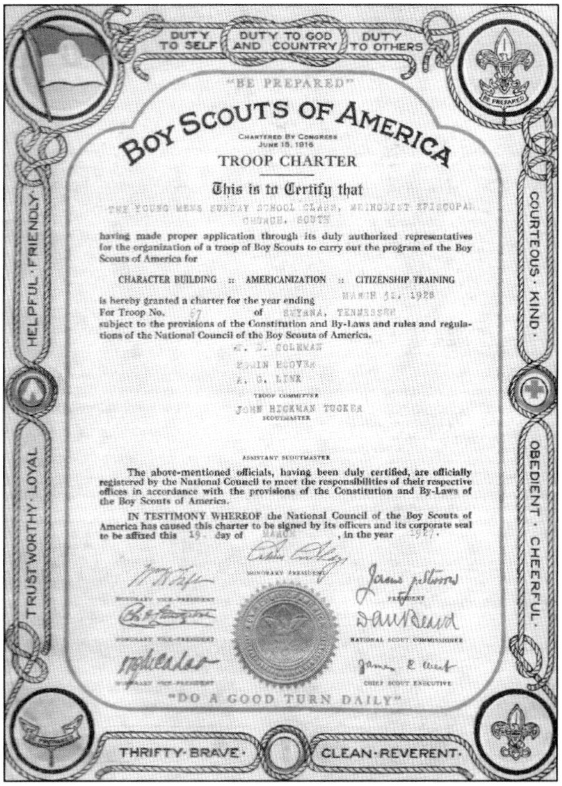

DUTY TO SELF · DUTY TO GOD AND COUNTRY · DUTY TO OTHERS

"BE PREPARED"

BOY SCOUTS OF AMERICA

CHARTERED BY CONGRESS JUNE 15, 1916

TROOP CHARTER

This is to Certify that

THE YOUNG MENS SUNDAY SCHOOL CLASS, METHODIST EPISCOPAL CHURCH, SOUTH

having made proper application through its duly authorized representatives for the organization of a troop of Boy Scouts to carry out the program of the Boy Scouts of America for

CHARACTER BUILDING :: AMERICANIZATION :: CITIZENSHIP TRAINING

is hereby granted a charter for the year ending MARCH 31, 1928
For Troop No. 67 of SMYRNA, TENNESSEE
subject to the provisions of the Constitution and By-Laws and rules and regulations of the National Council of the Boy Scouts of America.

W. D. COLEMAN
EDWIN HOOVER
A. G. LINK
TROOP COMMITTEE

JOHN HICKMAN TUCKER
SCOUTMASTER

ASSISTANT SCOUTMASTER

The above-mentioned officials, having been duly certified, are officially registered by the National Council to meet the responsibilities of their respective offices in accordance with the provisions of the Constitution and By-Laws of the Boy Scouts of America.

IN TESTIMONY WHEREOF the National Council of the Boy Scouts of America has caused this charter to be signed by its officers and its corporate seal to be affixed this 19 day of MARCH, in the year 1927.

HONORARY PRESIDENT
HONORARY VICE-PRESIDENT
PRESIDENT
HONORARY VICE-PRESIDENT
NATIONAL SCOUT COMMISSIONER
HONORARY VICE-PRESIDENT
CHIEF SCOUT EXECUTIVE

"DO A GOOD TURN DAILY"

HELPFUL · FRIENDLY · COURTEOUS · KIND · TRUSTWORTHY · LOYAL · OBEDIENT · CHEERFUL · THRIFTY · BRAVE · CLEAN · REVERENT ·

The Young Men's Sunday school class of the Methodist Episcopal church received a charter for the Boy Scouts of America troop No. 67 in March 1928. This charter came after Dr. J.S. Lowry attempted to organize a troop in 1916. With Edwin Hoover leading the boys, they went on many hikes and learned a great deal about nature. (Courtesy of Smyrna Public Library.)

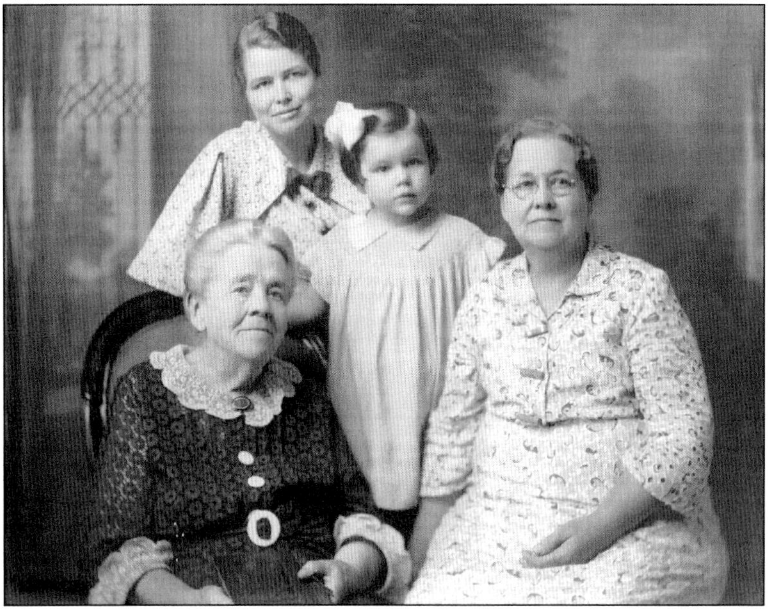

The Brittain women, sitting for a 1930s portrait, are, from left to right, Lucy Atkinson, Lena Miller Brittain, Joan Hall, and Grace Brittain Hall. Grace graduated from Smyrna High School in 1926. (Courtesy of Katherine Haynes Walkup and family.)

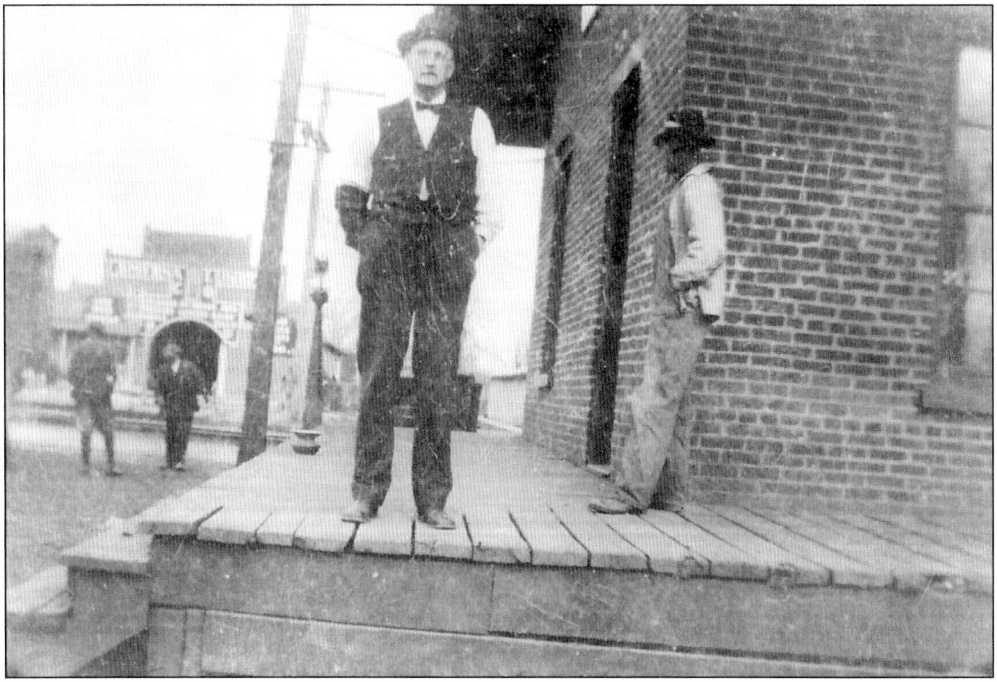

Nashville, Chattanooga & St. Louis Railroad (formerly the Nashville & Chattanooga) station agent William Washington Wright stands in front of the Smyrna Depot. William worked this job for 35 years and joined the Smyrna Church a few months before his death on Thanksgiving in 1923. (Courtesy of John Moore.)

Frances Dudley Smith (left) and Walaca Link enjoy a relaxing picnic at Jefferson Springs in 1929. The area became known for its resorts, and many hotels and spas popped up throughout the early half of the 1900s. (Courtesy of Smyrna Public Library.)

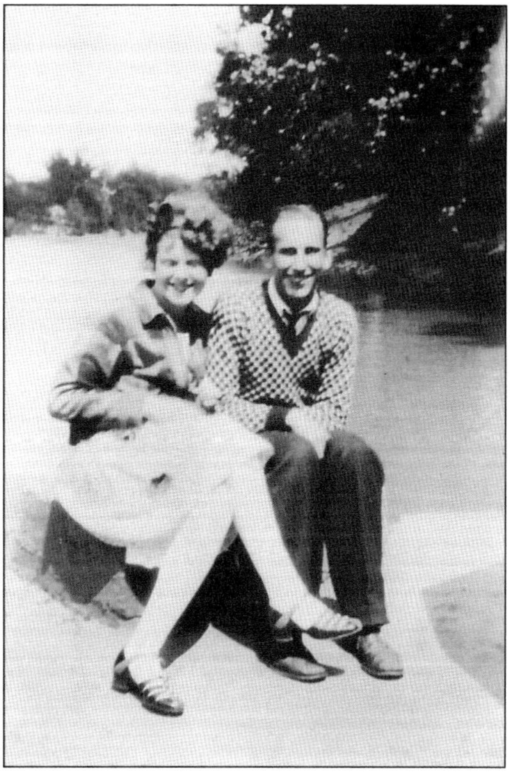

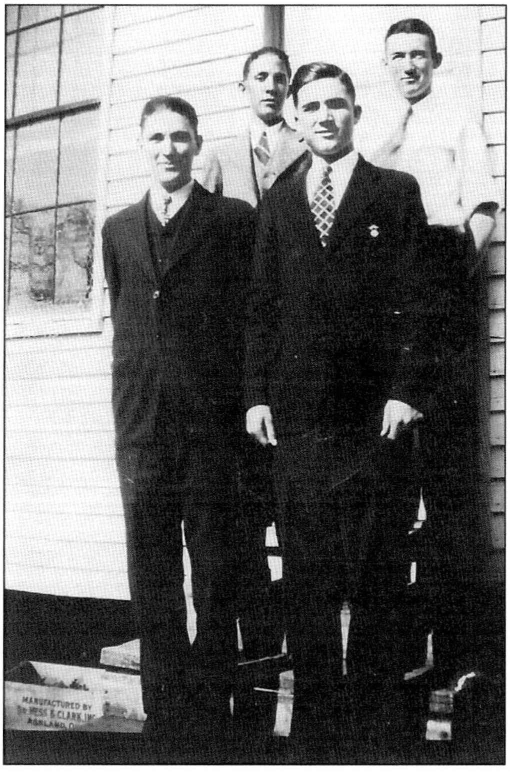

Rucker Raikes (left) and Herman Chumbly stand behind Vestal Raikes (left) and Rassie D. Fann in the early 1900s. Rucker worked at the air base in civil service on heavy equipment. Vestal later worked at Central State Hospital, a psychiatric hospital in Nashville. (Courtesy of Robert "Bud" Raikes.)

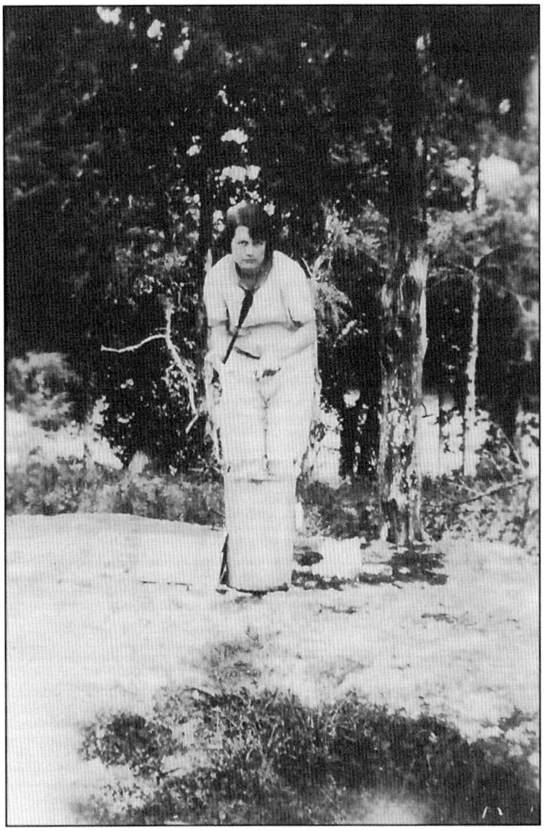

Sarah Hunter enjoys a class picnic at Old Jefferson Springs in 1929, the same year she graduated. Hunter was also a member of the Smyrna Methodist Church. (Courtesy of Smyrna Public Library.)

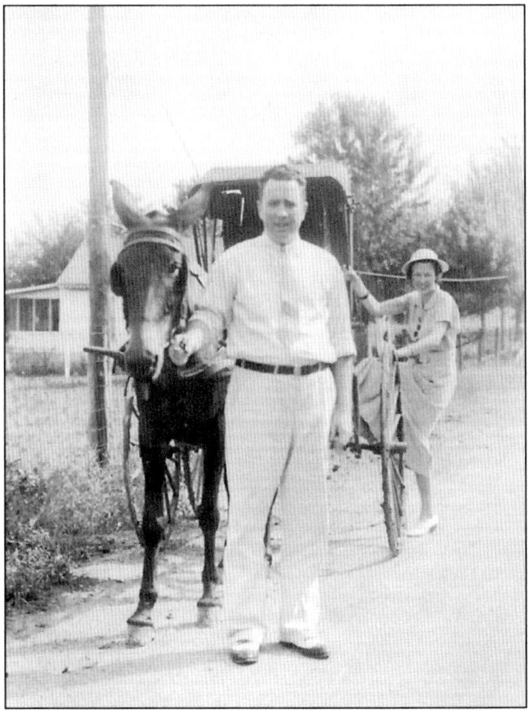

Ida King and Bob Batey load their buggy and head into Smyrna in the summer of 1934. Batey graduated from Smyrna High School in 1923 and joined the military after Pearl Harbor was attacked. He eventually became a major. While in the military, he spent time in China, Burma, and India. In 1960, he retired from Snyder & Black, Inc., a lithograph company in New York City. Batey died in 1982. (Courtesy of the Sam Davis Memorial Association.)

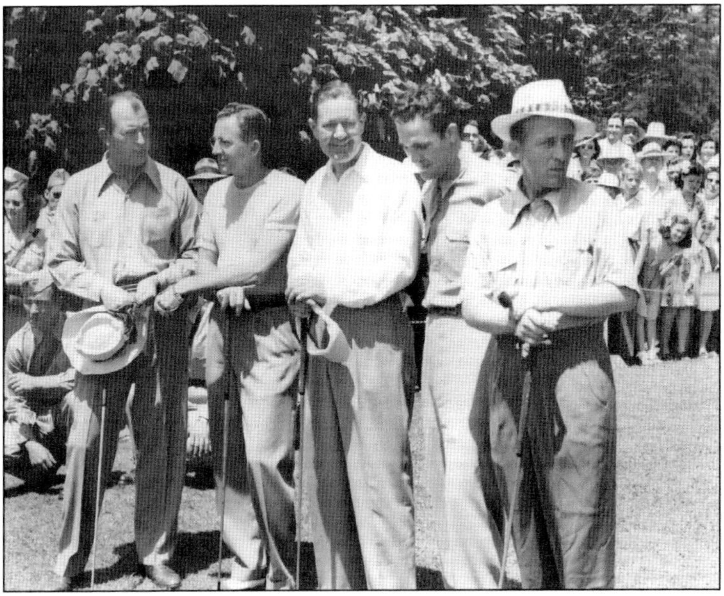

Pictured from left to right in 1943, Ed Dudley, unidentified, Byron Nelson, Billy Conn, and Bing Crosby play a nine-hole exhibition match in Smyrna as part of a United Service Organization and Red Cross effort to raise money for World War II. Smyrna was only one stop on their tour, which ran from 1940 until 1943. (Courtesy of Smyrna Golf Course.)

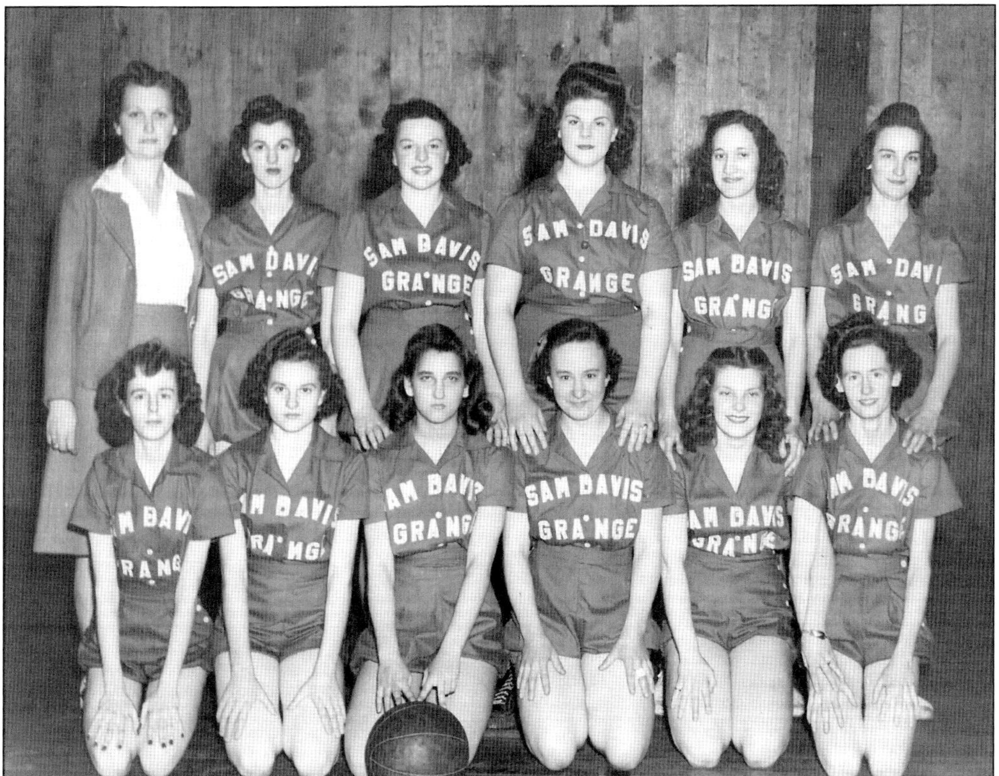

Players for the Sam Davis Grange basketball team in Smyrna pose for this photograph in 1946. The girls, led by Coach Lucille Dalton, played in an independent tournament from March 6 through March 9, 1946. (Courtesy of Smyrna Public Library.)

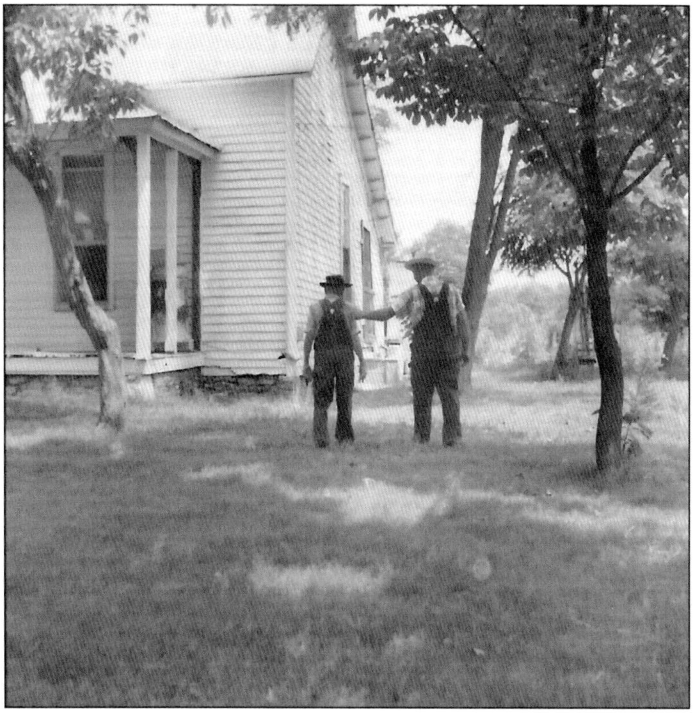

Brothers Malcolm (left) and Tommy Francis walk outside Malcolm's house in Jefferson on Sharp Springs Road in 1959. In the late 1950s, relatives built Tommy a cabin in the corner of Malcolm's yard. The cabin had one room but offered Tommy a comfortable life. After the Army Corps of Engineers purchased the land, the cabin was moved to higher ground on the Palmer farm a couple of miles south of Sharp Springs Road. (Courtesy of Toby Francis.)

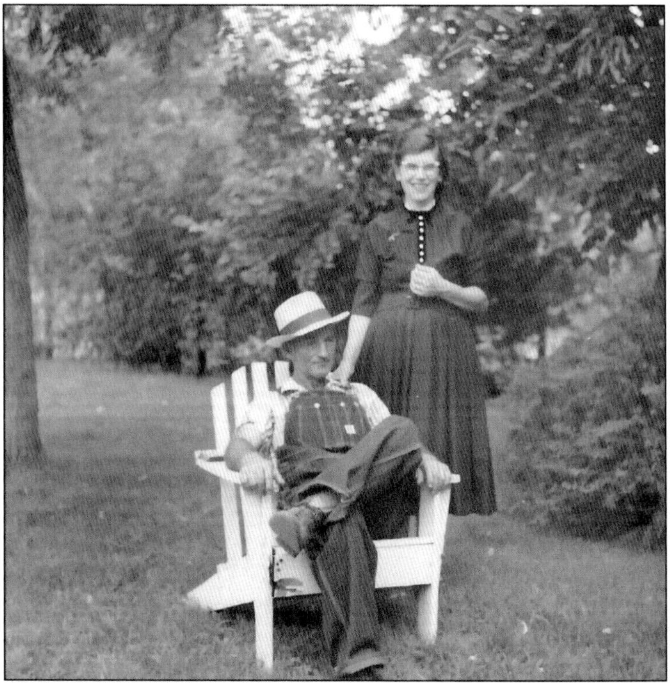

Malcolm Francis and Mary Sue Hendrix married in December 1931 and lived off Sharp Springs Road downstream of Jefferson in the 1901 home built by James C. McAdoo, which replaced an earlier log home. The Francis farm was 145 acres and part of a larger land grant once owned by John Sharp, who gave the road its name. The old log smokehouse and hen house survived until 1968. The couple is pictured here in 1959. (Courtesy of Toby Francis.)

Mary Kate and Rucker Raikes pose in front of their Smyrna house. Rucker served many years as a deacon of his church and worked at the Sewart Air Force Base. (Courtesy of Robert "Bud" Raikes.)

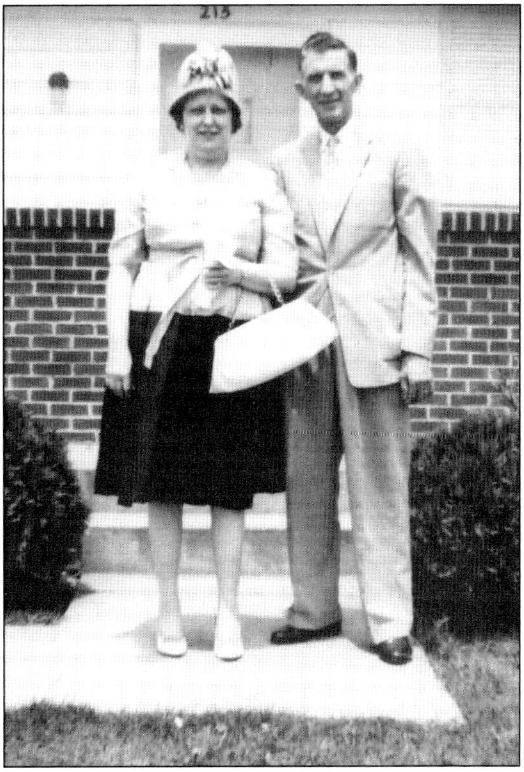

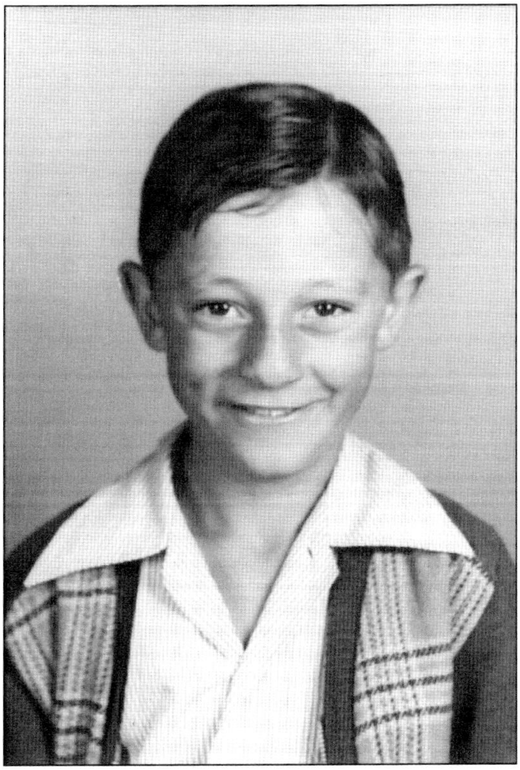

Robert Raikes, son of Mary Kate and Rucker Raikes, poses for a photograph as a young child. He later attended Smyrna schools and eventually became the principal of Smyrna High School. (Courtesy of Robert "Bud" Raikes.)

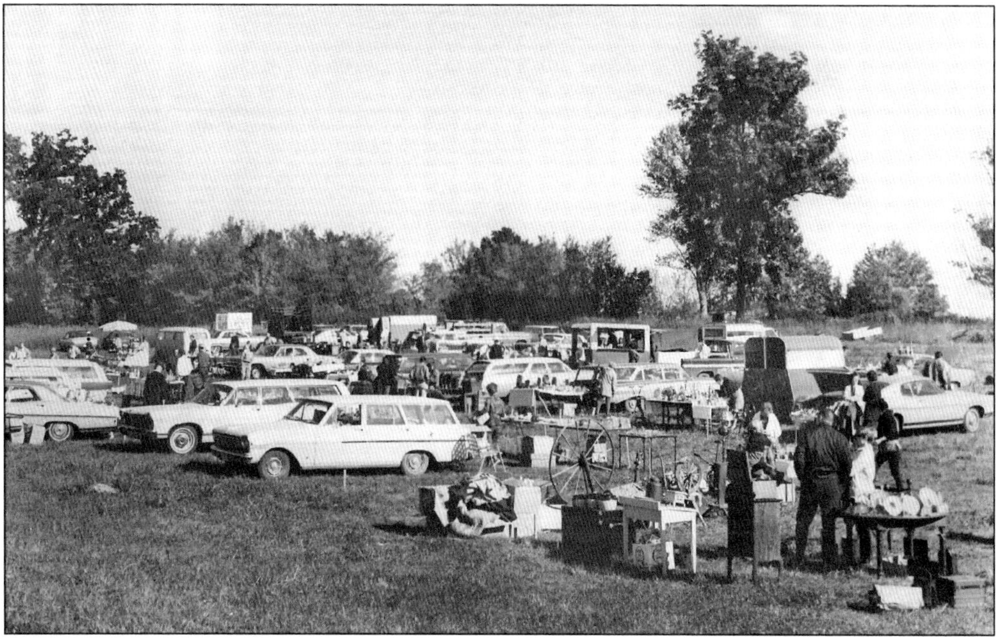

The Murfreesboro Flea Market, held on Murfreesboro Highway near Smyrna, sold antique and new items for households during this event held on October 4 and 5, 1968. It was sponsored by the Murfreesboro Antique Association. (Courtesy of Smyrna Public Library.)

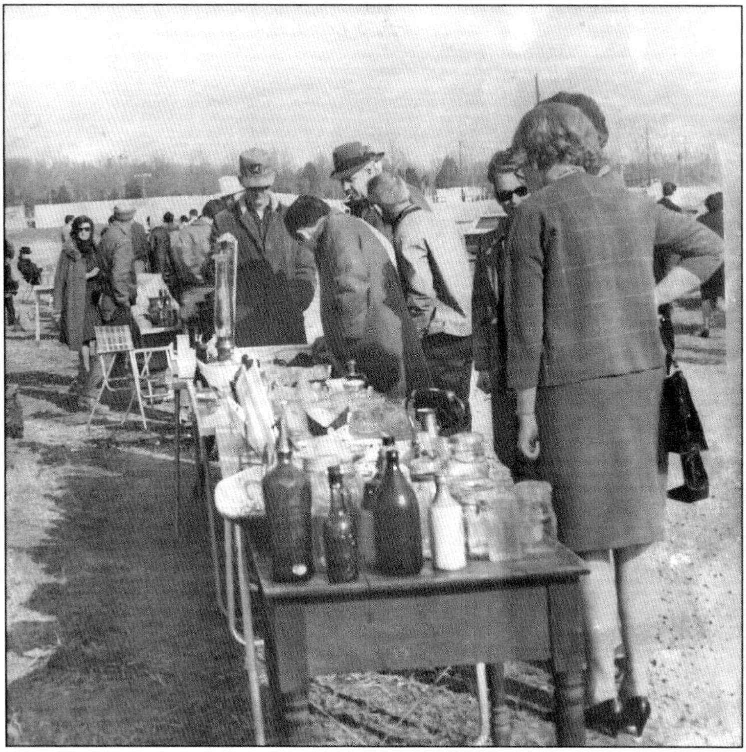

Mrs. Hughes (foreground) looks at various bottles while visiting the Murfreesboro Flea Market. Many Smyrna residents visited the monthly market, this one being held at the Murfreesboro Road Speedway. The men and women faced cold winds on this March day in 1969 while searching for goods. (Courtesy of Smyrna Public Library.)

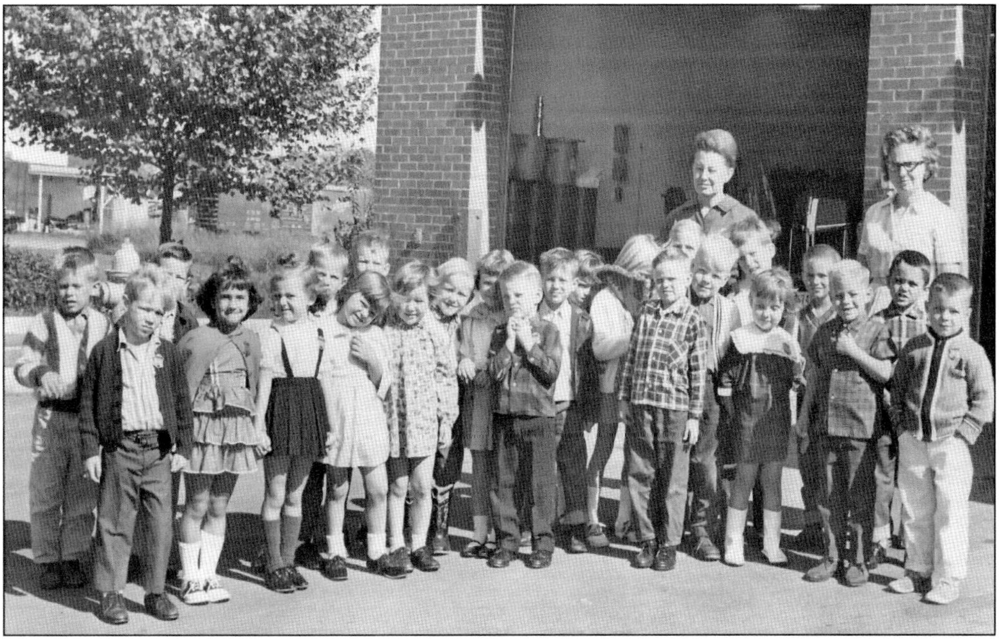

The Methodist Church Day Kindergarten students take a field trip to the Smyrna Fire Department in October 1966. The students were taking part in Fire Prevention Week and were led by teachers Mrs. Earnest Graves and Mrs. Kenneth Cole. (Courtesy of Smyrna Public Library.)

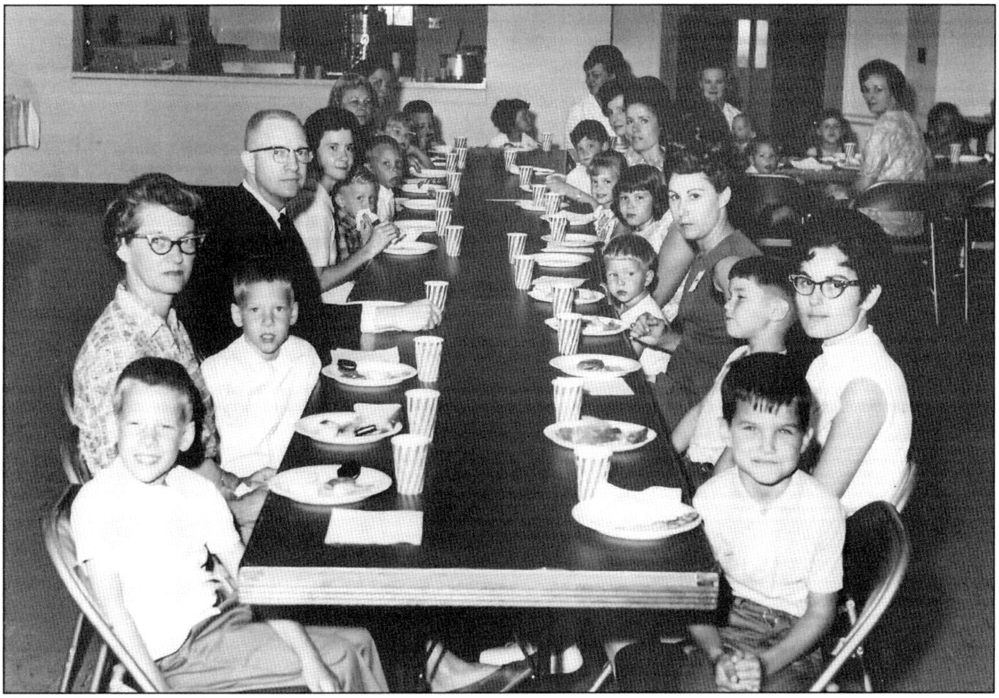

The Methodist Church Day Kindergarten students and their parents sit down for a meal on May 10, 1968. Mary Emma Graves served as the director of kindergarten at the time. Approximately 70 people attended the picnic in the church's fellowship hall. (Courtesy of Smyrna Public Library.)

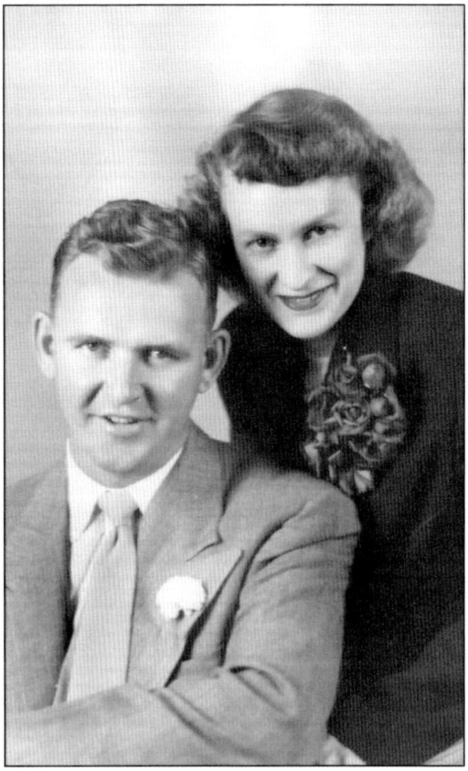

Gilbert Olerud and Mavis Nilsson married on September 21, 1950, and posed for this wedding photograph. The couple came to Smyrna in 1952 when Gilbert was with the military. He served in both World War II and the Korean Conflict. They fell in love with the town and decided to stay, founding several businesses, including Gilsville Family Center, Inc., Gil's Supermarket, and Gil's Ace Hardware. (Courtesy of Ginny Williams.)

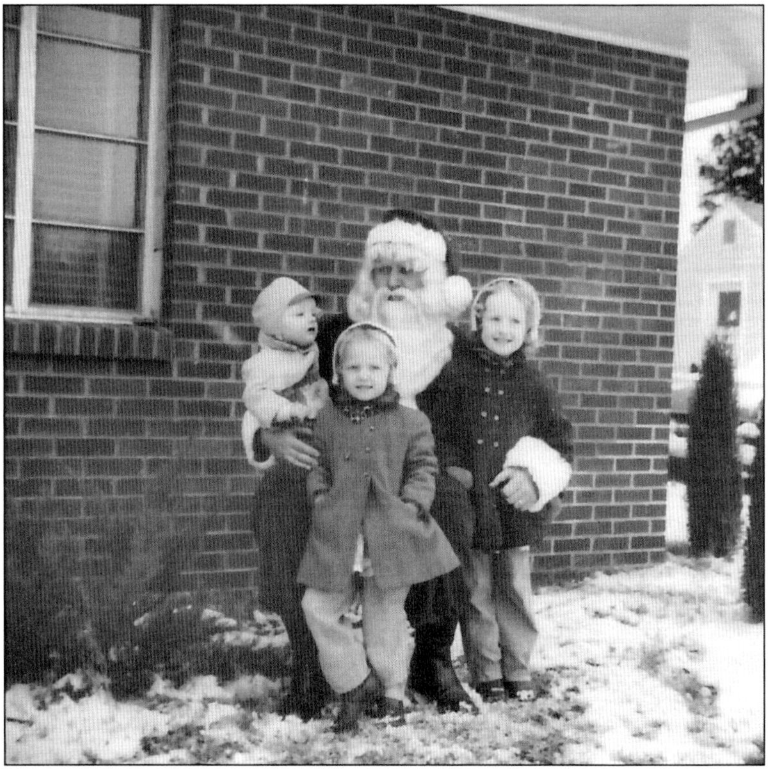

Gilbert Olerud played the town Santa for dozens of years, setting up a chair in the back of his store. When children came in, he would heartily greet them and hear their Christmas wishes. This December 1958 photograph shows Gilbert with his children, Gilbert III (left), Candy (center), and Ginny. Olerud was Santa in the town's first Christmas parade and reprised this role every year until his death in 1980. (Courtesy of Ginny Williams.)

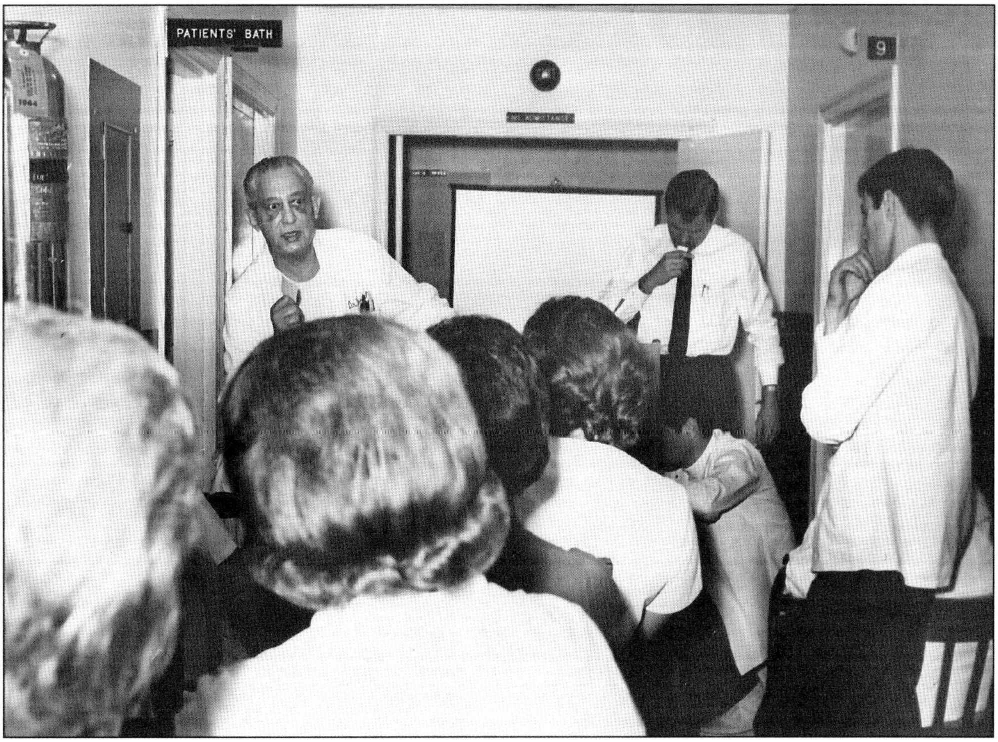

Paul Justice (center background, facing camera), representing Ayerst Laboratories of New York City, spoke to staff members at Goodall Clinic Tuesday, December 5, 1969, on the merits of a new drug, Atromid-S (Clofibrate). The drug showed promise of reducing cholesterol. Dr. George Goodall stands in the back left. (Courtesy of Smyrna Public Library.)

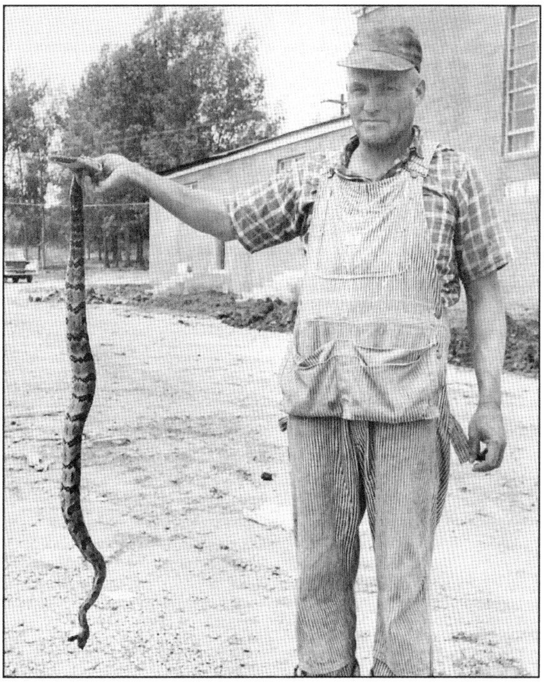

Bill Haynes stands with a snake he killed on his farm on Tuesday, August 8, 1969. He told a reporter from the *Rutherford Courier* that he was driving up his cows when he spied the four-foot rattler being chased by his dogs. He then picked up a stick and killed the snake with it. Haynes was a construction worker at Thurman Francis Jr. High School. The school later converted to an elementary school. (Courtesy of Smyrna Public Library.)

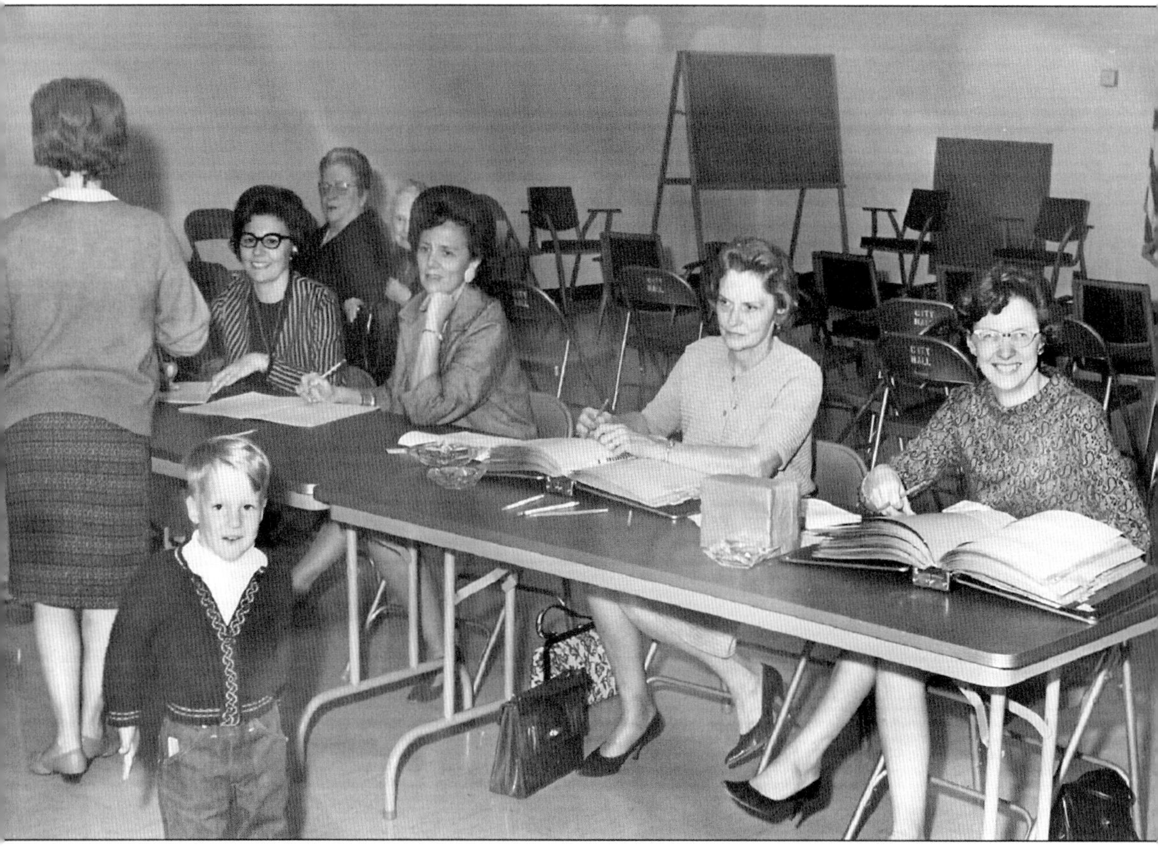

Smyrna election officials help residents vote in a 1960s election. (Courtesy of Smyrna Public Library.)

Mayor Sam Ridley issues a proclamation in recognition of National School Lunch Week (October 13–19, 1969). School cafeteria managers witness the mayor's signature. From left to right are Helen Leonard, Thurman Francis Jr. High School; Eunice Gillespie, Smyrna Primary; Claire Campbell, Rutherford County school food service supervisor; and Mattie Tucker, Smyrna Elementary. (Courtesy of Smyrna Public Library.)

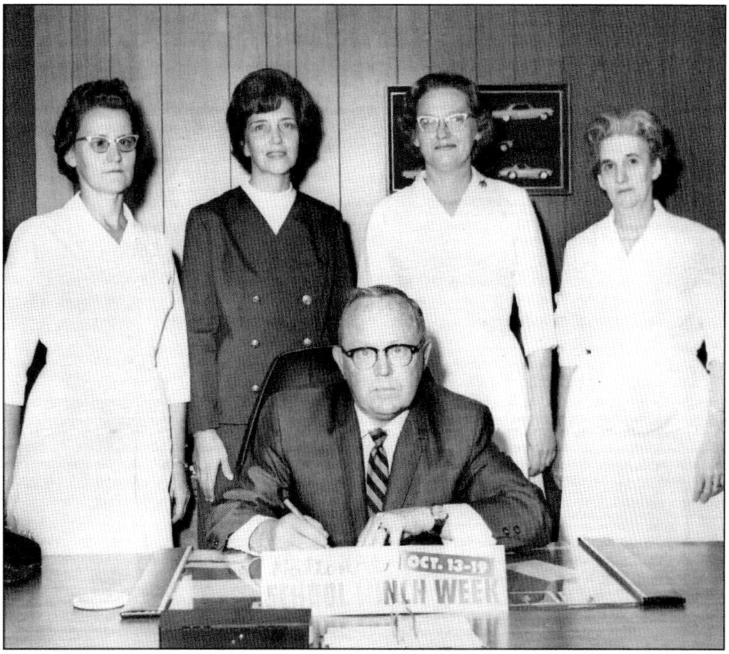

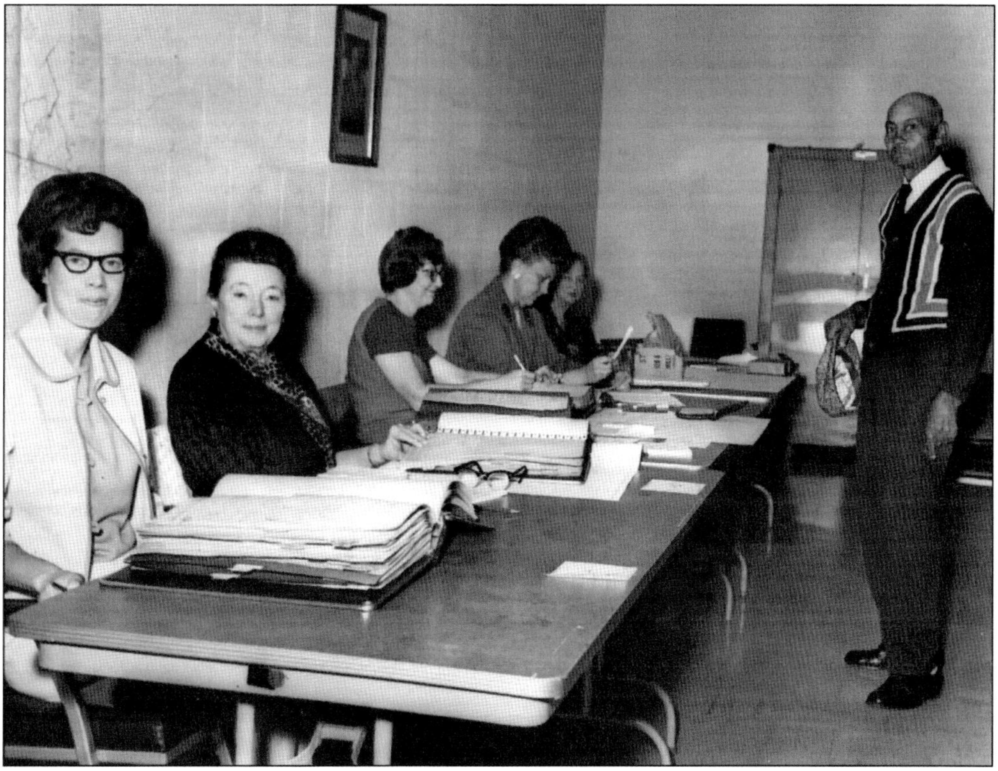

From left to right, Mrs. Albert Lawrence, Mrs. Lonnie Williamson, Mrs. Katherine Walkup, Mrs. Frank Barnett, and Mrs. John Hager help the voters of Smyrna in November 1969. Eugene "Jake" Johnson (far right) claimed at the time that he was the oldest voter born in Smyrna. (Courtesy of Smyrna Public Library.)

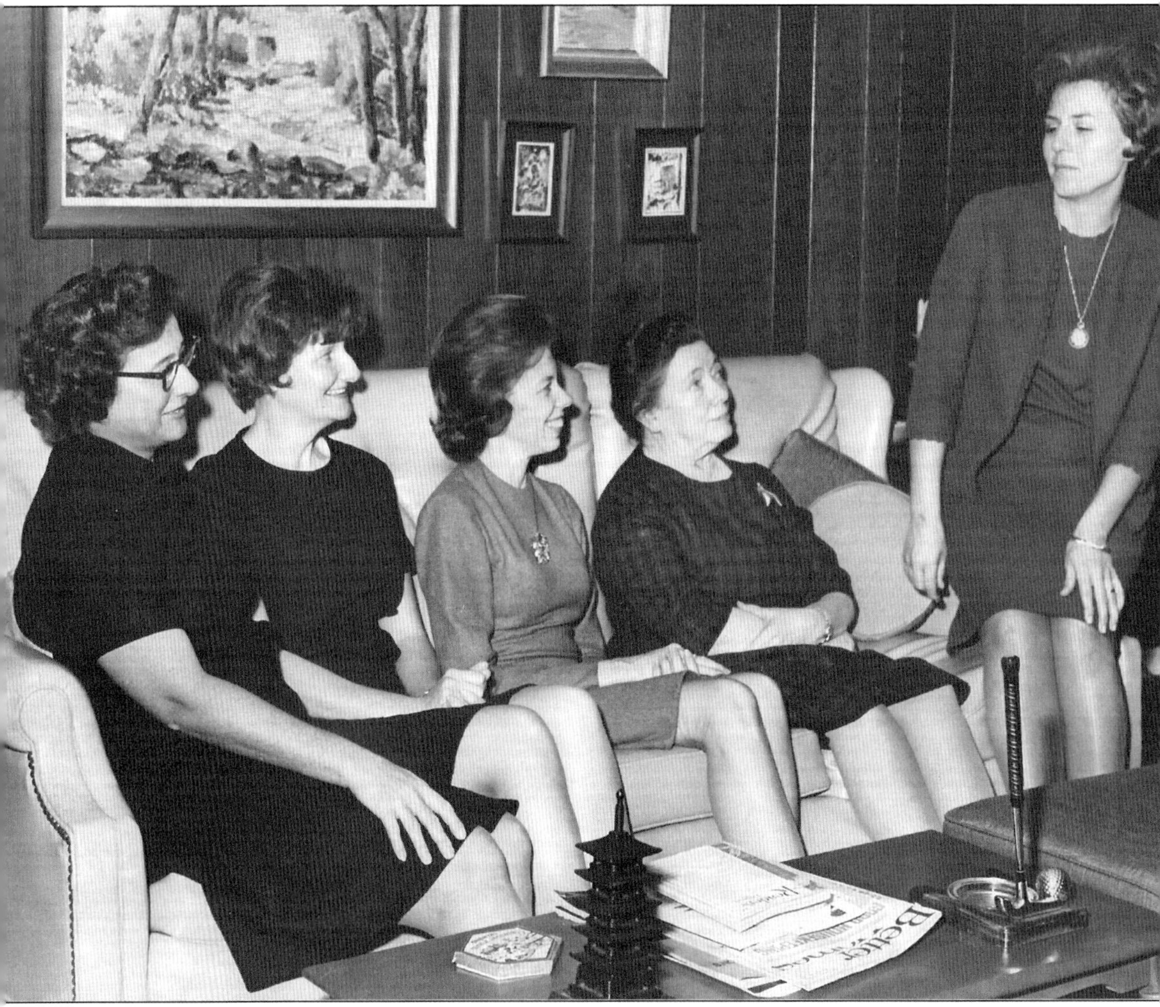

The officers of the Home Demonstration Club meet to discuss affairs in the 1960s. Home demonstration clubs were part of the 1914-established US Department of Agriculture program to aid families with little education in improving their homemaking. The first club meeting in Smyrna was held in 1936, and the group was active until the early 1950s. (Courtesy of Smyrna Public Library.)

From left to right, Mrs. Thomas Castillo, Patsy Brown, and Evelyn Felder celebrate the future arrival of Brown's baby with a party in August 1968. The ladies held a baby shower at Mrs. Felder's home as a meeting of the Smyrna Home Demonstration Club. (Courtesy of Smyrna Public Library.)

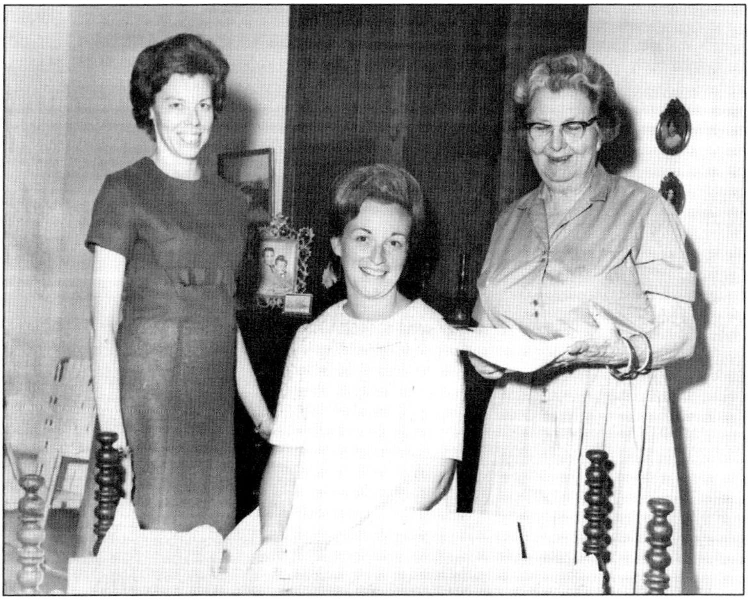

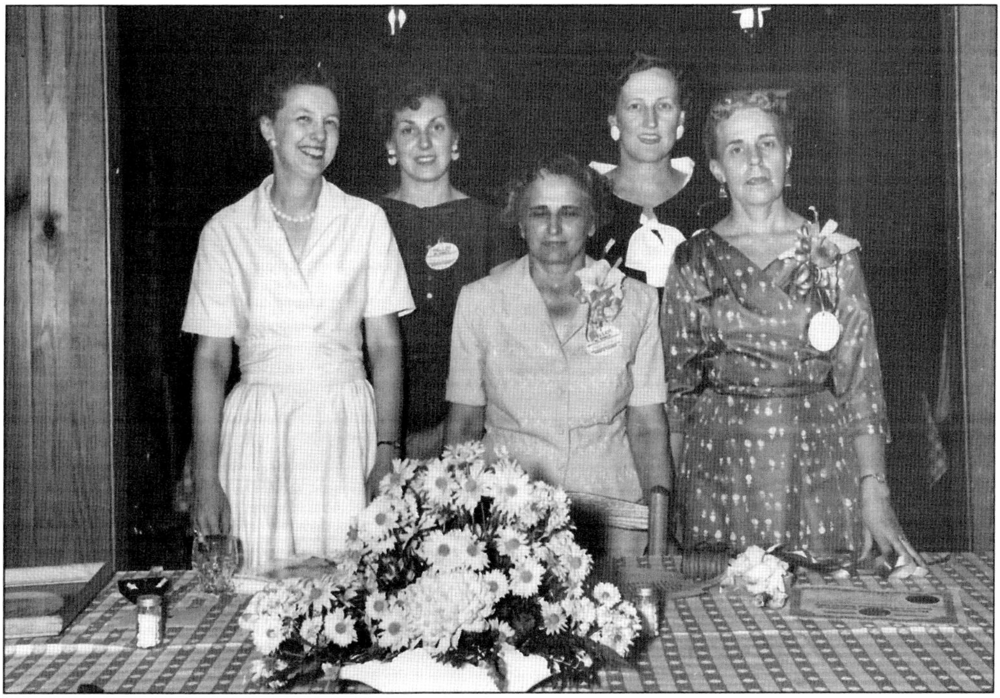

The Smyrna Business and Professional Women's Club is pictured at a meeting held at the Sam Davis Home Tea Room in the 1960s. The club was chartered in 1957 to promote women in the workforce. The group also held Christmas-lighting contests and laid the groundwork for organizing a library in Smyrna. (Courtesy of Smyrna Public Library.)

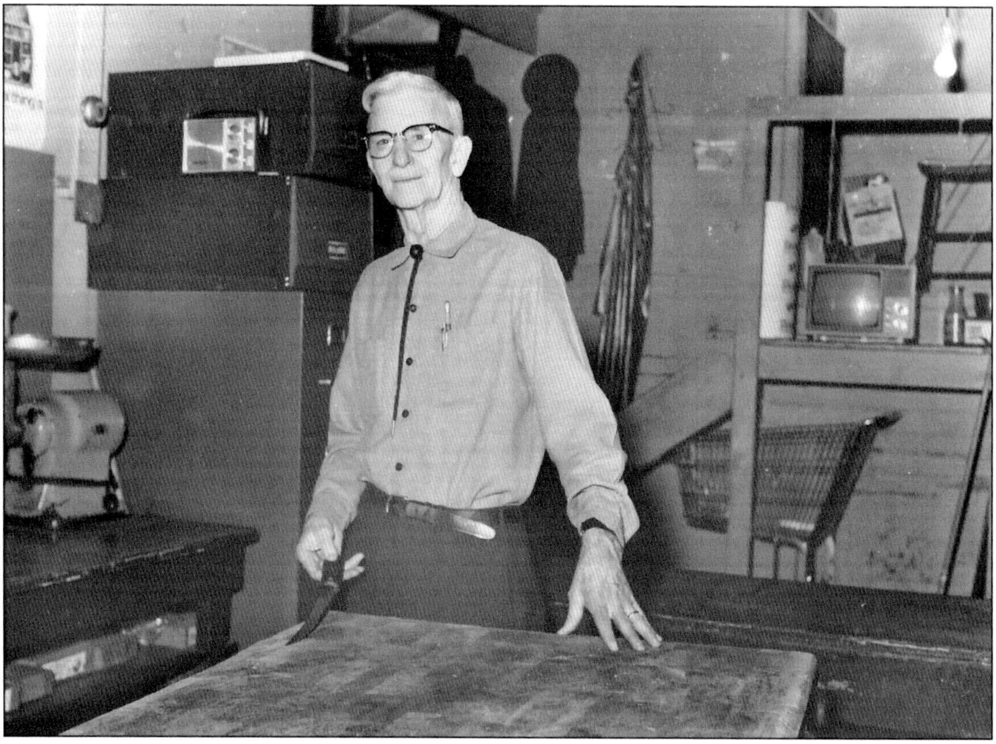

On his last day of work on December 31, 1970, Herbert Moore stands at the butcher block where he worked for so many years. (Courtesy of John Moore.)

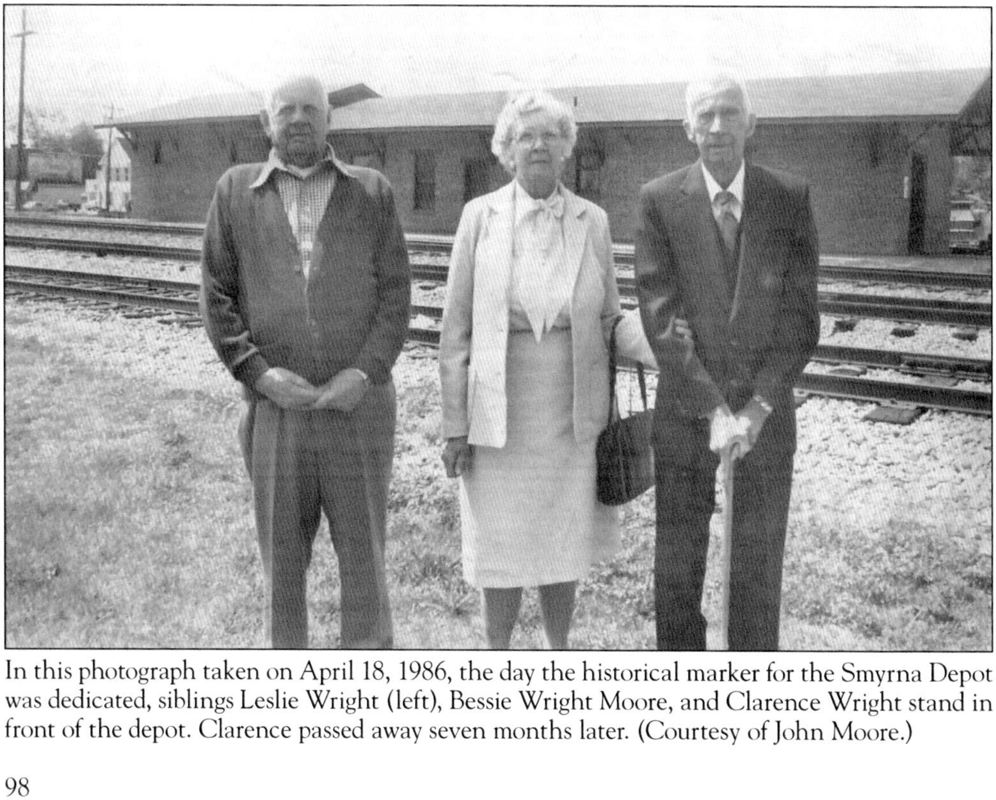

In this photograph taken on April 18, 1986, the day the historical marker for the Smyrna Depot was dedicated, siblings Leslie Wright (left), Bessie Wright Moore, and Clarence Wright stand in front of the depot. Clarence passed away seven months later. (Courtesy of John Moore.)

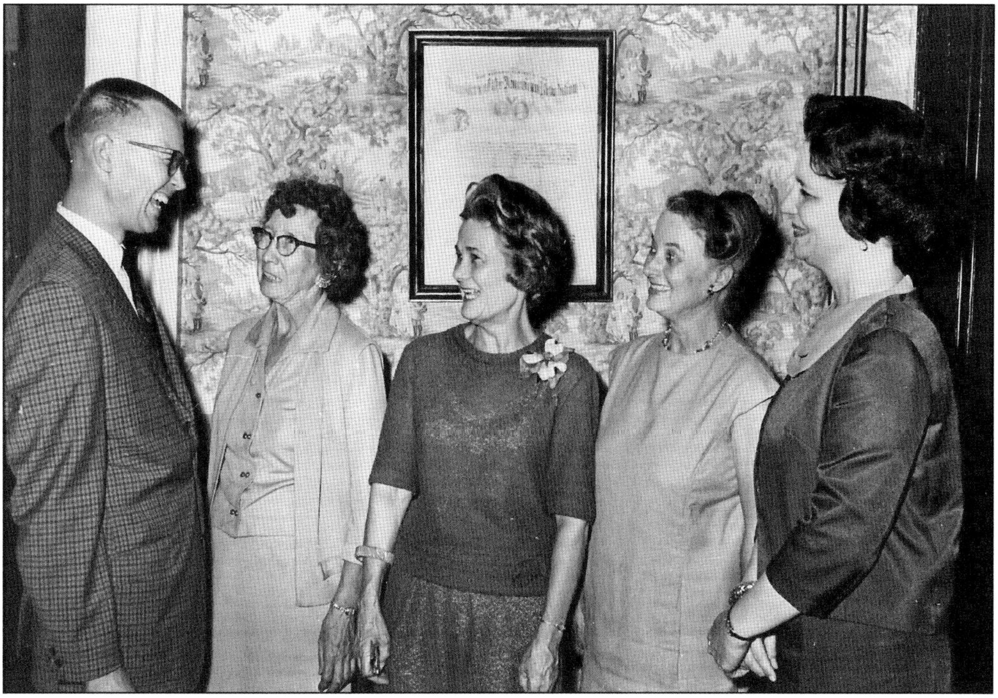

This is a 1960s meeting of the Daughters of the American Revolution, with member Sarah King seen on the far right. (Courtesy of Smyrna Public Library.)

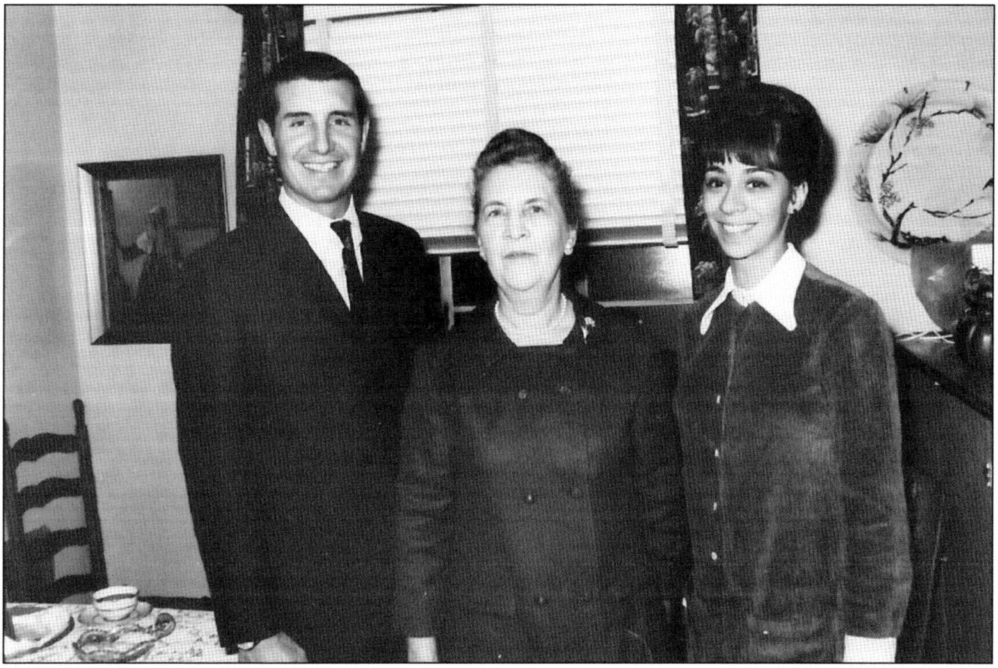

From left to right, Earnie Johns, Adeline King, and Florence Carnicelli pose for a photograph in February 1969. King wrote a good deal of the history of Smyrna and is well known for writing the script for *Son of This House*, a play retelling the story of Sam Davis. (Courtesy of Smyrna Public Library.)

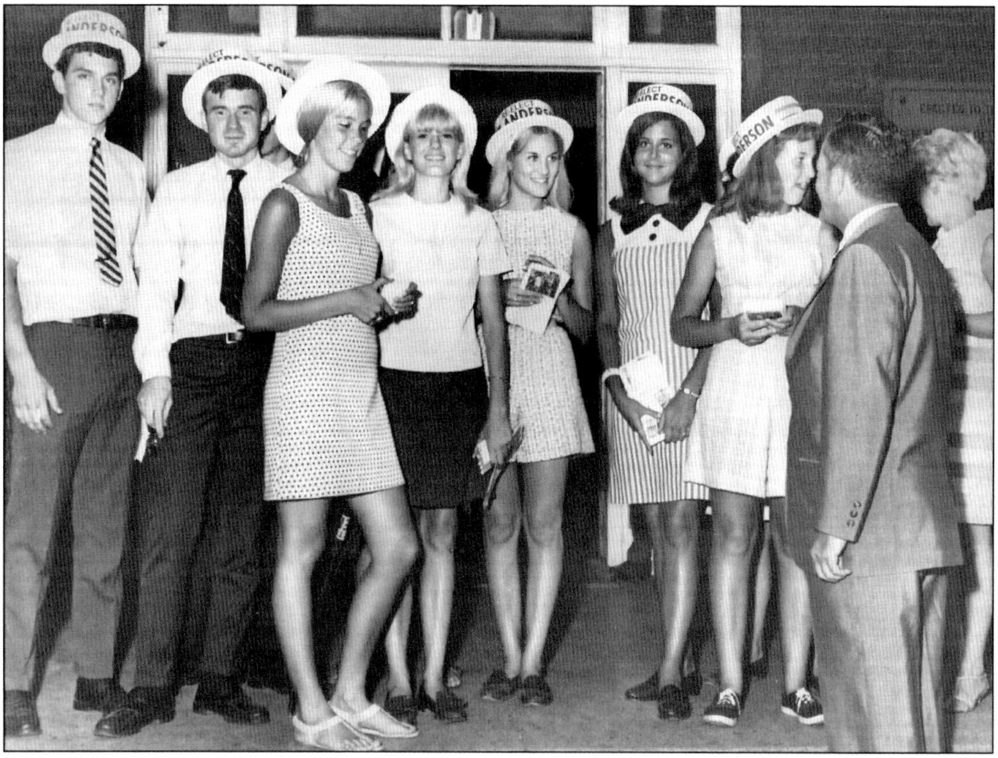

Volunteers rally for William R. Anderson, who was up for reelection to the US House of Representatives, serving the Tennessee Sixth District in 1968. He began his congressional career in 1965 after winning the 1964 election against Cecil Hill with 78 percent of the votes. (Courtesy of Smyrna Public Library.)

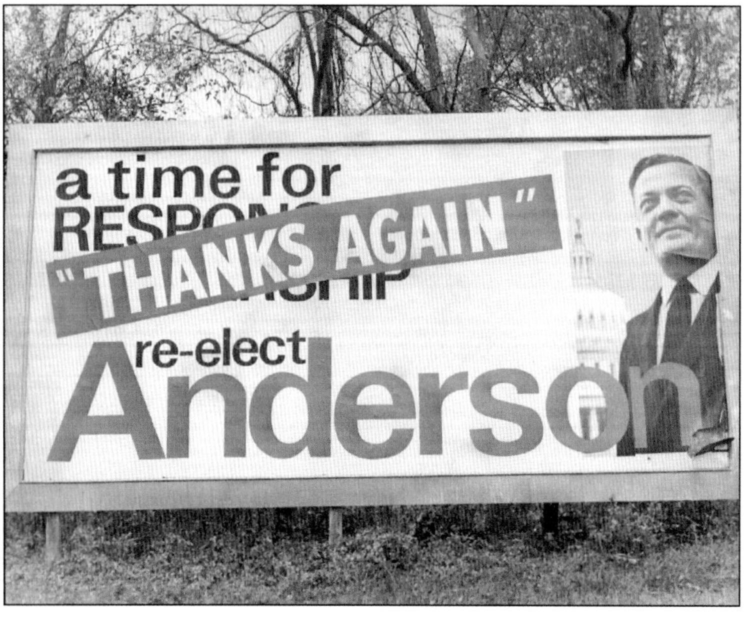

After a successful campaign, William R. Anderson thanks Smyrna residents for their votes. Anderson was born in Humphreys County and graduated from the US Naval Academy in 1943. He fought in World War II and won the Bronze Star. (Courtesy of Smyrna Public Library.)

Dr. George Goodall (far left), pictured here at a 1960s holiday party, attended school in Wilson County and continued his higher education in Alabama. In August 1949, Dr. Goodall came to Smyrna and served as the only doctor in town. By 1951, he had a modern clinic built and had 10 beds and surgical facilities. (Courtesy of Smyrna Public Library.)

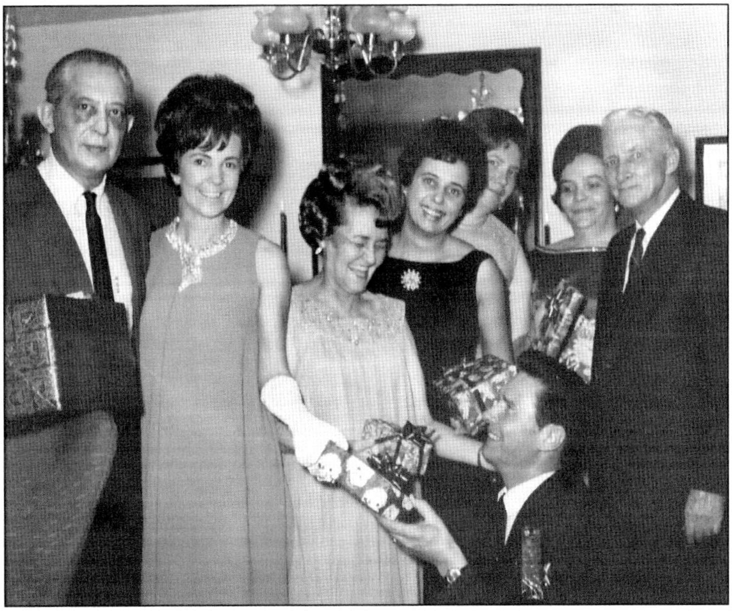

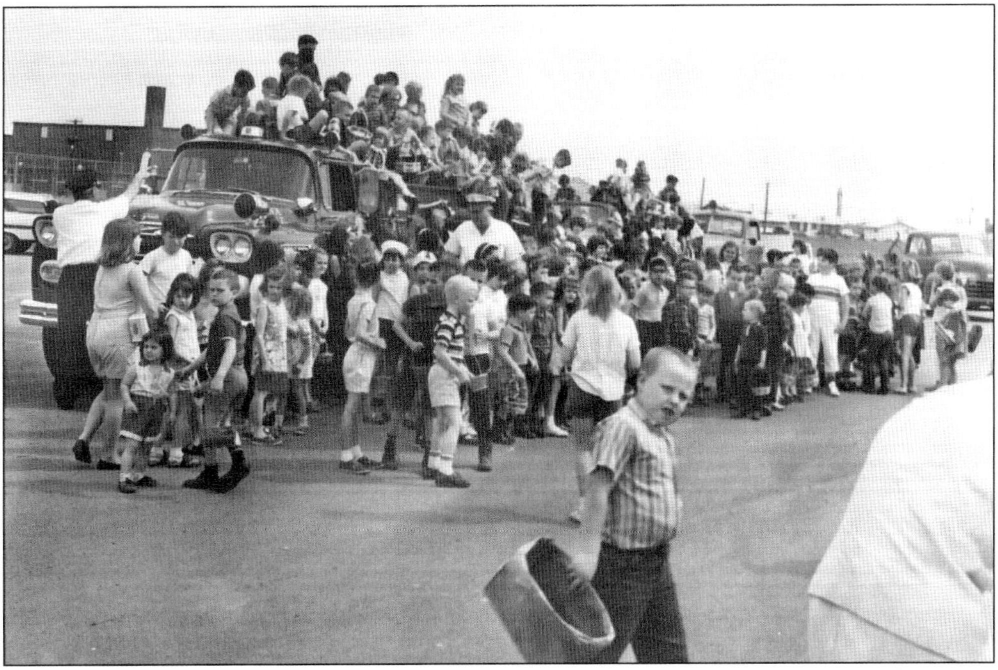

The Fireman's Easter Egg Hunt in Smyrna was extremely popular, as shown here in the 1960s. Many children attended the event year after year with their families. (Courtesy of Smyrna Public Library.)

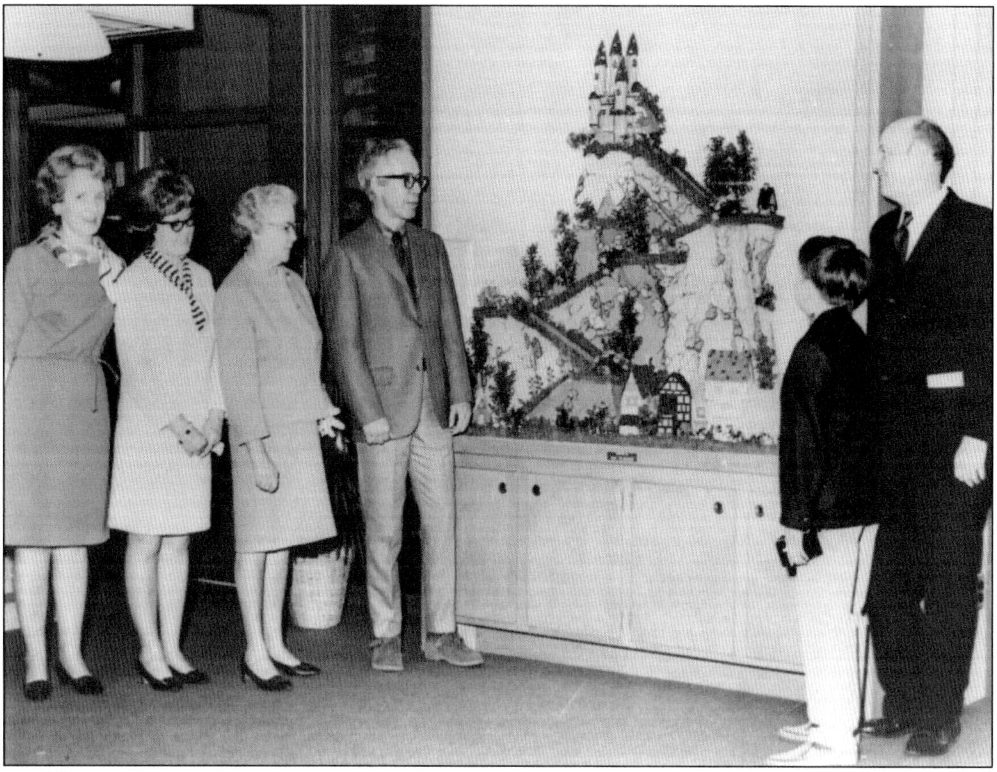

Well-known puppeteer Tom Tichenor built this colorful fairy-tale castle for the Smyrna Public Library in 1969. Pictured from left to right are Myla Parson, Mrs. Richard Hankins, Catherine Clark, Tichenor, Jimmy Stewart, and Marshall Stewart. The Smyrna Library was brand new to the community at the time of this gift from Tichenor. (Courtesy of Smyrna Public Library.)

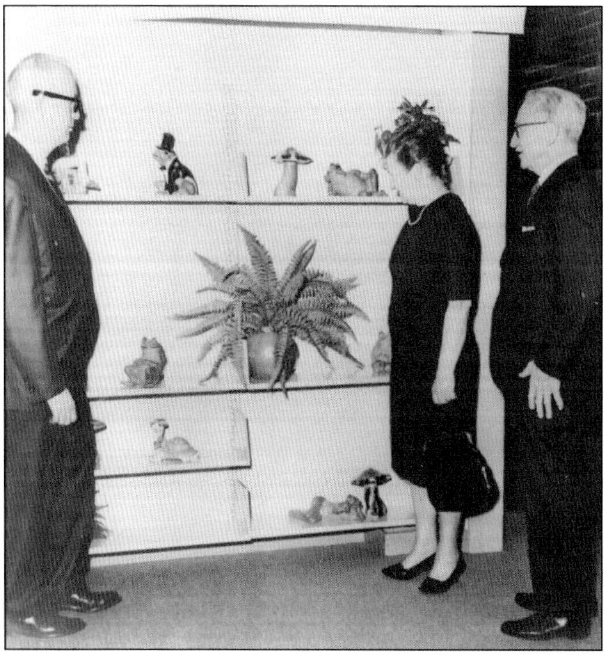

Patrons stand in the Smyrna Public Library in the 1970s when it was on Walnut Street. The library adjoined Smyrna High School and was within walking distance of Smyrna's junior high and primary schools. The library was built without any federal funds and featured a fireproof local history room to preserve books and manuscripts regarding Tennessee and Smyrna history. (Courtesy of Smyrna Public Library.)

Seven

Jefferson and Sky Harbor

Jefferson, a town that once neighbored Smyrna and now stands just outside of town limits, held the Rutherford County seat from 1804 until 1811. In August 1803, several citizens of Davidson and Williamson Counties petitioned the state legislature to create a new county. The legislature approved the measure; the next year, Rutherford County was set up, and a state committee chose Jefferson as the seat because of its location on the water. Robert Weakley and Thomas Bedford laid out the town with a town common. Soon, a courthouse, a county jail, a post office, taverns, and houses popped up. By 1811, the people of Rutherford County wanted a more centralized county seat and moved it to nearby Murfreesboro.

Jefferson remained a significant shipping port in the early and mid-1800s. Corn, tobacco, hides, cotton, and other crops went by way of flatboats to New Orleans markets. Soon, Jefferson was an inspection center for shipping products. The cedar glades covering the area allowed many to make a profit when they shipped wood upriver to Indiana and Ohio and downriver to Louisiana.

In the 1960s, the Army Corps of Engineers looked to raise water levels near Stewart's Ferry and create what is now J. Percy Priest Lake. Claiming the rising waters would cover Jefferson, it purchased around 15,800 acres and displaced many families. Creating the dam and the lake took several years and was completed in 1968; however, the water never reached the projected levels.

Sky Harbor was built in 1929 and served as the nearest airport for Nashville. It housed Interstate Air Lines planes and was about five miles southeast of Smyrna town limits. It had the latest technology of the time and measured the weather with barometers and other instruments used to keep the pilots informed. The US Post Office Department also used the airport to transport mail to Middle Tennessee. During World War II, Air Utilities, Inc., purchased the land and buildings for its plane-repair plant. The facility repaired Stearman PT-17s and PT-27s as well as Fairchild PT-23 planes. It later served as the location for the production of practice bombs for the war effort. After World War II, it closed, but the hangars and other buildings were not torn down until the late 1970s. By the 1990s, the land was used as a site for a boat-manufacturing plant.

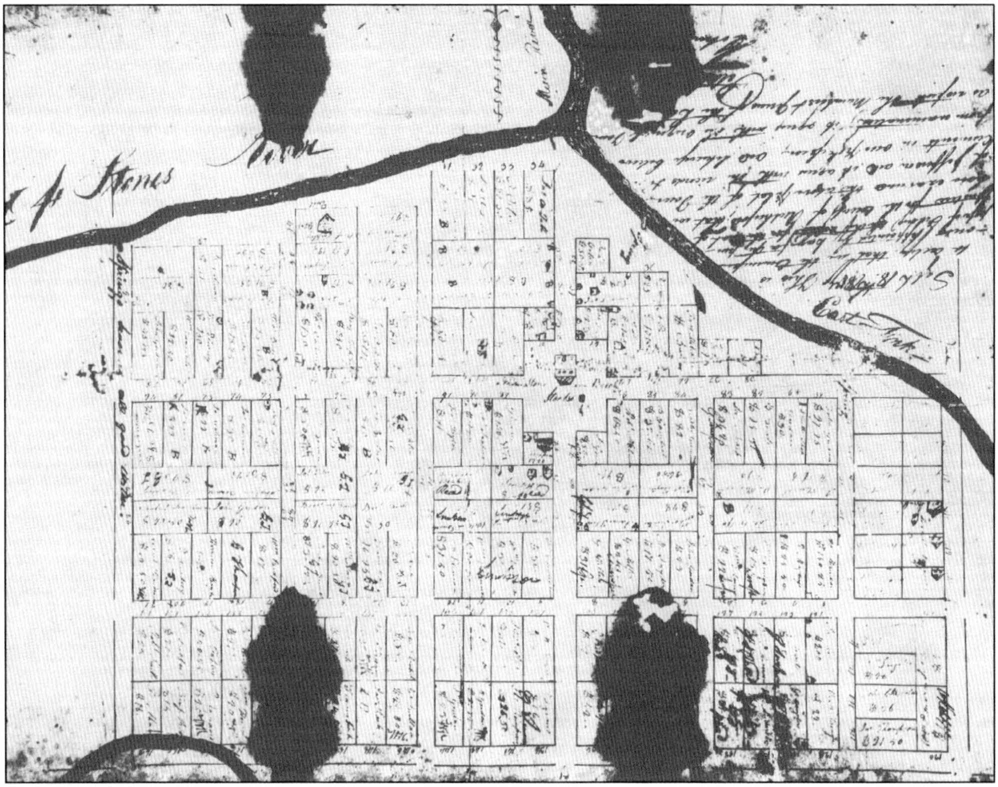

Named in honor of then-President Thomas Jefferson, the town of Jefferson popped up in the early 1800s and became the county seat of the newly formed Rutherford County. This 1804 map shows the layout of the town. Robert Weakley and Thomas Bedford planned the town around a centralized town common. (Courtesy of Rutherford County Office of Information Technology, GIS Division.)

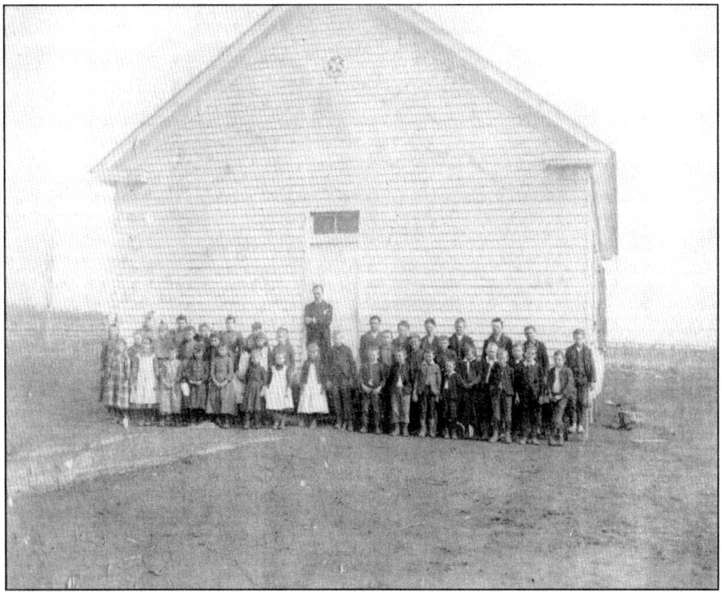

Found among the belongings of one-time student Anna Eliza Holloway, this photograph shows the Jefferson School around 1890. The wood-framed building was erected in 1888 and was replaced by a newer structure in 1930. After finishing school at Jefferson, Anna and her sister Nell Holloway attended a private school in the community. (Courtesy of Toby Francis.)

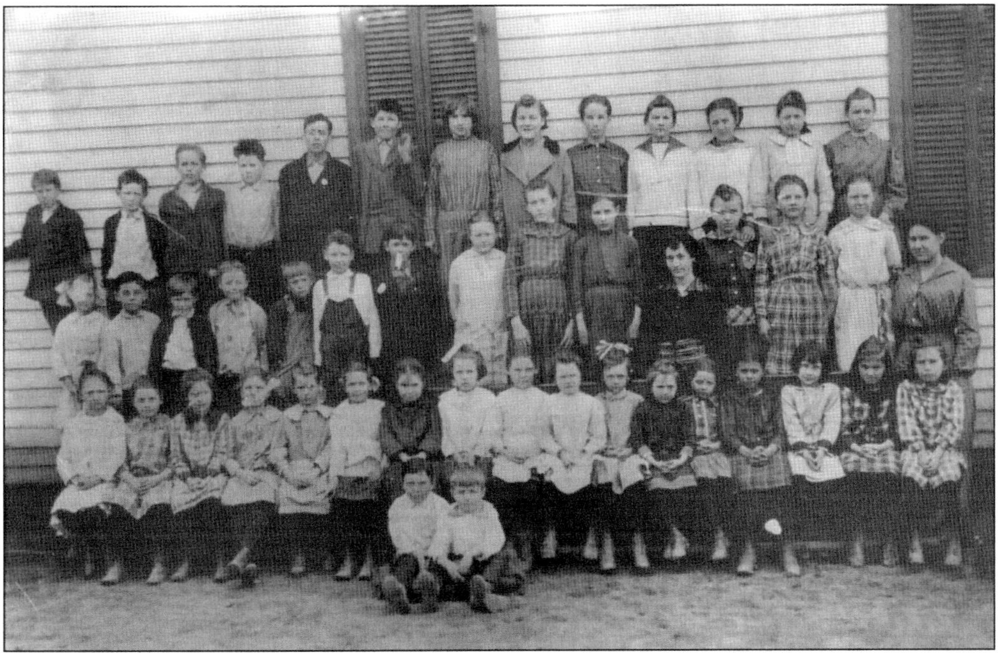

The students of Jefferson School are pictured here around 1911. This school in Jefferson was built in 1888 when Bettie Waller sold two acres of land she had inherited from her father for the use of a town school. In 1917, an addition was built on the back to provide more classroom space and a stage. (Courtesy of Toby Francis.)

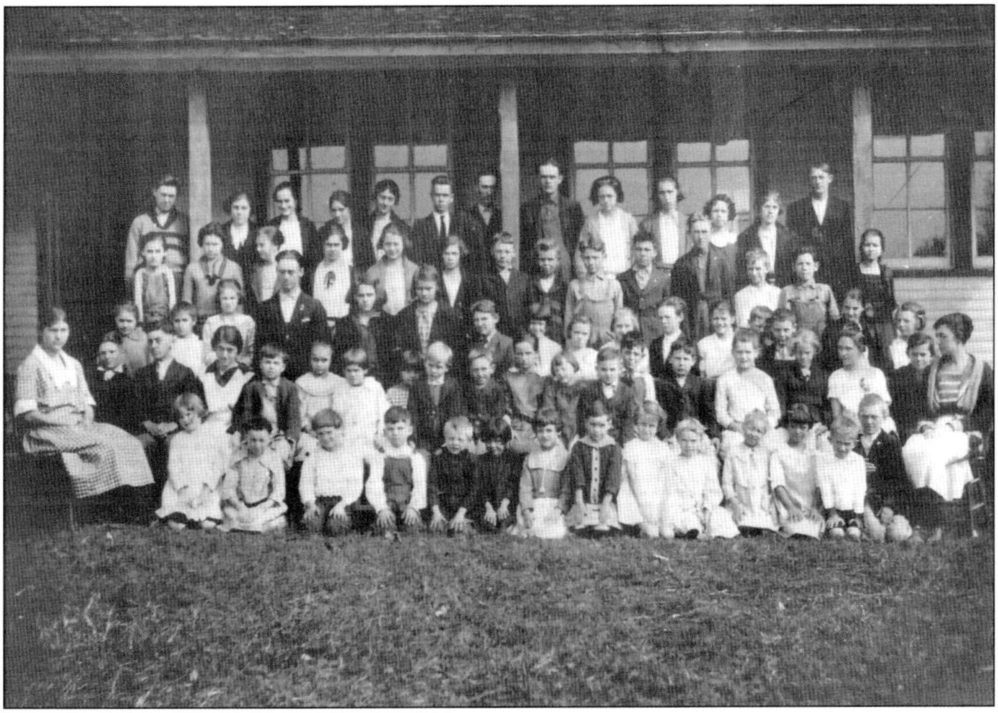

Teachers Tennie Halliburton, Margaret Ward, Dessie Nesbitt, and their students at Jefferson School are shown in this 1922 photograph. (Courtesy of Toby Francis.)

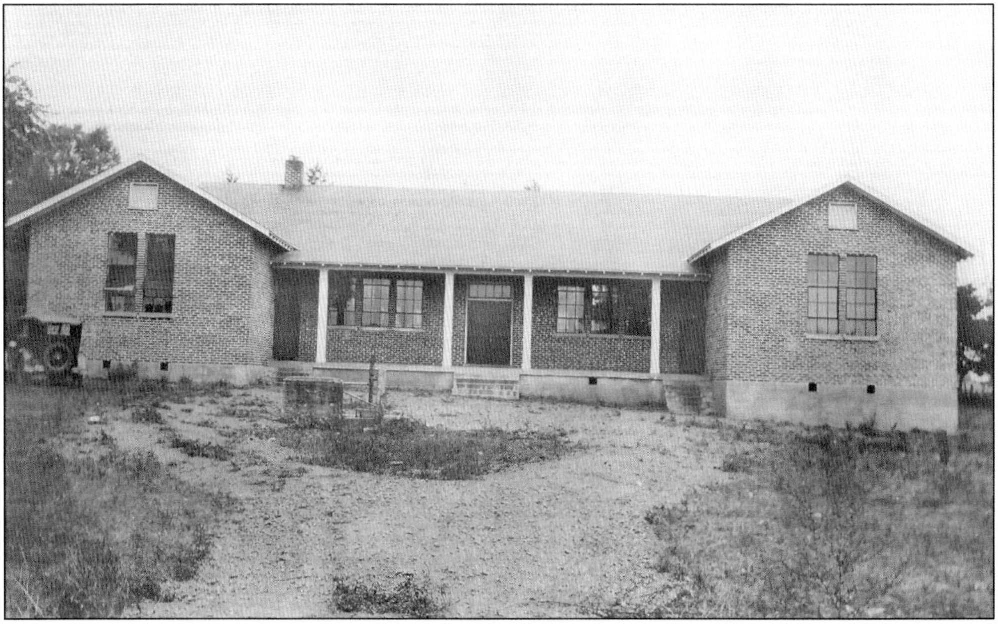

The 1888 Jefferson School caught fire, and despite the efforts of its students and teachers, who formed a bucket brigade, flames overtook the building. For the rest of the school year, classes were held at the Jefferson Church of Christ. This new brick school replaced the wooden structure and featured a concrete base and water fountain. (Courtesy of Toby Francis.)

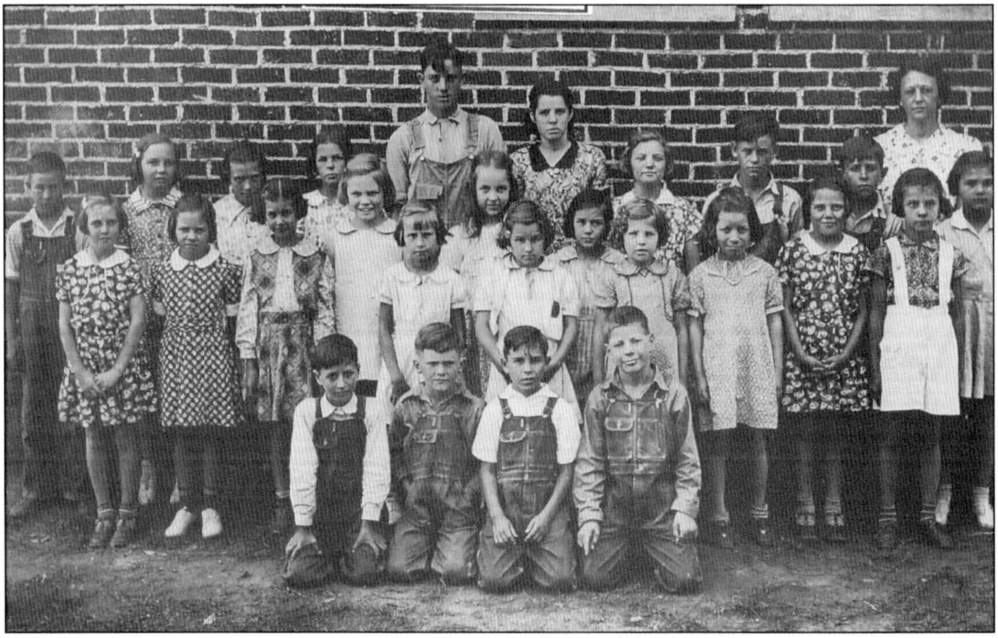

The 1938 third- and fourth-grade classes of Jefferson School, led by teacher Katherine Ward, are seen here. Katherine, daughter of Ben Hattie Lenoir Waller, came to Jefferson after teaching at nearby Rockdale School. (Courtesy of Toby Francis.)

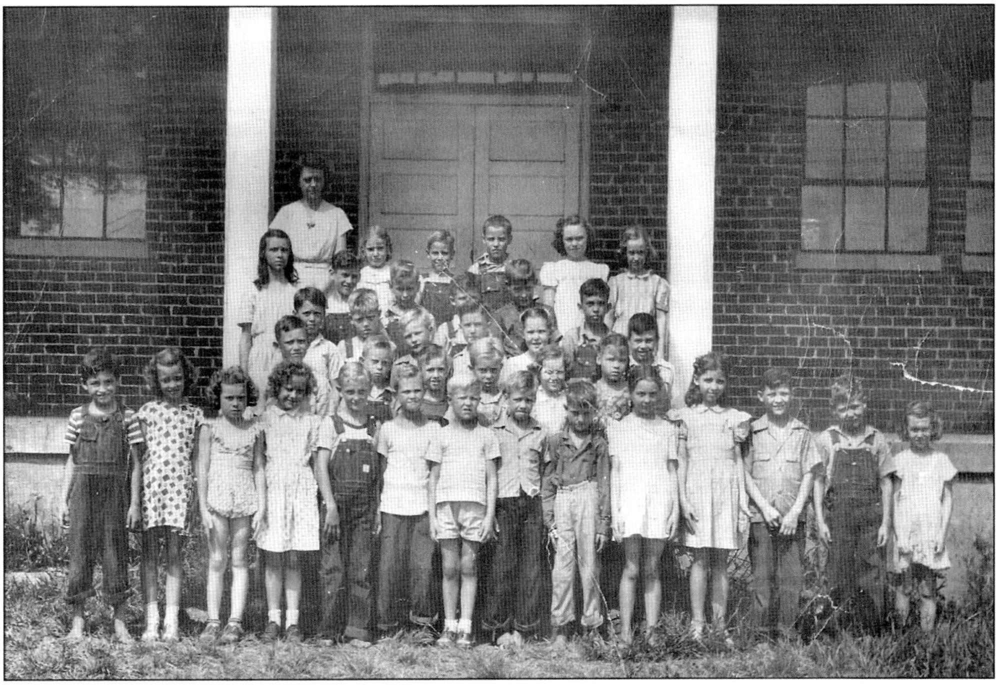

Katherine Ward and her third- and fourth-grade classes stand in front of the school building in 1948. Katherine had saved enough money after World War II to buy a new Chevrolet sedan. (Courtesy of Toby Francis.)

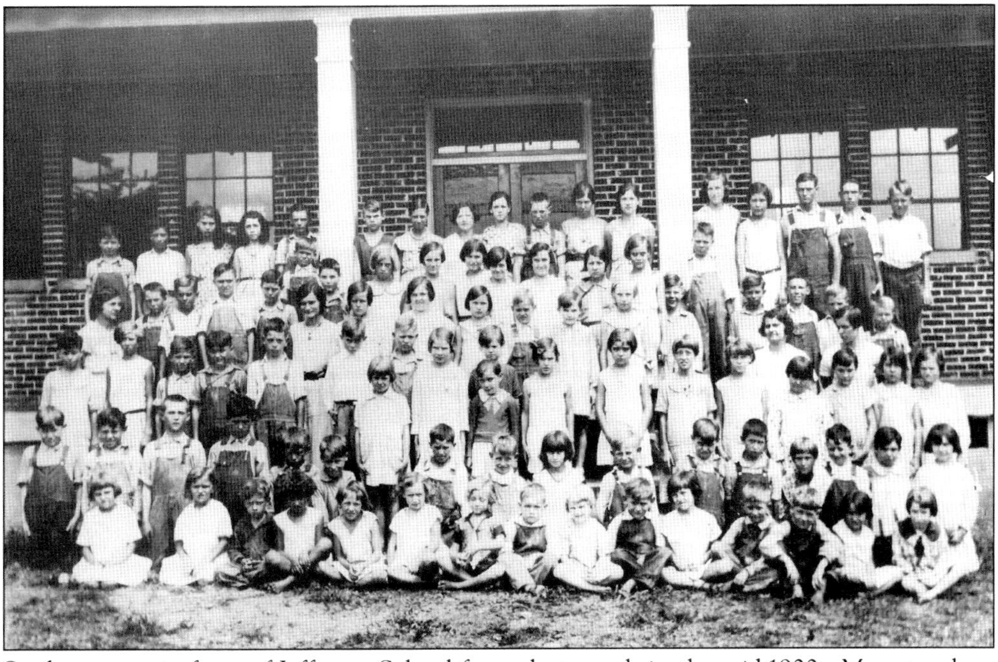

Students pose in front of Jefferson School for a photograph in the mid-1900s. Many teachers served the school in the early decades of the 1900s, including Virginia Tilford, Bessie Wright, Ray Coleman, Ophelia Elam, Frances King, Viola Tucker, Jesse Sanders, Mattie Becton, Everett Beasley, and Margaret Hazelwood. (Courtesy of Toby Francis.)

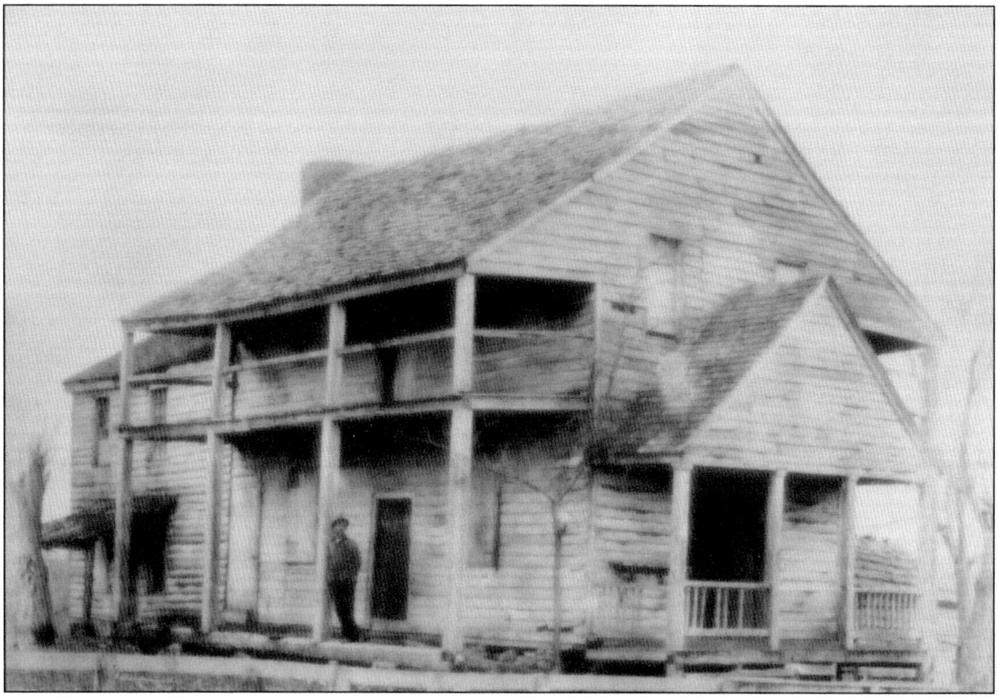

The Read Hotel in Jefferson was constructed after John Nash Read arrived in Rutherford County in 1806. The hotel stood until 1892 and was located on the east side of Jefferson's public square. Local legend claims that Andrew Jackson, Isaac Shelby, and Sam Houston stayed here when in the area. (Courtesy of Rutherford County Archives.)

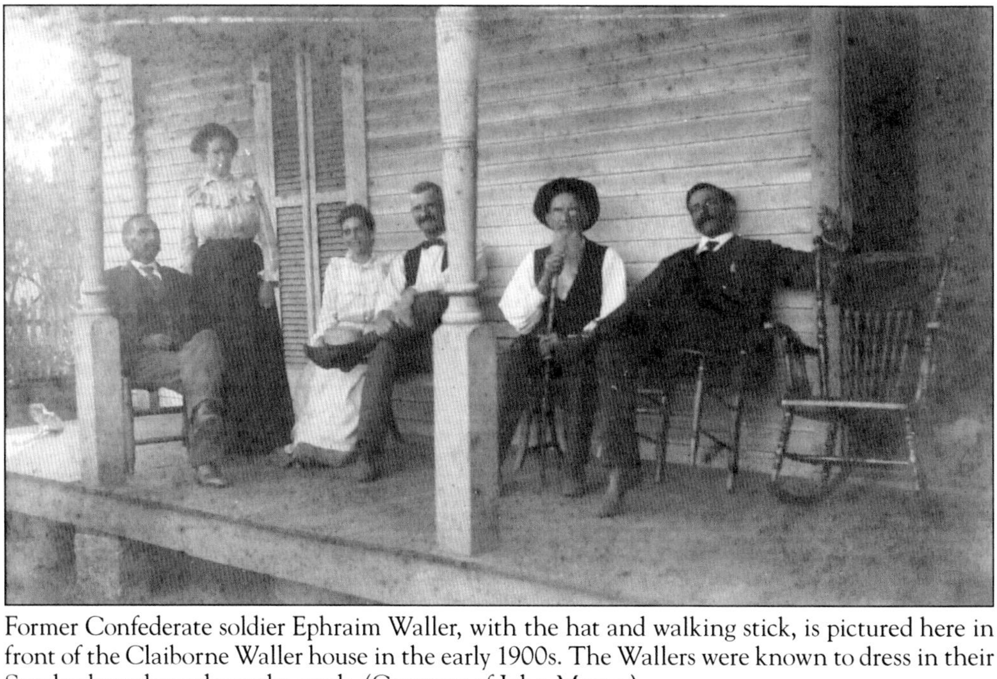

Former Confederate soldier Ephraim Waller, with the hat and walking stick, is pictured here in front of the Claiborne Waller house in the early 1900s. The Wallers were known to dress in their Sunday best throughout the week. (Courtesy of John Moore.)

William Washington Wright (seated) studied telegraphy and owned a mercantile business; he is seen here with his family in 1919. In 1888, he accepted a position with the Nashville, Chattanooga & St. Louis Railroad as an agent and operator at the Smyrna Depot. Standing behind him are, from left to right, son Frank Leslie Wright, wife Bettie Waller, daughter Bessie Wright, and son Clarence Waller Wright. (Courtesy of John Moore.)

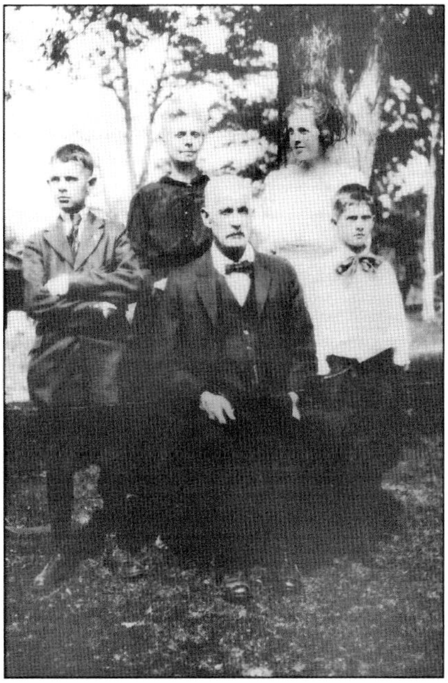

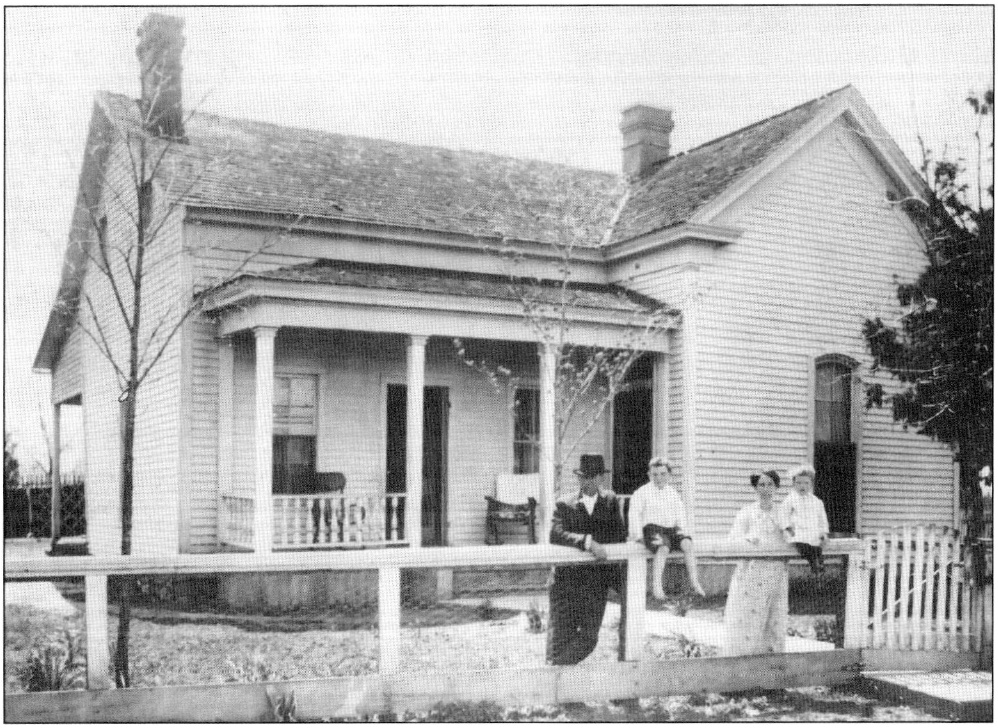

Claiborne Waller and his wife, Olivia Bell Carter, are shown here with their two sons, Bernice and Howard, around 1910. The house was built by Waller ancestor Eli C. Mitchell, a skilled woodworker. In 1878, Eli helped build the two-story mansion of William Davis, the older half brother of Sam Davis. He also worked on the Ridley/Davis Mill, located on the East Fork of Stones River. In addition, he constructed the houses for the Waller, Gooch, Nelson, and Dillon families. Eli had a wood shop in his yard and had a wood lathe driven by a mule. (Courtesy of John Moore.)

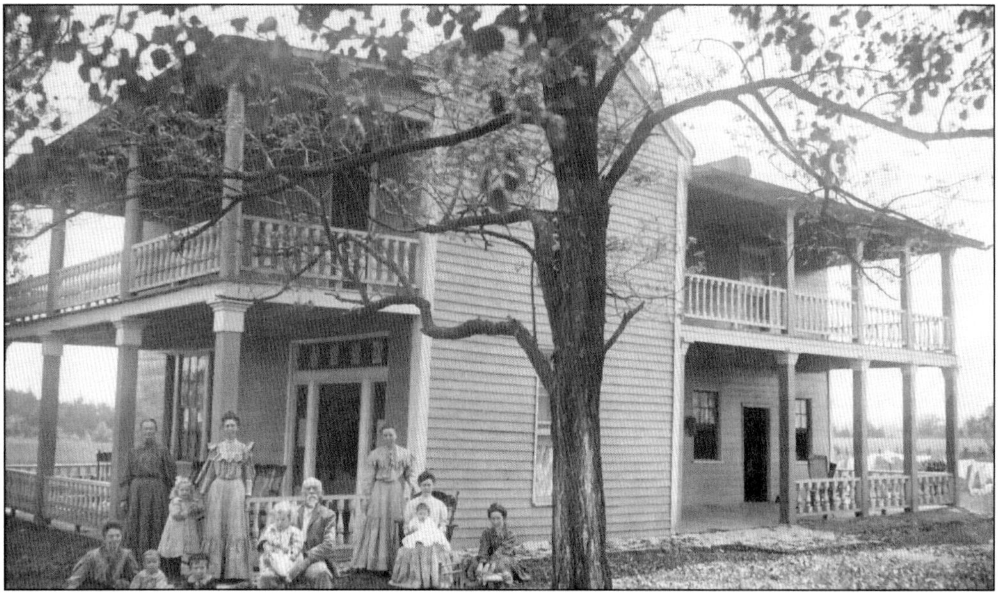

The Waller family is shown in front of their house around 1906. Ephraim Waller and his older brother George joined Joseph Wheeler's Confederate Cavalry at La Vergne on October 4, 1862. Their two brothers, William and James, also enlisted as Northern troops were advancing south toward Murfreesboro. (Courtesy of John Moore.)

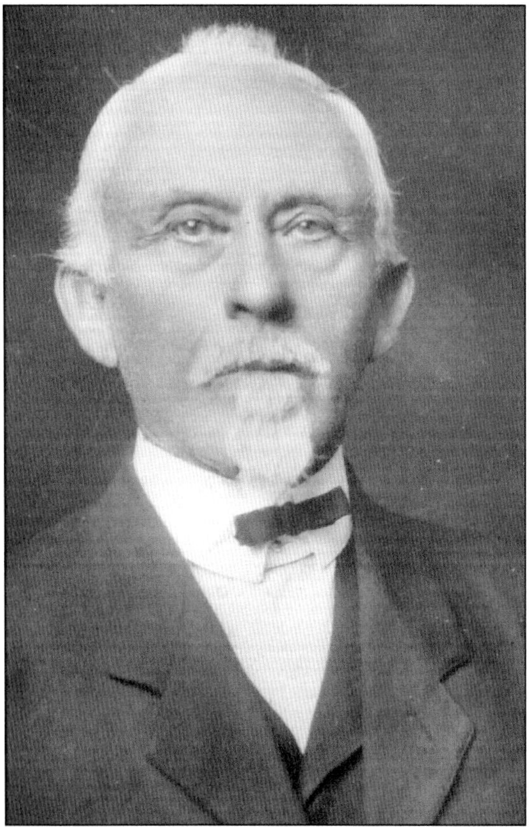

Ephraim Waller was a well-known figure in the Jefferson area during the late 1800s and early 1900s. His father, William Waller, worked as a millwright and built several water mills throughout the country. (Courtesy of Barry Lamb.)

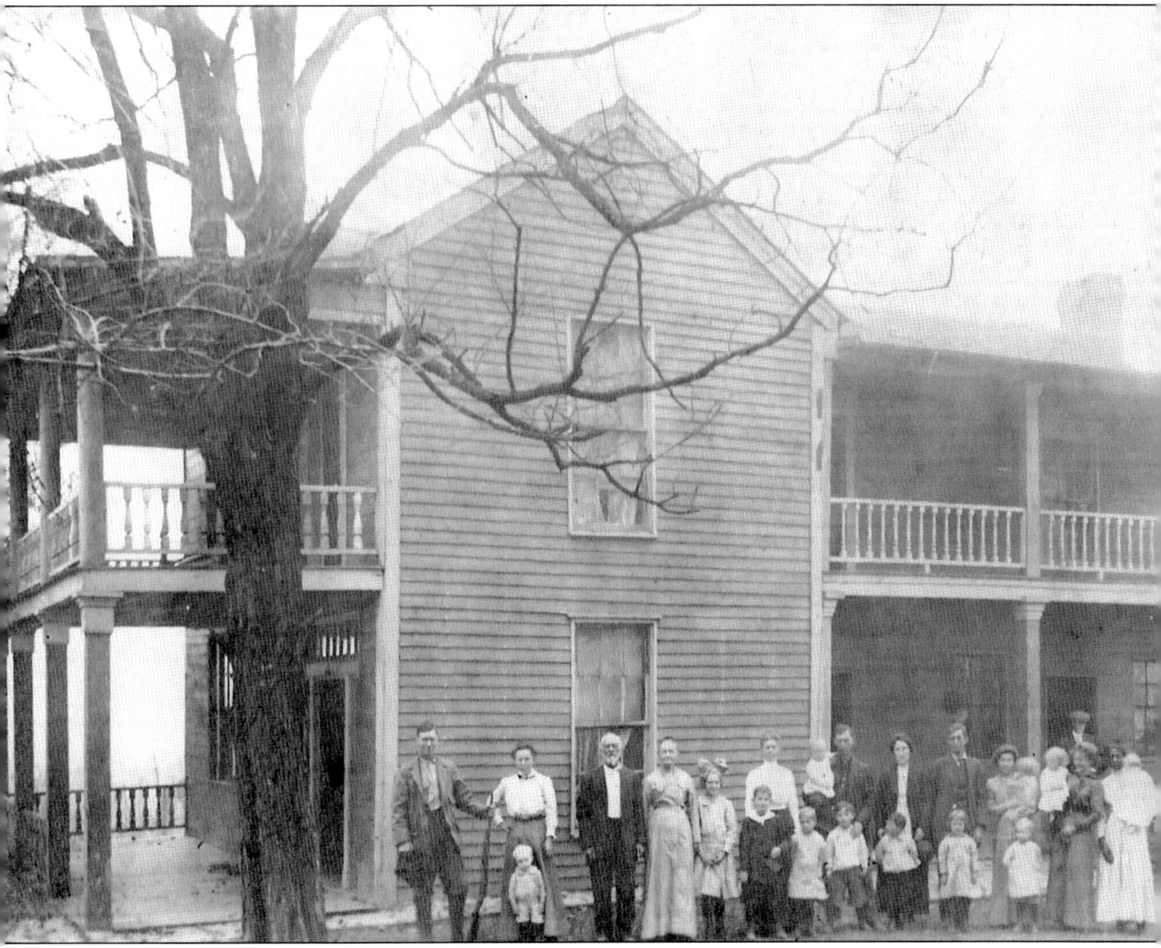

Ephraim and Mary Frances Mitchell Waller share Thanksgiving 1913 with their family. To the rear of the house is an adjoining small plot that served as the family cemetery. Ephraim and his wife lived in this house for many years before he passed away on September 12, 1918. Mary went to live with their daughter Emma Waller Ward, and the house was rented to the Ernest Mann family. (Courtesy of John Moore.)

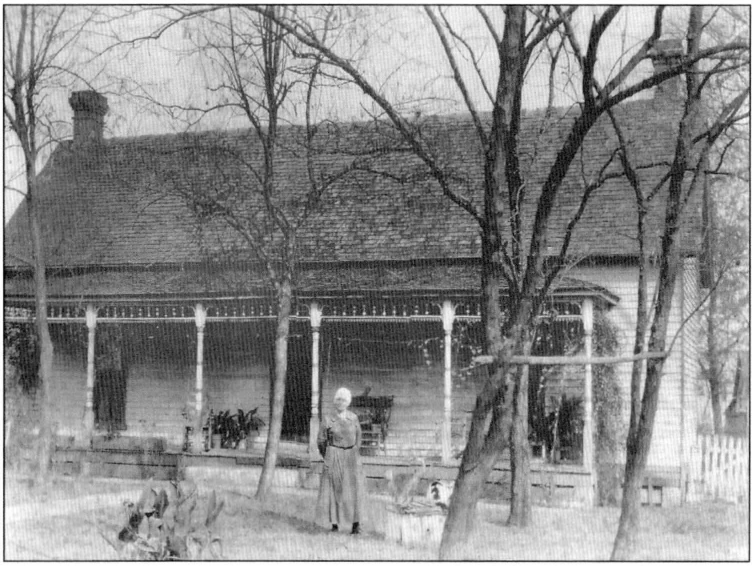

"Mammy" Maggie King Martin is seen here in front of her house in the early 1900s. She was the wife of James J. Martin, who built a storehouse on a lot near their home. He ran the store for a few years before it was taken over by Mr. Phipps. Eventually, Payton Smith bought the store and ran it until the 1940s. (Courtesy of Toby Francis.)

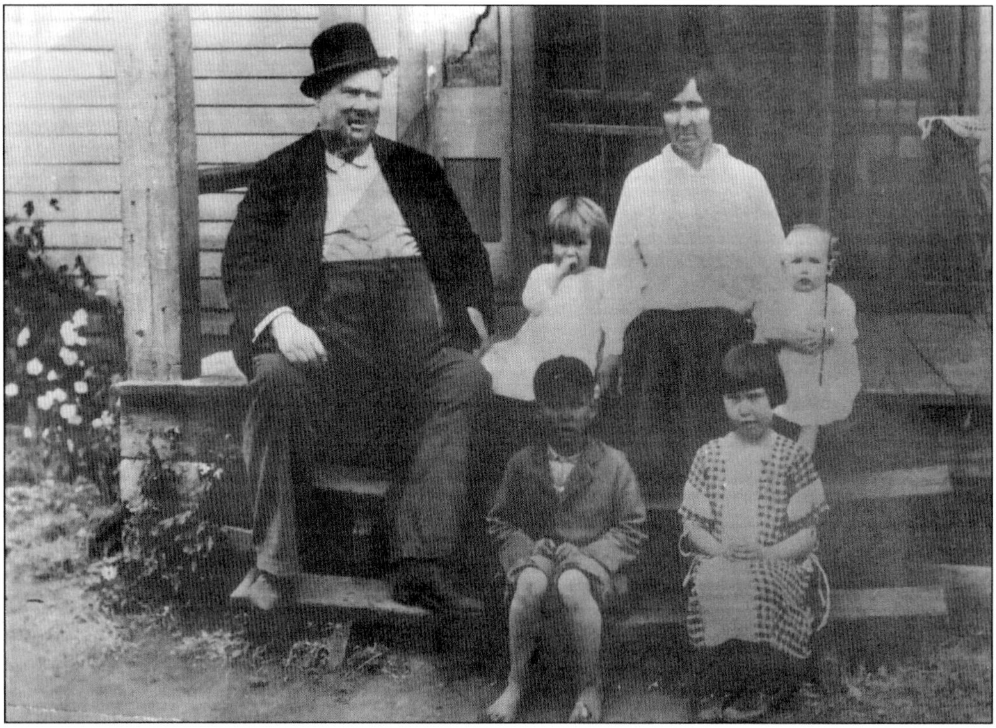

Dee and Vera "Ma" Mullins sit in front of their Jefferson home around 1925. Beatrice and Jack sit next to their mother, while Roy and Nell sit are in front of her. Ma Mullins continued to operate her husband's general store even after his death. The store stood on the north side of Jefferson Pike, east of the town square in Jefferson. As Mullins grew older, she ran the store from her wheelchair. She sold alcoholic beverages, which did not sit well with the locals. (Courtesy of Toby Francis.)

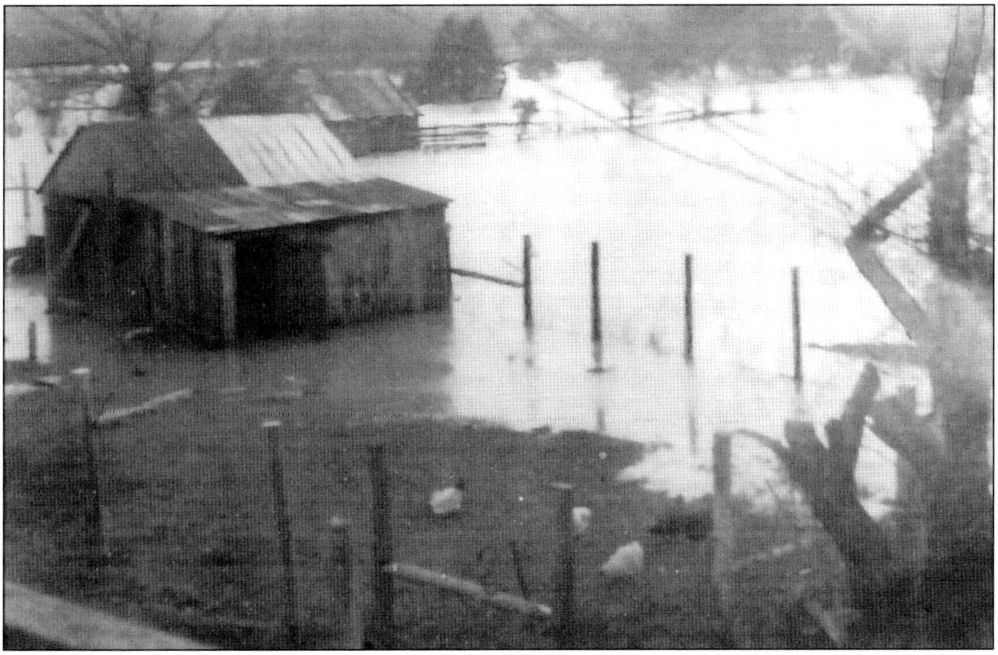

Floodwaters surround Jefferson in 1955, captured here by James Mullins. During this flood, the town was prepared, but the floods of 1902, the 1920s, the 1930s, and 1948 caught residents off guard. When unexpected flooding occurred, Jefferson was inundated with water for several days. (Courtesy of Toby Francis.)

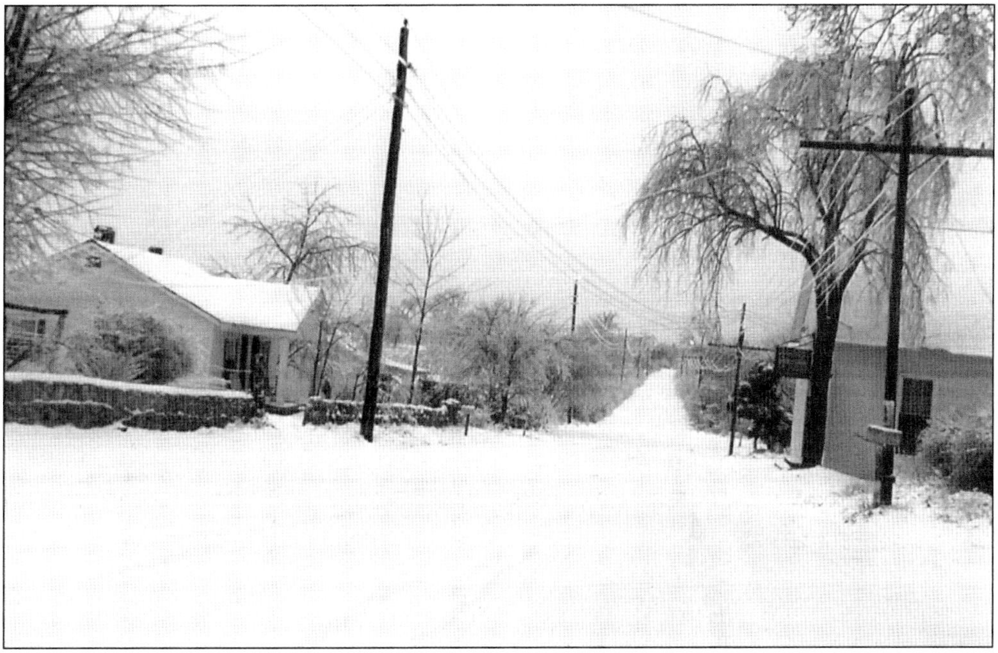

This image looks west on a snowy day in Jefferson. The Church of Christ is on the right. In later years, the church was moved back from the road, and classrooms were added. After the Army Corps of Engineers purchased the land, Ernest Eades bought the main section of the church and moved it across the river, where he used it as a storage building. (Courtesy of Toby Francis.)

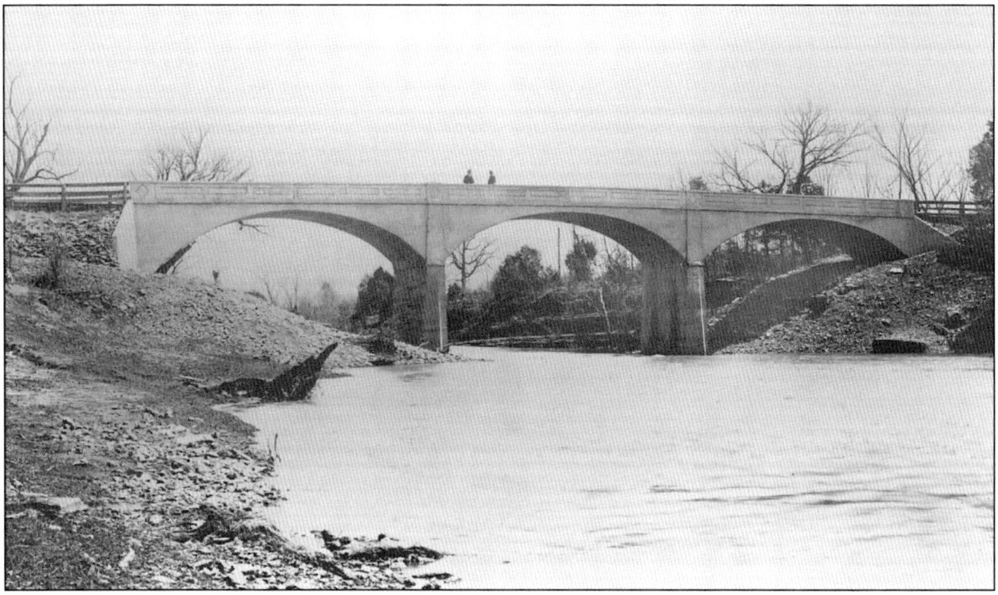

Two men are seen standing on Jefferson Pike Bridge over Stones River in winter around 1922. When the river was higher, flatboats were loaded with products from forests and farms and sent downstream. The operators manipulated the curves in the waterway and traveled down the main branch of the Stones River to the Cumberland and on to Nashville. Even after train tracks and roads were constructed, boats used the Stones River for transportation. (Courtesy of Shacklett's Photography.)

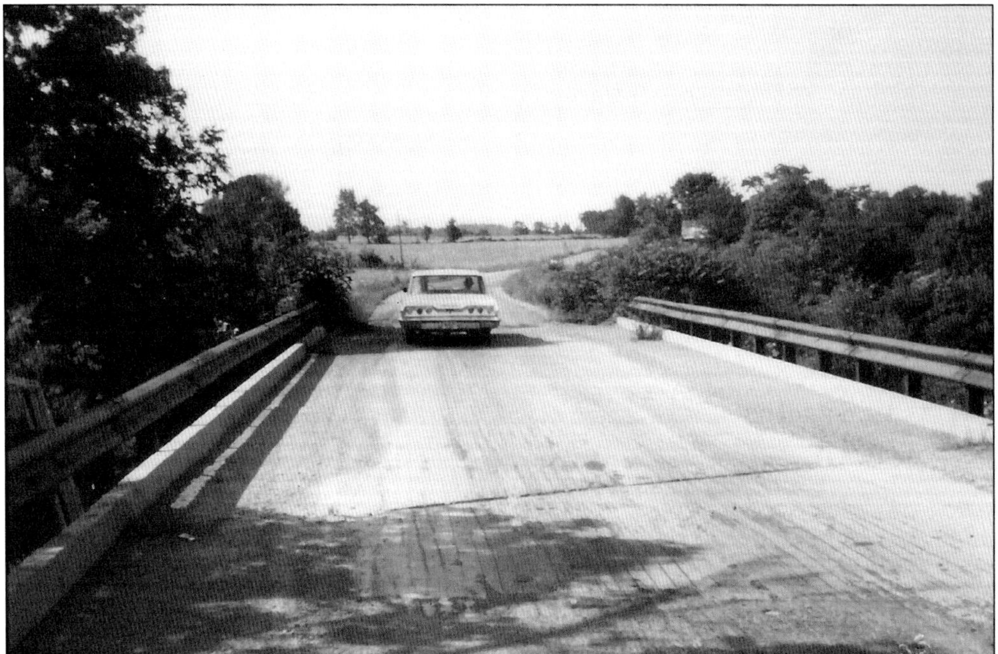

This photograph shows the new Spring Creek Bridge in 1966. The bridge had been built just a few years before but was destroyed by the Army Corps of Engineers shortly after this photograph was taken. (Courtesy of Jimmy Francis.)

When Jimmy Francis learned of the closing of his town of Jefferson, he, Everett Waller, and Wilson Francis went around taking photographs of their favorite spots. Here, Roy Hunter (left), Everett (center), and Wilson stand in front of a store near Sulfur Springs in 1966. The store was operated by Robert and Ruth Rion and had gasoline pumps, rooms for rent, and a bowling alley. (Courtesy of Jimmy Francis.)

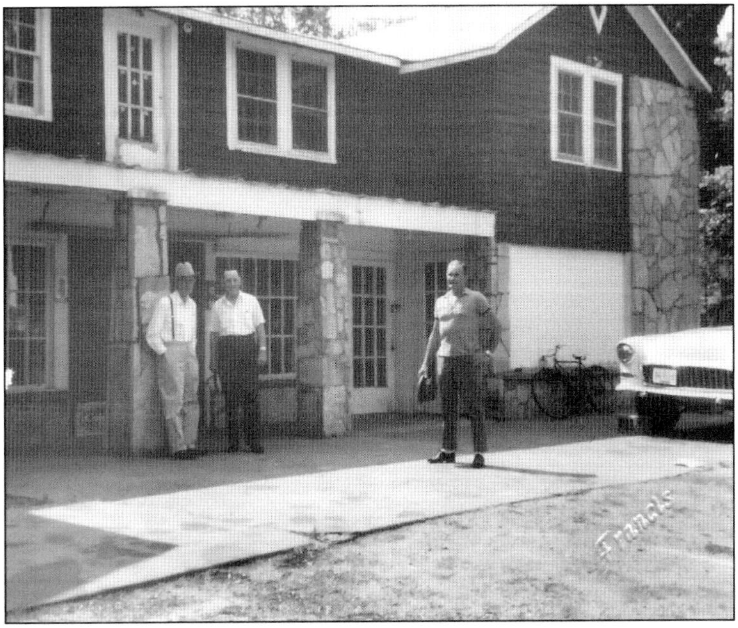

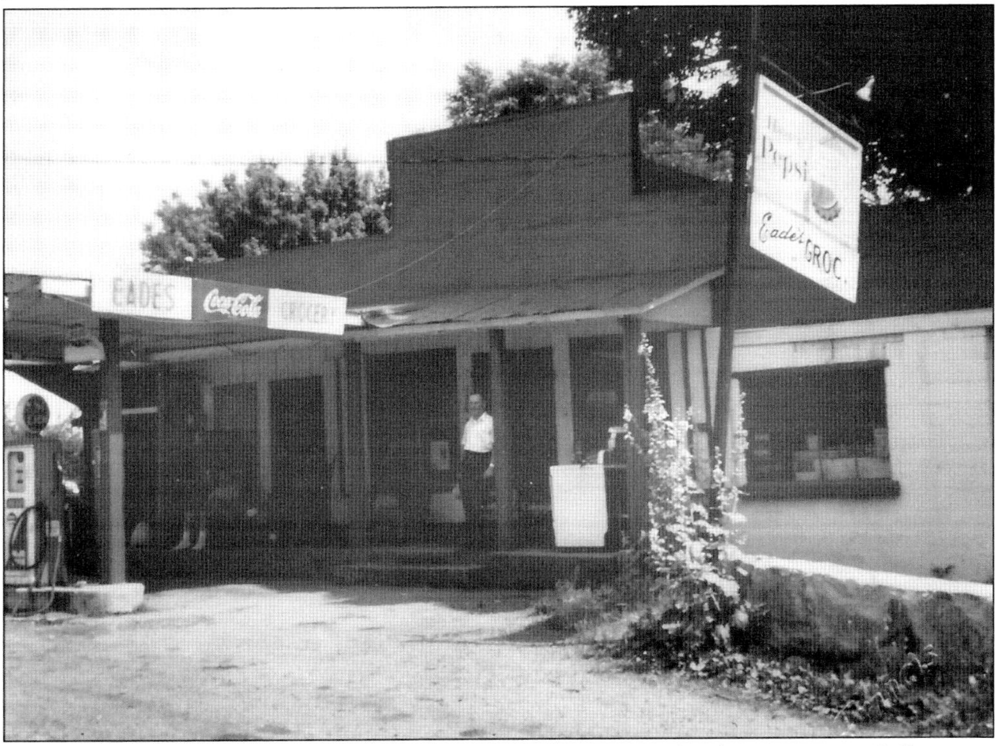

Everett Waller (left) and Danny Francis are pictured in front of Eades Grocery in Jefferson in 1966. The Eades Store provided passersby with a bite to eat and a cold drink. Conversation was free and plentiful with the store owner and clerks. Patrons could purchase a loaf of bread, a jug of milk, a box of nails, or some seeds for planting. Jefferson had no rural mail delivery, so residents had to pick up their mail from mailboxes sitting beside the lane near the store. (Courtesy of Jimmy Francis.)

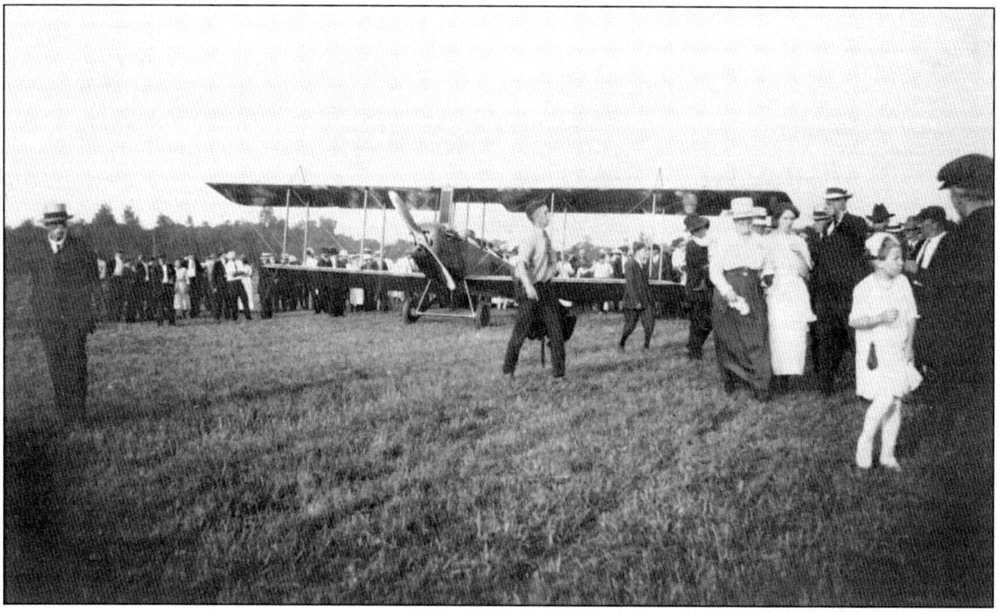

Men and women look at the latest in aviation technology on opening day of Sky Harbor in October 1929. Sky Harbor, the region's first airport, was sandwiched between Old Nashville Highway near Florence Road and the railroad tracks. Jimmy Doolittle, the famed military pilot, attended the ceremony and performed for the crowd. (Courtesy of Shacklett's Photography.)

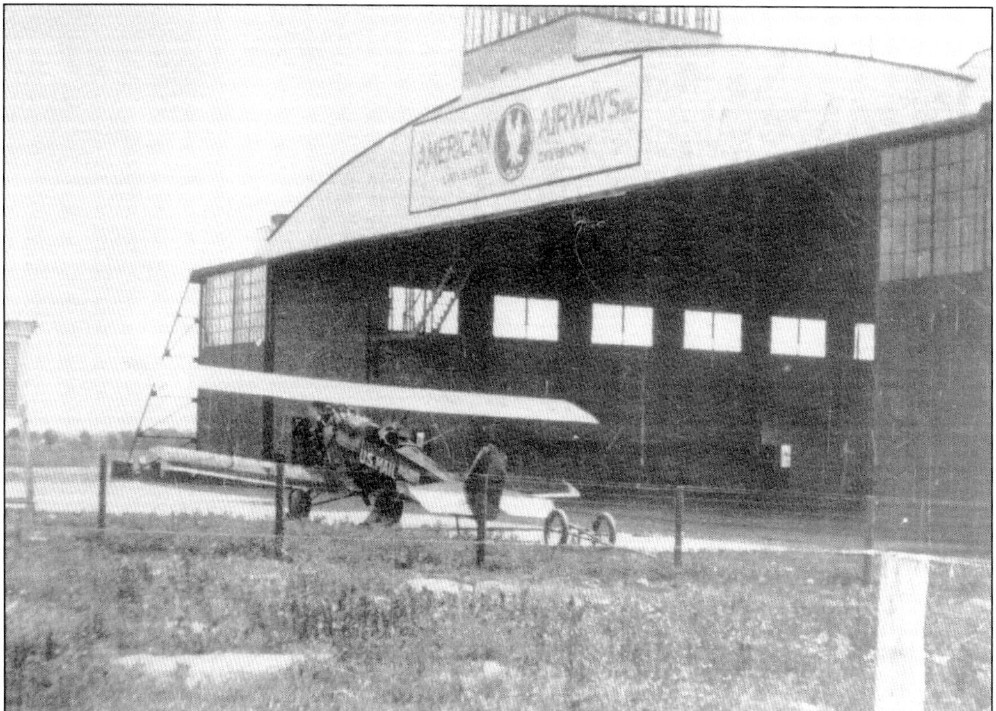

Sky Harbor served as the local base for commercial and airmail planes with regular routes to Atlanta and Chicago. A mail plane sits in front of the hangar in the late 1920s or early 1930s. (Courtesy of Shacklett's Photography.)

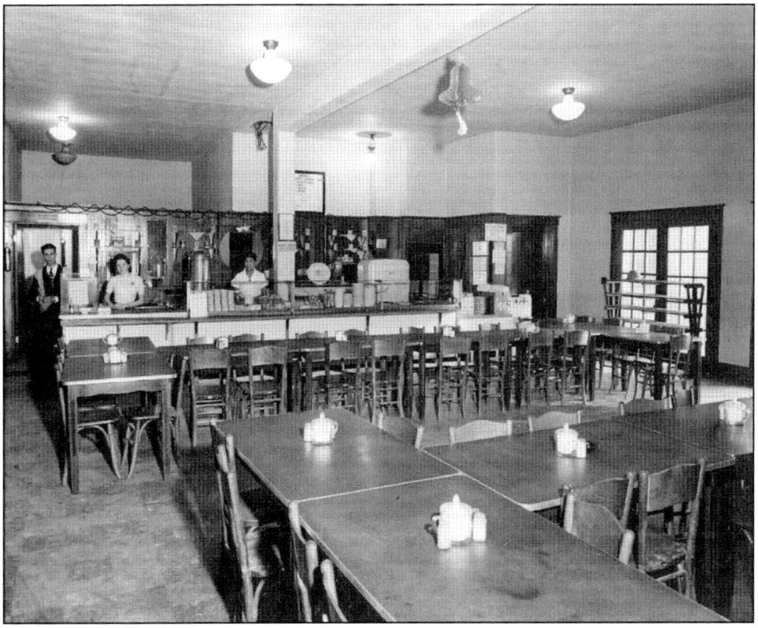

When not at work or in the air, Sky Harbor employees and visitors could grab a bite to eat in the lunchroom, seen here around 1940. The airport served as a hub for the area and offered daily flights with Anderson Airways, later known as American Airlines. (Courtesy of Rutherford County Archives.)

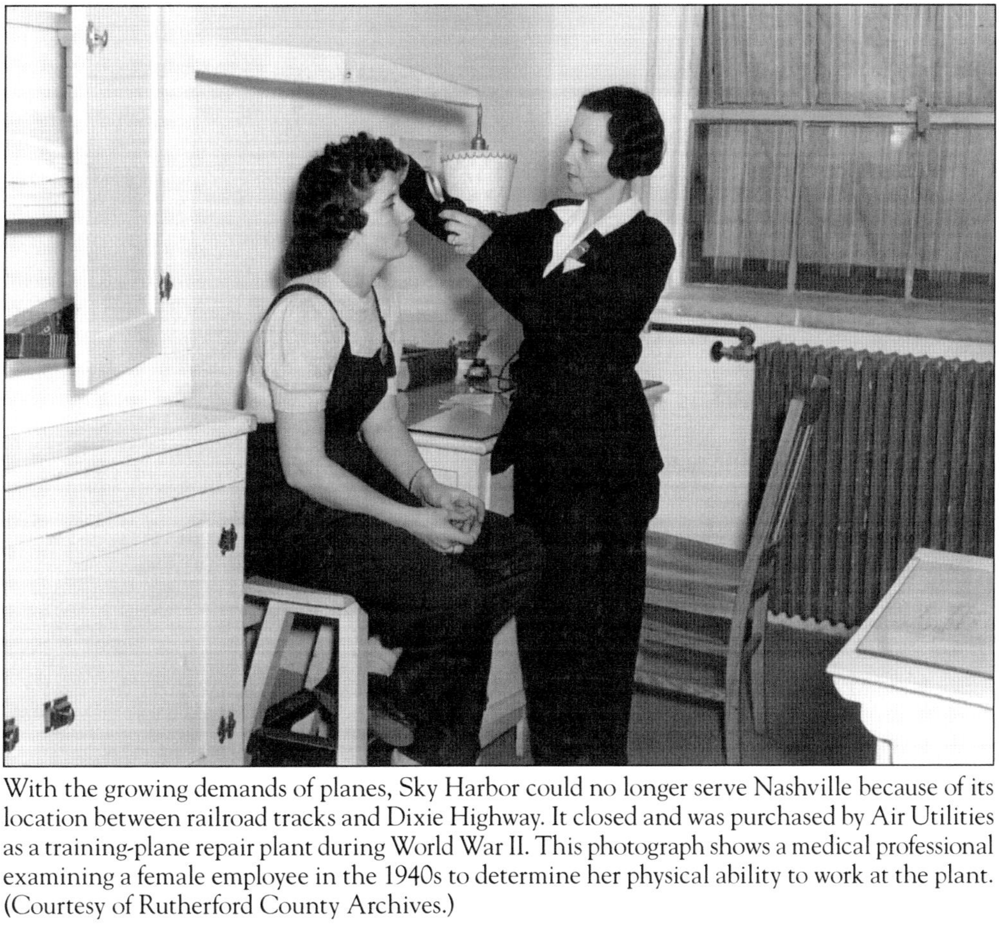

With the growing demands of planes, Sky Harbor could no longer serve Nashville because of its location between railroad tracks and Dixie Highway. It closed and was purchased by Air Utilities as a training-plane repair plant during World War II. This photograph shows a medical professional examining a female employee in the 1940s to determine her physical ability to work at the plant. (Courtesy of Rutherford County Archives.)

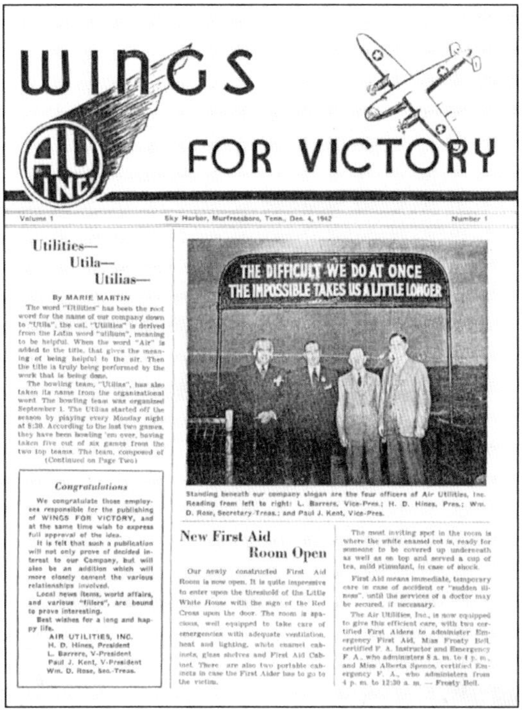

WINGS FOR VICTORY

AU INC.

Volume 1 | Sky Harbor, Murfreesboro, Tenn., Dec. 4, 1942 | Number 1

Utilities— Utila— Utilias—

By MARIE MARTIN

The word "Utilities" has been the root word for the name of our company down to "Utila", the cat. "Utilities" is derived from the Latin word "utilium", meaning to be helpful. When the word "Air" is added to the title, that gives the meaning of being helpful to the air. Then the title is truly being performed by the work that is being done.

The bowling team, "Utilias", has also taken its name from the organizational word. The bowling team was organized September 1. The Utilias started off the season by playing every Monday night at 8:30. According to the last two games, they have been bowling 'em over, having taken five out of six games from the two top teams. The team, composed of

(Continued on Page Two)

Congratulations

We congratulate those employees responsible for the publishing of WINGS FOR VICTORY, and at the same time wish to express full approval of the idea.

It is felt that such a publication will not only prove of decided interest to our Company, but will also be an addition which will more closely cement the various relationships involved.

Local news items, world affairs, and various "fillers", are bound to prove interesting.

Best wishes for a long and happy life.

AIR UTILITIES, INC.
H. D. Hines, President
L. Barrere, V-President
Paul J. Kent, V-President
Wm. D. Rose, Sec.-Treas.

Standing beneath our company slogan are the four officers of Air Utilities, Inc. Reading from left to right: L. Barrere, Vice-Pres.; H. D. Hines, Pres.; Wm. D. Rose, Secretary-Treas.; and Paul J. Kent, Vice-Pres.

New First Aid Room Open

Our newly constructed First Aid Room is now open. It is quite impressive to enter upon the threshold of the Little White House with the sign of the Red Cross upon the door. The room is spacious, well equipped to take care of emergencies with adequate ventilation, heat and lighting, white enamel cabinets, glass shelves and First Aid Cabinet. There are also two portable cabinets in case the First Aider has to go to the victim.

The most inviting spot in the room is where the white enamel cot is, ready for someone to be covered up underneath as well as on top and served a cup of tea, mild stimulant, in case of shock.

First Aid means immediate, temporary care in case of accident or "sudden illness", until the services of a doctor may be secured, if necessary.

The Air Utilities, Inc., is now equipped to give this efficient care, with two certified First Aiders to administer Emergency First Aid, Miss Frosty Bell, certified F. A. Instructor and Emergency F. A., who administers 8 a. m. to 4 p. m., and Miss Alberta Spence, certified Emergency F. A., who administers from 4 p. m. to 12:30 a. m. — Frosty Bell.

Sky Harbor closed before the outbreak of World War II, and the buildings became a training facility for plane production to support the war effort. This 1942 newsletter tells of the efforts of staff, as well as of the newly formed bowling team. (Courtesy of Rutherford County Archives.)

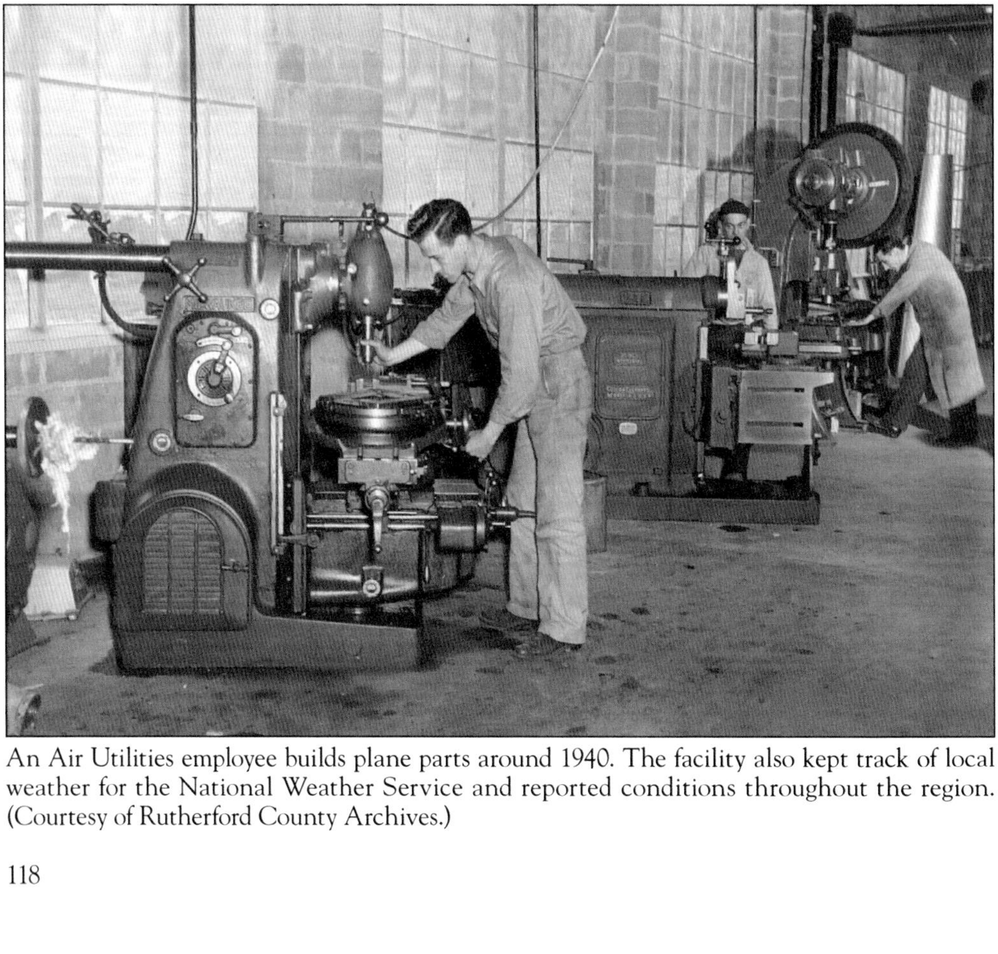

An Air Utilities employee builds plane parts around 1940. The facility also kept track of local weather for the National Weather Service and reported conditions throughout the region. (Courtesy of Rutherford County Archives.)

Local "Rosie the Riveters" work on airplane wings at Sky Harbor around 1940. A few of the planes produced during World War II include the Boeing P-12, Bell P-39, Brewster F2A Buffalo, Douglas P-70 Havoc, Lockheed P-38 Lightning, and many others. (Courtesy of Rutherford County Archives.)

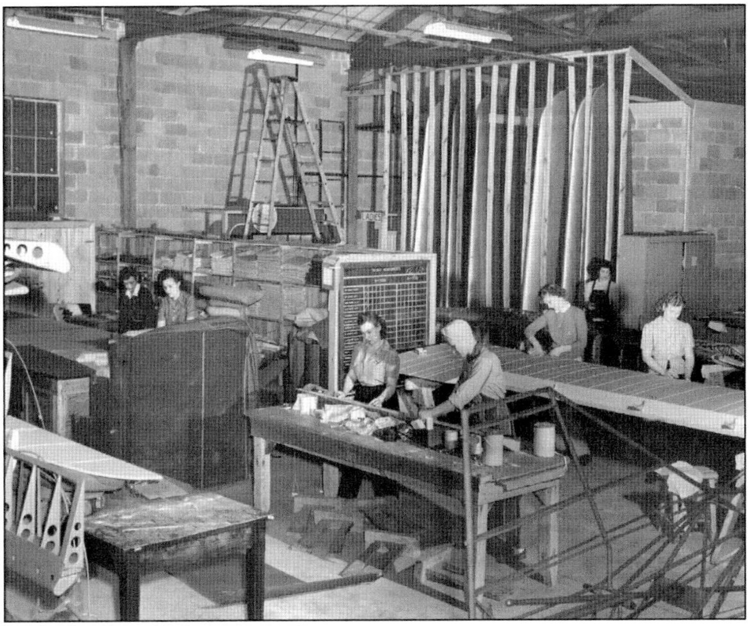

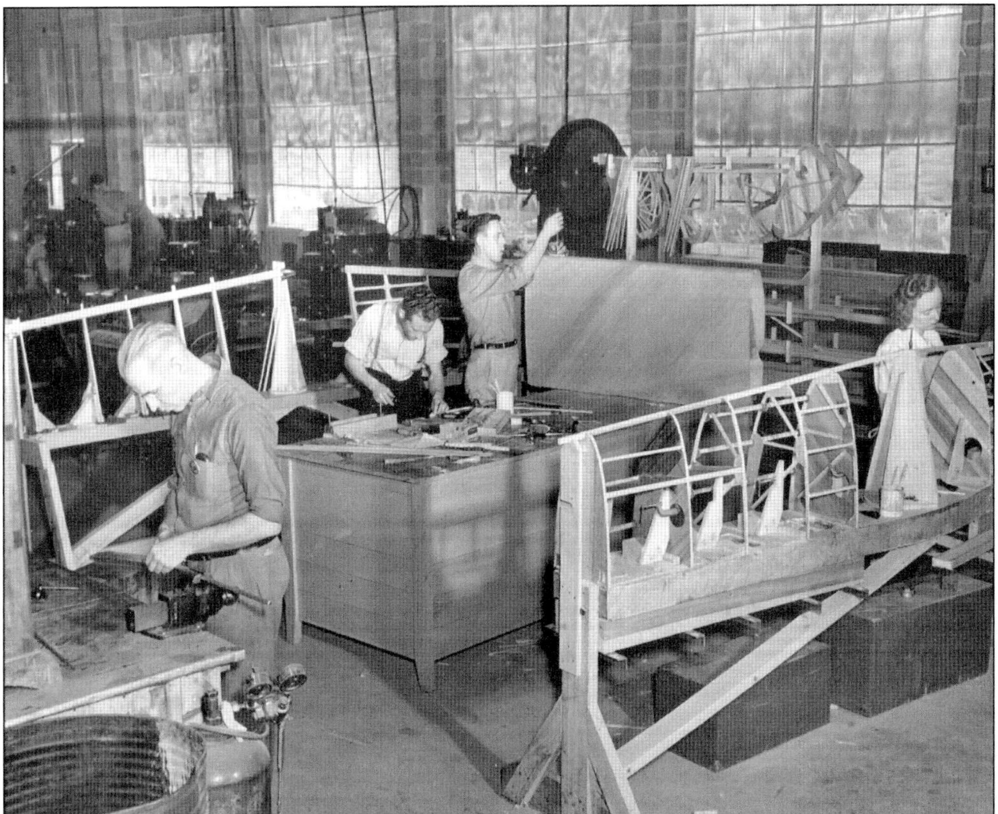

These men and woman are assembling airplane wings at Sky Harbor around 1940. Even after the Nashville airport moved to Berry Field in 1937, Sky Harbor saw a few of the same planes as it had when it was a commercial flight field. (Courtesy of Rutherford County Archives.)

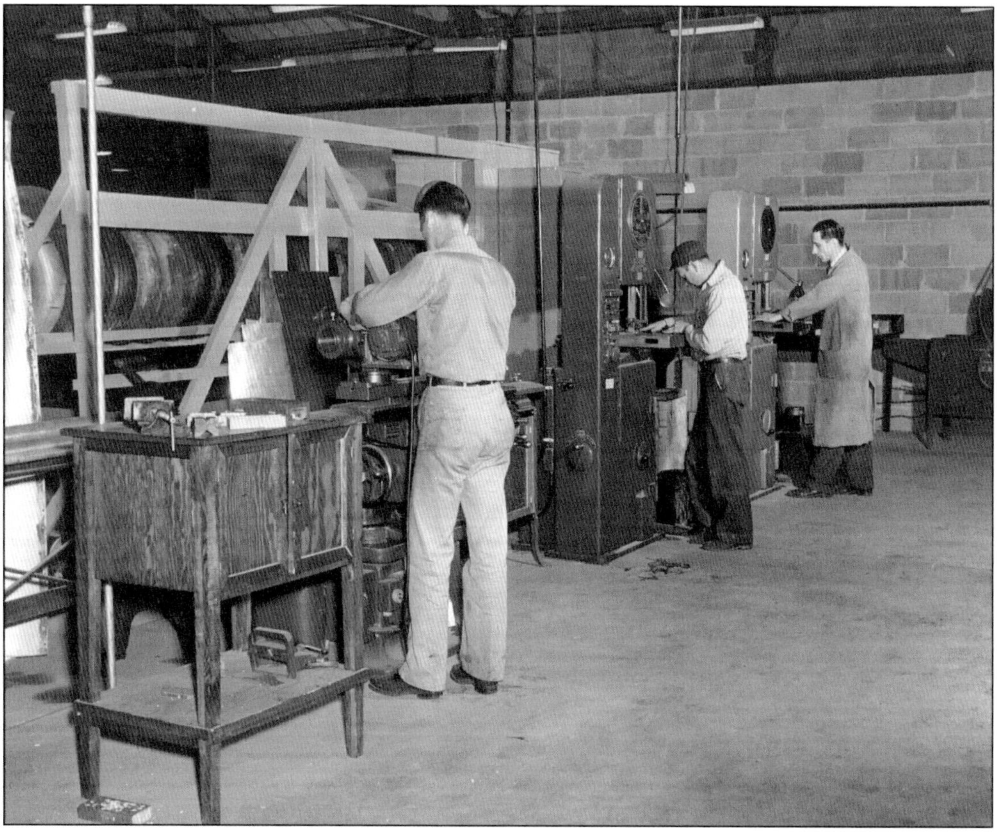

Air Utilities employees examine plane parts in the 1940s. Assistant plant supervisor F.B. Manlove checked their work during his time there in 1943. (Courtesy of Rutherford County Archives.)

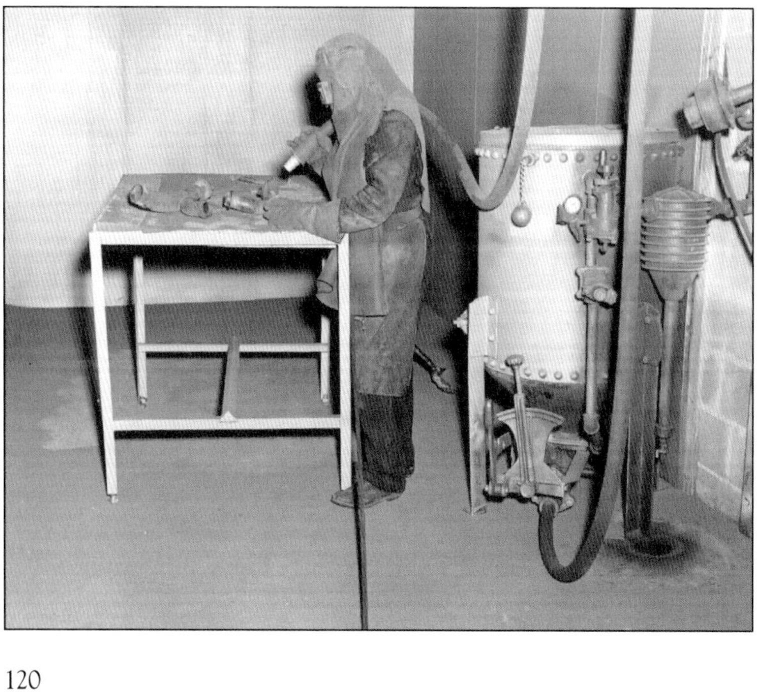

An employee works with toxic chemicals while repairing airplane parts at Sky Harbor around 1940. (Courtesy of Rutherford County Archives.)

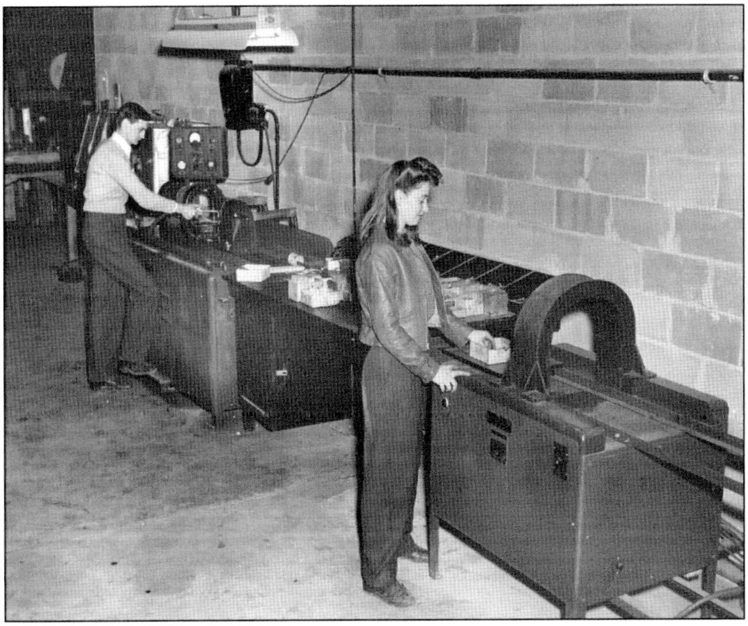

This man and woman check the smaller parts for planes, including the Stearman PT-17 and the Fairchild PT-23 at the Air Utilities plane-repair plant. (Courtesy of Rutherford County Archives.)

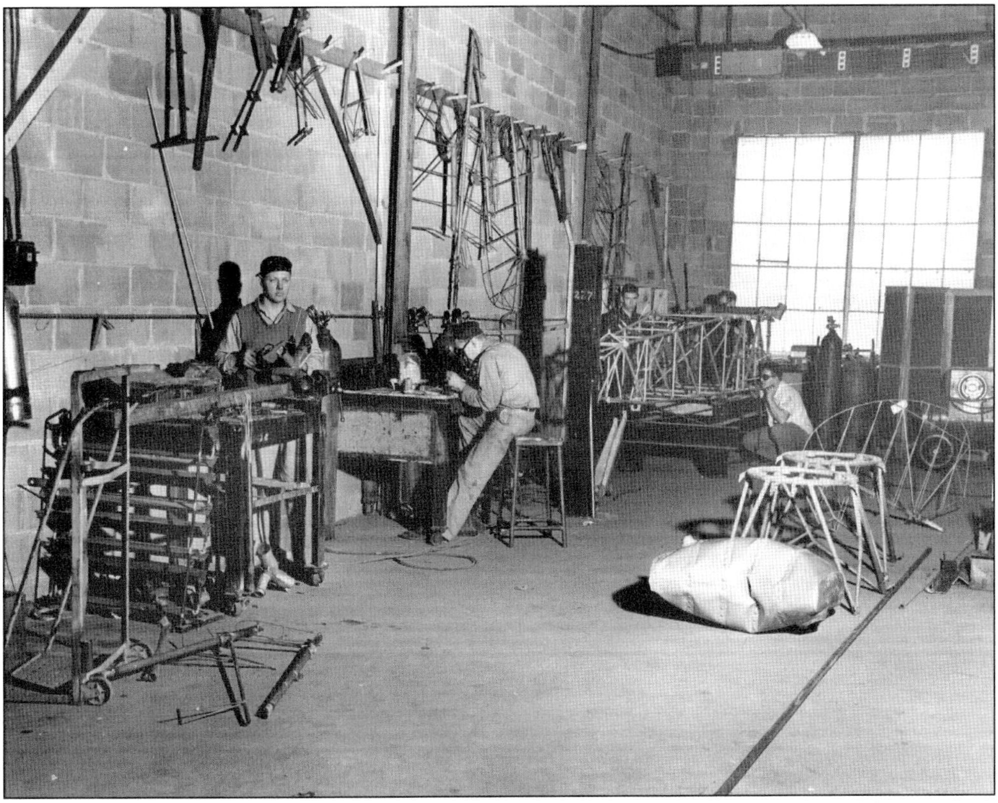

The man on the left welds plane components while the men on the right assemble a portion of the plane. The plant included several departments, including the wing department, sewing department, subassembly department, and final-assembly department. (Courtesy of Rutherford County Archives.)

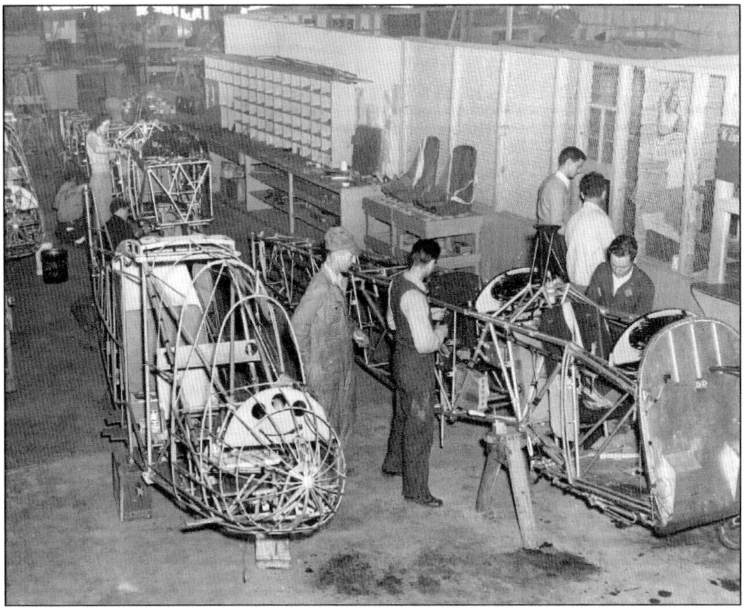

Men and women assemble the bodies of planes at Air Utilities, Inc. The subassembly department installed seats, throttles, sticks, and other airplane necessities. The company allowed women to work alongside the men, as shown in this photograph from the mid-1940s. (Courtesy of Rutherford County Archives.)

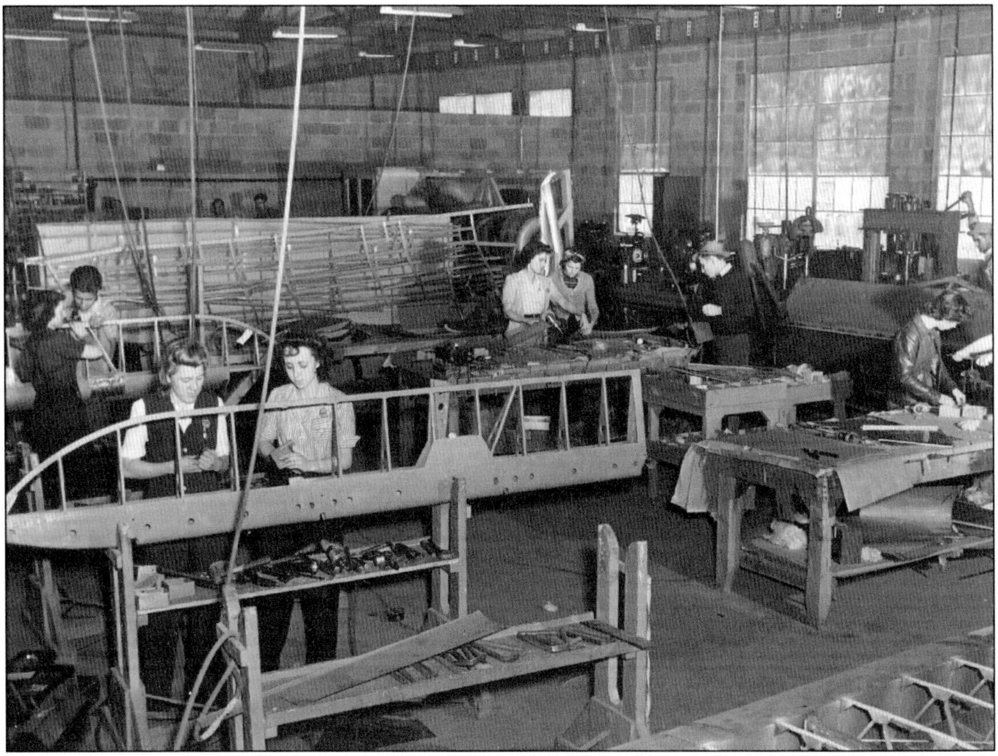

In his 1940s image, the women on the left are inspecting a partially built airplane wing, while the group on the right is repairing plane parts. With men on the battlefields, the government decided to launch a propaganda campaign to bring women into the workforce. They created Rosie the Riveter, who became popular in 1942 and even more admired when Normal Rockwell painted an image of her on the cover of the *Saturday Evening Post* in May 1943. (Courtesy of Rutherford County Archives.)

Men finish the assembly of airplane wings in this 1940s photograph. The final-assembly department was where the wings were covered, the major stabilizers were installed, and the landing gear was put into place. (Courtesy of Rutherford County Archives.)

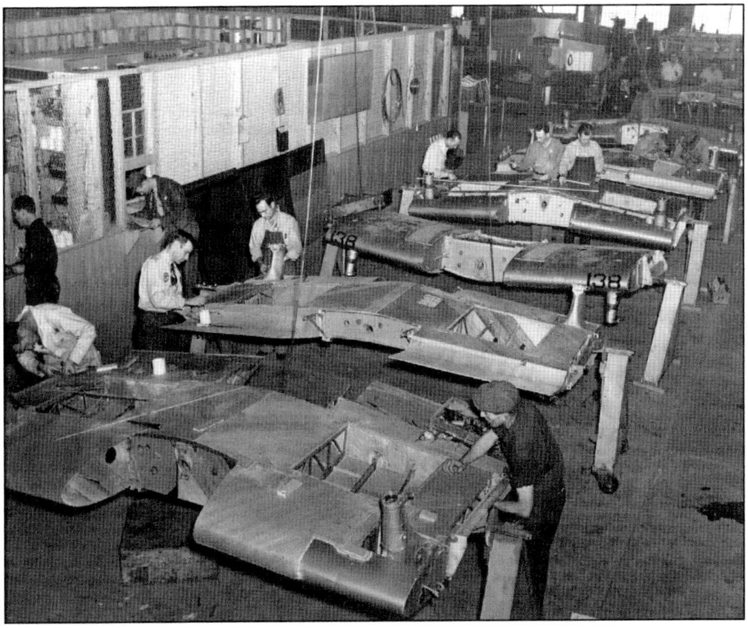

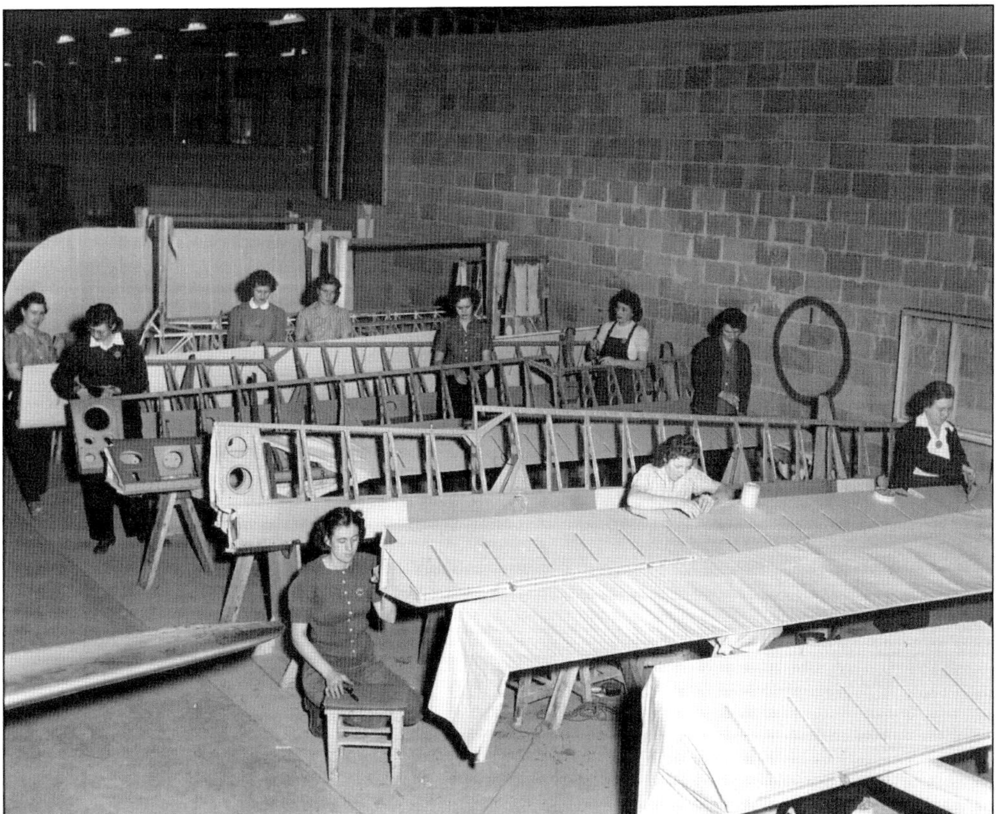

Women assist the war effort at Sky Harbor in the 1940s. The sewing department consisted of many women who were in charge of sewing the wing coverings, placing them on the wing frame, and covering the other wing parts, such as the ailerons. (Courtesy of Rutherford County Archives.)

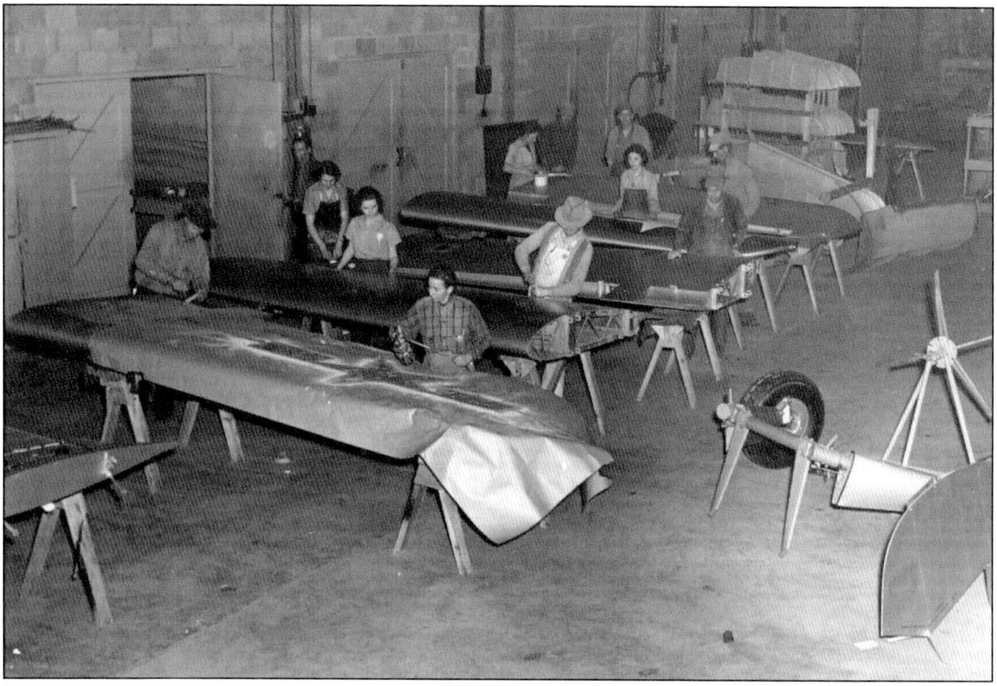

The woman in front spray paints a star onto a completed airplane wing in the 1940s at Air Utilities plane-repair plant. This was one of the stops in the final-assembly department before the planes were sent out for use. (Courtesy of Rutherford County Archives.)

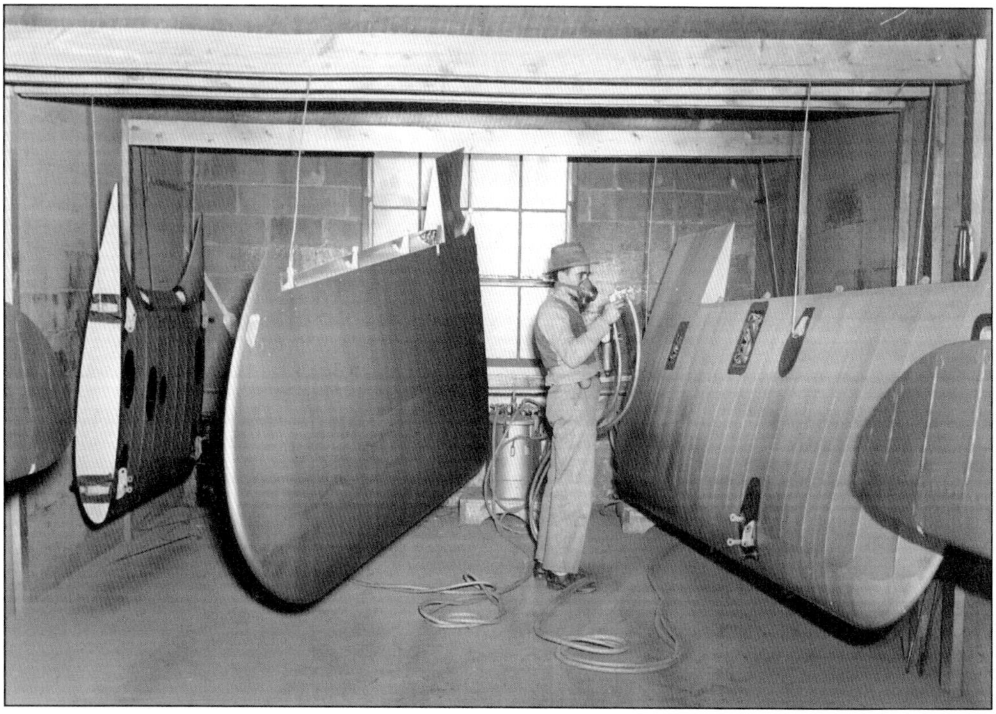

This 1940 photograph shows a man spraying a finished airplane wing before it is attached to the rest of the plane. (Courtesy of Rutherford County Archives.)

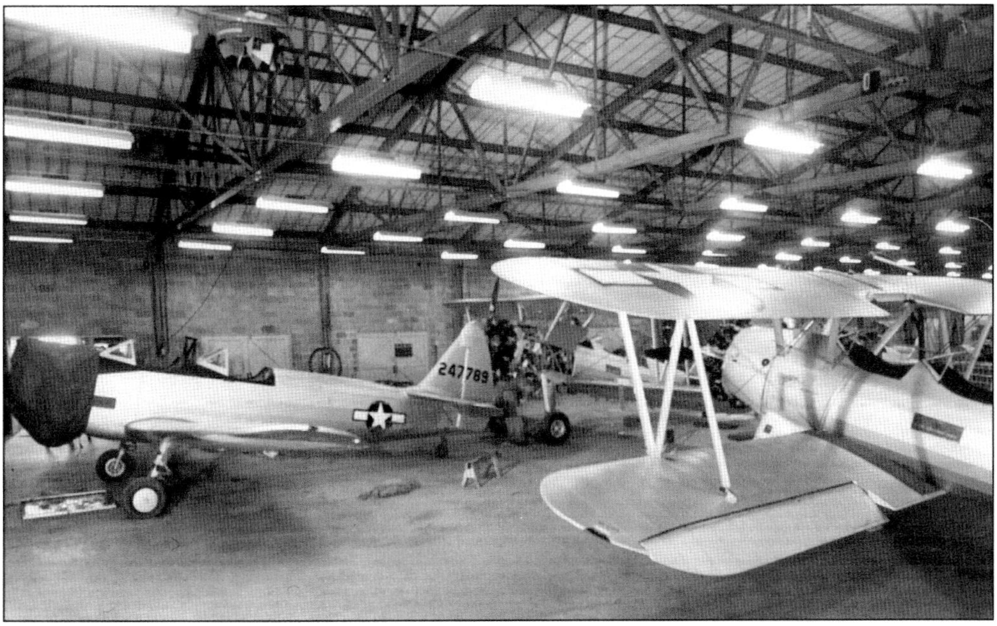

Finished airplanes sit at the old Sky Harbor Airport awaiting their test runs in this mid-1940s photograph. Air Utilities took over and could be reached by phone at the number 1416. (Courtesy of Rutherford County Archives.)

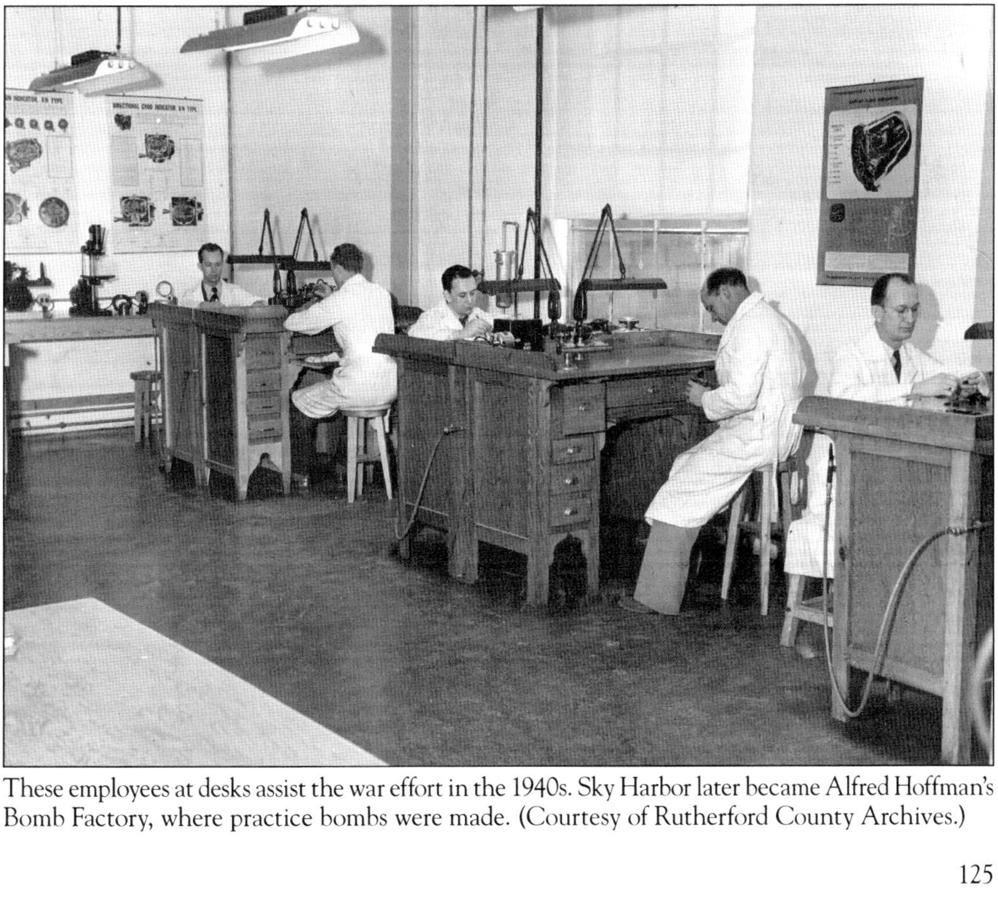

These employees at desks assist the war effort in the 1940s. Sky Harbor later became Alfred Hoffman's Bomb Factory, where practice bombs were made. (Courtesy of Rutherford County Archives.)

Index

About the Organization

The Sam Davis Memorial Association (SDMA) graciously provided information for several photographs in this book, along with the historical references for many of the chapter titles and captions. SDMA was formed in 1930 when the State of Tennessee gave the charter to the newly formed organization to preserve the memory of Sam Davis. Sam's niece Andromedia Sinnott, or "Ms. Medie" as she was known, was a driving force behind the efforts to preserve the house as a historic site. Ms. Medie became the first regent of the historic site and gave tours of the property well into the 1950s.

Today, the SDMA preserves the Historic Sam Davis Home & Plantation to keep alive the story of Sam Davis, his family, and the people who labored on the Middle Tennessee farm before, during, and after the Civil War. Through museum exhibits, the historic home, preserved farmland, and quality education programs, the SDMA imparts to its visitors the importance of learning about their past and its relevance to their present.

The site sits on 168 acres, 100 of which are cultivated for cotton, which the Davises would have grown when they lived there. The main house was built between 1810 and 1820, and Charles Davis, Sam's father, added on to it in 1850 for his growing family. The property also boasts a modern visitor center and 2,775-plus-square-foot museum opened in November 2003, as well as many original outbuildings, including a kitchen, a smokehouse, and an overseer's cabin. Three single-pen cabins and one dogtrot cabin for enslaved workers were moved to the property in the 1940s to interpret the lives of enslaved African Americans on the plantation.

Each year, the museum hosts a variety of activities that appeal to the diverse community of Smyrna. The site is supported by the revenue produced by events and daily tours, monetary donations, membership to the Sam Davis Memorial Association, and private facility rentals. For more information on the site or to make a donation, please visit www.samdavishome.org or call 615-459-2341.